EXOTIC ENCOUNTERS

Borgo Press Books by BRIAN STABLEFORD

Against the New Gods, and Other Essays on Writers of Imaginative Fiction
Algebraic Fantasies and Realistic Romances: More Masters of Science Fiction
Alien Abduction: The Wiltshire Revelations
The Best of Both Worlds and Other Ambiguous Tales
Beyond the Colors of Darkness and Other Exotica
Changelings and Other Metamorphic Tales
A Clash of Symbols: The Triumph of James Blish
Complications and Other Stories
The Cosmic Perspective and Other Black Comedies
Creators of Science Fiction
The Cure for Love and Other Tales of the Biotech Revolution
The Devil's Party: A Brief History of Satanic Abuse
The Dragon Man: A Novel of the Future
The Eleventh Hour
Exotic Encounters: Selected Reviews
Firefly: A Novel of the Far Future
The Gardens of Tantalus and Other Delusions
Glorious Perversity: The Decline and Fall of Literary Decadence
Gothic Grotesques: Essays on Fantastic Literature
The Great Chain of Being and Other Tales of the Biotech Revolution
The Haunted Bookshop and Other Apparitions
Heterocosms: Science Fiction in Context and Practice
In the Flesh and Other Tales of the Biotech Revolution
The Innsmouth Heritage and Other Sequels
Jaunting on the Scoriac Tempests and Other Essays on Fantastic Literature
Kiss the Goat
The Moment of Truth: A Novel of the Future
Narrative Strategies in Science Fiction, and Other Essays on Imaginative Fiction
News of the Black Feast and Other Random Reviews
An Oasis of Horror: Decadent Tales and Contes Cruels
Opening Minds: Essays on Fantastic Literature
Outside the Human Aquarium: Masters of Science Fiction, Second Edition
The Plurality of Worlds: A Sixteenth-Century Space Opera
Prelude to Eternity: A Romance of the First Time Machine
The Return of the Djinn and Other Black Melodramas
Salome and Other Decadent Fantasies
Slaves of the Death Spiders and Other Essays on Fantastic Literature
The Sociology of Science Fiction
Space, Time, and Infinity: Essays on Fantastic Literature
The Tree of Life and Other Tales of the Biotech Revolution
The World Beyond: A Sequel to S. Fowler Wright's The World Below
Yesterday's Bestsellers: A Voyage Through Literary History

EXOTIC ENCOUNTERS

SELECTED REVIEWS

by

Brian Stableford

THE BORGO PRESS

An Imprint of Wildside Press LLC

MMX

I.O. Evans Studies in the Philosophy and Criticism of Literature
ISSN 0271-9061

Number Fifty-Two

Copyright © 1992, 1993, 1994, 1995, 1996, 1997, 1998, 1999, 2000, 2001, 2004, 2006, 2010 by Brian Stableford

All rights reserved.
No part of this book may be reproduced in any form without the expressed written consent of the publisher.

www.wildsidebooks.com

FIRST EDITION

CONTENTS

Introduction 9

PART ONE:
Reviews from *The New York Review of Science Fiction*

Cosm by Gregory Benford, and *Rogue Star* by Michael Flynn,
    #118 (June 1998) 13
Deepdrive by Alexander Jablokov, #125 (January 1999) 18
The Boss in the Wall by Avram Davidson & Grania Davis,
    #126 (February 1999) 20
Stardust by Neil Gaiman, #127 (March 1999) 23
Northern Stars by David G. Hartwell & Glenn Grant, #128
    (April 1999) 26
Stinger by Nancy Kress, #129 (May 1999) 28
Starfarers & *Operation Luna* by Poul Anderson, #139
    (February 2000) 31
Foreign Bodies by Stephen Dedman, #141 (May 2000) 36
Rings (Charles L. Harness), #142 (June 2000) 39
Prophets for the End of Time by Marcos Donnelly, #145
    (September 2000) 45
Alexandre Humboldt-Fonteyne: La Collection Interdite by
    Michel de Spiegeleire, #146 (October 2000) 48
Oceanspace by Allen Steele, #148 (December 2000) 53
Kingdom of the Grail by Judith Tarr, #151 (March 2001) 55
*Music of Many Spheres: The Essential Hal Clement, Volume
    2*, #153 (May 2001) 62
Summers at Castle Auburn by Sharon Shinn, #160
    (December 2001) 66
The Space Opera Renaissance edited by David G. Hartwell
    and Kathryn Cramer, #215 (July 2006) 69

PART TWO: Reviews from *Interzone*

The Death Guard by Philip George Chadwick, #69 (March 1993) 89

"The Wrong Tree": *The Ascent of Wonder: The Evolution of Hard SF* ed. David Hartwell and Kathryn Cramer, #88 (October 1994) 91

"The Seductions of Undeath": *A Dance in Blood Velvet* by Freda Warrington, *"What Sweet Music They Make...."* by Thee Vampire Guild, *Sopor Aeternus* by Sopor Aeternus and the Ensemble of Shadows, *SunDown SunRise* by Jackie Askew & *Vampire: The Complete Guide to the World of the Undead* by Manuela Dunn Mascetti, #90 (December 1994) ... 94

"Monsters of the 20th Century": *Il Fantasma dell'Opera* by Ataraxia, & *Motherfuckers* by David Britton, #114 (December 1996) 96

"Another Case of Conscience": *The Sparrow* by Mary Doria Russell, #116 (February 1997) 101

"Babes in the Wilderness": *The Wood Wife* by Terri Windling, *Dradin in Love* by Jeff VanderMeer & *The Fall of the House of Usherettes* by Forkbeard Fantasy, #116 (February 1997) 103

"But the Platitudes Linger": *A Scientific Romance* by Ronald Wright, *Jack Faust* by Michael Swanwick, *Diaspora* by Greg Egan & *Child of the River* by Paul McAuley, #125 (November 1997) 106

"The Endurance of Edgar Allan Poe": *The Murder of Edgar Allan Poe* by Sophia Kingshill, #127 (January 1998) 112

"Phantasmagoria Revisited": *The Barbers of Surreal* by Forkbeard Fantasy, #131 (May 1998) 115

PART THREE: Reviews from *Foundation*

Meeting in Infinity by John Kessel, #56 (Autumn 1992) 119
The Barber of Aldebaran by William Moy Russell, #63 (Spring 1995) 123
Voyage by Stephen Baxter, #68 (Autumn 1996) 125
The Gaia Websters by Kim Antieau. #70 (Summer 1997) 128
Earthquake Weather by Tim Powers. #70 (Summer 1997) 133
The Twentieth Century by Albert Robida, #92 (Autumn 2004).. 137
The World as It Shall Be by Emile Souvestre, #96 (Spring 2006) 141

PART FOUR: Miscellaneous Reviews

"What Sweet Music They Make...." by Thee Vampire Guild,
   Other Dimensions #3 (Winter 1996) 147
Incubus by Ann Arensberg. *Magill's Literary Annual 2000*,
   edited by John D. Wilson 168

Index 173
About the Author 195

INTRODUCTION

Most of the reviews reprinted here were produced in the twilight of the most prolific phase in my "career" as a reviewer, in the late 1990s, during which period I received a steady flow of review copies from *The New York Review of Science Fiction* and was briefly numbered among *Interzone*'s regular reviewers. *Foundation* also supplied review copies on a regular basis, but at a much slower rate than the *NYRSF*, being a quarterly rather than a monthly publication. Of the three suppliers, *Interzone* was the only one that actually paid money for the reviews, but the editor dropped me when I started reviewing books one at a time rather than artfully combining review of three or four books in a single article, because he paid a flat fee per column, thus making the latter system more economical for him and less so for me. This sacrifice on my part was probably reckless, not because the pittance was worth chasing, but because *Interzone* had always been hospitable to the ridiculous whims that led me occasionally to review idiosyncratic items of my own selection, including esoteric CDs of Gothic rock music and eccentric theatrical performances.

I was forced to abandon prolific book reviewing—and, indeed, almost all book reviewing—shortly after the turn of the Millennium, when the gradual decline of my eyesight began to make reading such a chore that I could only justify it, in connection with what I continued to think of as my "work"—long after it stopped producing anything remotely comparable to the officially-recognized "minimum wage"—when it constituted necessary research. I had spent most of my life anticipating that when I retired from writing I would be able to spend more time reading, but circumstances dictated that it would be the other way around. In the meantime, as the most recently-dated items on the contents page reveal, I still beg the occasional review copy of a book that I am desperate to acquire because it is essential to my unfortunately-esoteric interest in the early development of French scientific romance, and occasionally succeed in receiving such alms.

Like my previous collection of reviews, *News of the Black Feast*, this volume is illustrative of my woeful long-term misunderstanding of the true purpose of book reviewing, which is to provide free ads for publishers, in supposed spirit of reciprocal altruism; it was not until I had given up that I realized, belatedly, that one should never, under any circumstances, employ a book review to say what one really thinks rather than merely lavishing praise, hypocritically if necessary. By then, alas, it was far too late; although they are in a small minority, there are a handful of items herein whose intemperate hostility offended publishers very deeply—although I must confess that many publishers had never shown the slightest inclination to avoid offending me, even before I stepped out of line. (Another thing I was slow to realize is that there is one rule for the privileged and another for the unprivileged in the literary world, just as there is in every other walk of life.)

Fortunately, because commercial publishers are far too vain, as well as far too wealthy, to hang around in the places that authors are constrained to frequent, I have very rarely had to account for my misdeeds in a personal capacity, but readers of this volume might be interested to know that I once ran into the late James Turner, the then-proprietor of Arkham House, not long after publishing the review of John Kessel's *Meeting in Infinity* reproduced here. Mr. Turner was kind enough to inform me on that occasion that he had been commissioned by Mr. Kessel to "beat me up," but was even kinder in showing no sign of any intention of actually carrying out the mission. In fact, however, I did not believe that he had been given any such instruction, and explained to him that Mr. Kessel had already made his unhappiness clear to me in a letter of complaint, to which I had replied in moderately diplomatic terms. I also remarked that I had reviewed other books that Arkham House had recently published in much kinder terms, and that I felt sure that, for instance, Alexander Jablokov had been much happier with my assessments.

"He cried," said Mr. Turner.

I did not believe that either, but was about to pass on, leaving the matter there, when Mr. Turner put in a heartfelt complaint of his own, to the effect that every time I reviewed one of his books, even when I was complimentary about the fiction they contained, I made rude comments about the jacket copy. He, of course, was the person who wrote the jacket copy for all his books. I had not been conscious of doing this, but on subsequent consultation of my records, I found that he was correct; on the three occasions when I had reviewed Arkham House books produced under his aegis, I had, in fact, offered uncomplimentary asides regarding the jacket copy. It is probably not my fault that Mr. Turner was the world's worst blurb-writer, but it was certainly insensitive of me to point it out repeatedly without even being aware of what I was doing, and I regret it, even while simultaneously feeling that there is something essentially absurd about my having given an ad-writer an acute sense of grievance by writing ads that referred to his ads in a less than complimentary fashion.

When I replied to Mr. Kessel's complaint, incidentally, I suggested that, as he had just been appointed book reviewer for *The Magazine of Fantasy & Science Fiction*, he could easily get his own back by reviewing one of my books in less than complimentary terms. He refused, thus tacitly admitting that any publicity is better than no publicity, and that even the most vicious review in the world (and there are three included here that are considerably nastier than my review of *Meeting in Infinity*) cannot possibly injure the sales of a book. Indeed, my hard-won knowledge of human perversity suggests that a venomous review might even help sales of a book, were it to appear in a place where anyone was actually likely to read it—a category that excludes, alas, such small-time publications as *The New York Review of Science Fiction, Interzone* and *Foundation*. Indeed, until I met Mr. Turner, I had been under the impression that no one actually read book reviews except the people whose books were being reviewed, and if our encounter served no other purpose, it reminded me that small-press publishers are likely to read them too, just in case anyone happens to mention their jacket copy.

While on this subject, it might be appropriate to reiterate the point made in the body of the review in question, that the most sustained demolition featured herein, of David Hartwell and Kathryn Cramer's *The Space Opera Renaissance*, was sent to me by one of the editors, in the full knowledge that I would dissent strongly from his thesis, who then proudly published it in his own magazine. As a man who knows the value of controversy, Mr. Hartwell was probably hopeful that it would stir up some debate—but that proved unduly optimistic, probvably because the only person who ever bothered to read my brilliant exposé of his faults and misunderstandings was him. I cannot suppose for a moment that he did so sympathetically, and cannot blame him for that.

On the other hand, I have heard from a third party—the publisher of this book, as it happens—that Tim Powers was quite fond of my review of *Earthquake Weather*, and I am glad to know that I have occasionally been capable of playing an angelic role as well as that of Devil's Advocate. It is, on the whole, probably the nobler of the two callings.

PART ONE

Reviews from *The New York Review of Science Fiction*

Cosm **by Gregory Benford, Avon, January 1998**
Rogue Star **by Michael Flynn, Tor, April 1998**

We read different kinds of texts in different ways, with different consequences. Texts that offer us serious food for thought require connoisseur reading according to the dictates of gourmet tastes; their produce requires careful digestion and makes a proteinaceous contribution to our intellectual nourishment. On the other hand, mere literary confections can be wolfed down as snacks for the sake of a momentary sweetness; they do not tax our mental digestive juices in the least and—always provided that we take regular mental exercise—we burn off their empty calories almost as soon as we have thrown away their gaudy wrappers.

The legacy of serious texts is built into the structures and sinews of our experience, while lightweight popular fiction is important to us only while we are immersed within the text. For this reason, it does not matter much how quickly lightweight fiction becomes dated, or even that it becomes dated at all. Nor does it matter overmuch whether lightweight fiction makes sense, or finds a good fit with the knowledge, sentiments and attitudes that are permanently accommodated within our experience. Lightweight science fiction, therefore, runs into few problems of reception on account of employing ideas that are out of date or flagrantly nonsensical. Serious science fiction, by contrast—science fiction that tries with all its might to produce visions of the future that are clear, coherent and convincing—delivers itself into a catch-22 situation by virtue of the fact that the imaginary futures with which it attempts to nourish connoisseur readers are bound to go out of date long before their intended effect is exhausted.

Whereas the most substantial fiction about the past has an inbuilt shelf-life of centuries, even the very best fiction about the near future will be shunted off into the mercurial mists of alternative history within five or ten years at the most. What a heroic quest it is, then, to embark upon the writing of an ultra-hard near-future-set science fiction novel! What special bravery it must require to undertake a future history series that will probably take longer to write than it will to go out of date! *Cosm* and *Rogue Star* are two of the finest products of contemporary hard science fiction, written by masters of the art at the very peak of their form, but what will become of them in ten years time, let alone a hundred? They will, of course, still offer to the most sensitive and best-educated palates a tantalizing recollection of the lost hopes and betrayed expectations of their own day, but no narrative can entirely resist depletion by that kind of marginalization. What justice is there in the perversity which rules that a book of this kind can only retain its timeliness to the extent that it over-reaches its grasp, dabbling in possibilities that will forever remain the rations of Tantalus?

Of the two books under consideration, *Cosm* is likely to enjoy a slightly longer shelf-life, unless cosmic irony really kicks into gear and produces an experimental result closely akin to the one described, whereby smashing uranium atoms together inside a Relativistic Heavy Iron Collider produces a mini Big Bang and a window into a virgin universe, which continues to expand into its own private space. Were that to happen in the real world, the evolution of the real cosm would quickly expose any flaws in Benford's account—but while the unrealized possibility lasts, his text will date only to the extent that its snapshot of the Byzantine workings of the contemporary scientific community loses its color and sharpness.

Rogue Star, by contrast, already has the termites of time gnawing away at its foundations, by virtue of being a sequel to *Firestar* (1996), which offered a fairly detailed account of historical exploits taking place on the world stage in the years 1999 and 2000. Assuming that there is at least one more volume yet to come (a fair guess, considering the number of issues left teasingly unsettled), the story will still be approaching its climax while real time is swallowing up its points of origin. Flynn's greatest strength as a writer of hard sf is his ability to characterize individuals operating within a hypothetical near-future context—the year 2009, in this instance—with minute exactitude. There is a peculiar tragedy in the fact that the first and foremost result of his brilliance is that he delivers exceptionally well-rounded hostages to fortune and the vagaries of ever-advancing history.

By comparison with the four viewpoint characters employed in *Rogue Star*, Gregory Benford's characterization of Alicia Butterworth, the sole viewpoint character of *Cosm*, seems a trifle garish, but there are precious few other sf novels which could be juxtaposed with it to similar effect. To some extent, at least, the heightened color is admirable ambition fringed with political correctness; although Alicia's position is not so very far removed from the one Benford actually occupies at the University of California, Irvine, her identity—as a single black female—is so far removed from his as to constitute a considerable challenge to the creative imagination. How she will seem to other single black females I cannot tell, but I was on her side from page one—which, considering that her behavior does raise some awkward ethical questions, turned out to be of some consequence with respect to the story's power to grip me. As with any top-flight hard sf story, however, even a reader who didn't like or believe in its heroine could probably take an absorbing interest in her achievement, given that it represents the ultimate wet dream of contemporary particle physics: not the acquisition of a Grand Unified Theory (which sensation would inevitably be more visceral than orgastic) but the chance to do cosmology in the lab.

Cosmology has, to date, been one of those awkward sciences whose theoretical edifice has to be built upon a single set of observations; we know of only one universe, and are limited to the observations we can make of it at this particular moment in time. Alicia's misfired experiment opens up the glorious possibility of manufacturing universes wholesale and observing the entire course of their lifetimes in a matter of weeks. The observations in question are, by necessity, a trifle impressionistic, but cosmologists are primarily interested in the Big Picture, and it only requires the production of two new cosms—the second being necessary to prove that the first one wasn't a fluke and that all cosms aren't exactly alike—to get the gist of the Biggest Picture of All: the one that explains how come our universe is so nice and dandy for folks like us. (Like most other cosmology-fixated sf novels of recent years, *Cosm* is prepared to assume that Brandon Carter's cosmic anthropic principle is not quite as trivial as it may seem.)

As with any novel that deals with the everyday lives of professional scientists, *Cosm* does have to work hard to maintain its pace. Having taken good care to mention all the tedious tasks that distract university teachers from the serious business of hard thinking, Benford is careful to send his story skipping like a stone across the surface of Alicia's quotidian existence. We catch only a single glimpse of her teaching, and the time that she spends actually taking readings from her observational apparatus are so ruthlessly crammed into the text-breaks that it sometimes seems that her poor research assistant Zak is doing all the work for none of the credit. Even when essentially tedious events have been ruthlessly omitted, that which remains is still so lacking in conventional melodrama that the author has to throw in an entirely gratuitous and utterly pointless attempted kidnapping, as well as arranging that the only thing the cosm actually does during the early stages of its development contrives to cause a fatality.

Given that Alicia is hounded so mercilessly by her rivals (who consider that she has stolen the cosm) and her own employers (who are determined that she will have to take all the blame for anything and everything) these further attempts to stoke up the narrative boiler may seem to some readers of *Cosm* to be a trifle over the top, but a novel that has no option but to include some ferocious theoretical disquisitions—complete with equations, graphs and diagrams—cannot be expected to take any chances. Benford has done this sort of thing before—most notably in *Timescape*, which many people (me included) consider to be his masterpiece—and he takes full advantage here of all his experience and native wit; *Cosm* may well displace *Timescape* in the affectionate regard of those readers who have long thought it unlikely to be bettered.

In *Rogue Star* Michael Flynn makes no such attempt to maintain the fever pitch of his narrative. Indeed, he is so utterly unconcerned with conventional melodrama that some readers might well find themselves wondering, half way through the book, whether anything is ever going to happen to any of his four main characters. However interested readers may be in the career of "Flaco" Mercado, who is ardently ambitious to support his new family by obtaining work as a fitter on the LEO space station, and no matter how fond they might become of the troubled poet and crusading environmentalist Roberta "Styx" Carson, they might well find their patience being tested by the time devoted to the trivial details of their day-to-day routines. Astronaut Forrest Calhoun, making rendezvous with a stray asteroid, spends most of his time thinking about what he and his companions are doing rather than actually doing it, and even Mariesa van Huyten—the prime mover in the political/industrial conspiracy that moves the levers of the plot—spares no effort in agonizing over her decisions.

Flynn revels in exactly the kind of low-gear narrative labor that Benford either avoids altogether or tries hard to step up to a higher pitch. This makes his work wonderfully convincing, but at the cost of being rather less captivating than it might be. Such a strategy is always a risk, and that risk is aggravated here by the fact that the story's real beginning was some 570 pages before the opening of chapter one of *Rogue Star*, and the corollary fact that we will have to read at least one more novel to find out why asteroids are being mysteriously realigned to take pot-shots at the Earth, and what defenses can be erected against the bombardment. By way of compensation, the reader does have a future-set narrative that is every bit as dense, complex and convincing as the most earnest and exact present-set narratives of recent provenance.

When the threats of death that are everpresent in *Rogue Star* finally turn into actual casualty figures, the damage is on a perfectly believable scale. When the corrosive psychological stresses and strains that incessantly grind away at the various characters finally generate actual breakages, the crack-ups in question are restrained by decency as well as common sense. Everything here is awkwardly and painfully normal, with the single exception of the mysteriously shifting asteroids and the hastily-obscured footprint left behind in the very distant past on the only one available for inspection. There is no cosm-substitute here: no wet dream for anyone, whether he (or she) be a particle physicist, an engineer or a hardened science fiction reader. That might not matter so much were the food for thought contained in the text guaranteed to last and linger, but even those who read it with the best will in the world must do so knowing that, by the time the year 2009 actually arrives, the whole narrative is likely to seem direly and dreadfully quaint.

The fact that these books will date so quickly will not, of course, render them unreadable or uninteresting, any more than the fact that 1984 was nothing like *Nineteen Eighty-Four* robbed George Orwell's nightmare of all its power and relevance. It does mean, however, that they will very soon require a hyperconscious kind of connoisseur reading and an oddly-contorted kind of imaginative appreciation. For a few fugitive years, however, they will retain an expectant vitality and challenging piquancy that no other kind of text can possibly offer. For a little while, they will feed their hungry readers images of an imminent future which are wholly compelling. Provided, therefore, that they are consumed while fresh, they will offer a gourmet experience which only produce of this kind can excite. Some might reckon it all the more valuable for being so valiantly evanescent—and so they should.

Deepdrive by Alexander Jablokov, Avon Eos; August 1998

When I reviewed Alexander Jablokov's *Carve the Sky* in these pages some years ago I began by pointing out that sf writers suffer more than writers in other genres from the problem of McGuffin inflation (although I used a different spelling of Hitchcock's neologism). The world in which our children's children will live out their lives will be very different from ours, and those desiderata that are sufficiently powerful to drive the plots of thrillers set in the present day—fortunes in gold bullion, the blueprints of secret weapons, and so on—may no longer be adequate to the task.

Carve the Sky solved this problem by invoking the most traditional of sciencefictional McGuffins, the myth of cosmic breakout, but Jablokov was compelled by the necessity to outdo its previous users to hype up the magnitude and existential significance of the breakout in question. Humankind having long since climbed out of Earth's gravity well, the next great hurdle to be overcome in furthering the destiny of the species in the world within that text was the development of a star-drive, and it was the search for that mislaid secret which motivated those characters who could not be content with lives devoted to mere art-work.

Some time afterwards, I had occasion to review, again in these same pages, Jablokov's short story collection *The Breath of Suspension*, which moved me to observe that the more serious works contained therein were inclined to "reflect upon....the question of what drives people to transform and transcend their limited circumstances". I also commented on the manner in which the tales in question "call attention to the significant role played in such achievements by stubbornly symbolic gestures" and "carry [an]....intimate and desolate sense of psychological imprisonment".

Jablokov's latest novel, *Deepdrive*, picks up all these threads and spins them out further. The McGuffin that levers the plot into hectic motion is the eponymous breakout technology, which is fundamentally similar to but markedly sexier than the star-drive in *Carve the Sky*. In the hope of getting one step nearer to that technology, Sophonisba Trost (Soph to her friends) joins a team of mercenaries in a desperate attempt to recover a renegade Vronnan named Ripi—supposedly the only member of his species in the solar system—from captivity on Venus.

One such expedition, led by the enigmatic and charismatic space-pirate Tiber, has already come unstuck, and when Soph's mission is chaotically aborted she has no alternative but to try to join forces with the stranded Tiber. While she moves toward that preliminary objective her fate becomes entangled with those of Ambryn Chretien, a haruspex who affects to obtain inspiration from alien entrails, and a professional enforcer named Elward Bakst. These three are forced into a temporary alliance, which eventually proves anything but temporary, as their long chase takes them to the Trojan asteroids via Mercury, the Moon, the space habitat Mesh-Matrix Krystal and various other dangerous locations. As the novel's climax approaches, they discover that the vessel which carried Ripi into the solar system was not, in fact, equipped with a deepdrive—but that the vessel that has brought avenging angels of his own species in hot pursuit most certainly is.

It is pointed out in the early stages of this plot that the significance of the deepdrive is by no means merely utilitarian. So many vividly exotic and profoundly enigmatic aliens have set up outposts in the solar system—most significantly the Gunners, the Bgarth and the Ulanyi—that many humans have begun to feel like remote South Sea islanders newly confronted with the knowledge that the ironclad ships continually passing by are part of a great civilization. Humans have become cargo cultists, and will remain that way unless and until they acquire the means to join the galactic game themselves. This confession helps to bring into clearer focus the fact that the true subject-matter of the novel is another kind of "deepdrive": the inner motivation that all sapient beings, human or alien, must possess in order to add ideative meaning to the Schopenhauerian will to survive.

Carve the Sky added a relatively straightforward early-Nietzschean gloss to Schopenhauer, equipping its human characters with a supplementary "will to power" whose proper exercise is in art-work rather than oppressive politics. *Deepdrive* is more adventurous, following Nietzsche in attempting to find a Dionysian solution to the existential predicament, which can accommodate and subsume, rather than merely opposing, the contrasted Apollinian approach. The reader learns more than the characters by virtue of obtaining far more information about Ripi's background: the peculiar biology of his species, the nature of his rebellion, and—most important of all—the intricate ecology that links his species very intimately to others, including those human beings who already constitute a facet of the greater galactic civilization. With this context available, the reader is able to see the actions, ambitions, lusts and obsessions of the main characters in a broader context than they are able to apply to themselves, thus gaining a far better appreciation than they ever do of the awkward quality of their psychological imprisonment and the symbolic significance of their stubborn but mostly futile gestures.

Jablokov has always tried to construct his plots so as to obtain the best of two literary worlds; he has written furiously-paced thrillers brimming over with exotic action, but he has always tried to skim that action over the surface of measurable philosophical depths. The plot of *Deepdrive* is driven at a faster pace than any of its predecessors, save for a few pauses for breath, but it also contrives to cut deeper and more vertiginously into the existential questions that support its plot. Although it is slightly rambling and suffers several abrupt changes of direction—tendencies that are neither unnatural not inapt in a work that covers so much territory—Jablokov's plot is as intelligent as it is colorful, and it is very colorful indeed. If Jablokov has never quite succeeded in bringing off this trick before—as, in my opinion, he never quite has—the practice he put in certainly did him a deal of good. It is by no means easy to equip a wild and gaudy space opera with real food for thought, and few writers have ever contrived to master the trick, so the achievement of *Deepdrive* is by no means small.

The Boss in the Wall: A Treatise on the House Devil, by Avram Davidson and Grania Davis (with introductions by Peter S. Beagle and Michael Swanwick). Tachyon, 1998

In the course of its long and distinguished career, *The Magazine of Fantasy & Science Fiction* has supplied a useful harbor to many a literary mariner adrift in a self-made craft so eccentrically exotic that it could not contrive to obtain regular berths in other ports. Avram Davidson, who made his debut in the magazine in 1954 with "My Boyfriend's Name is Jello", so obviously belonged nowhere else that he eventually served a term as its editor in 1962-64. He did launch a determined attempt to establish himself as a writer of conventional commercial fiction thereafter, but it fell apart soon enough. Between 1964 and 1966 he published seven sf novels—most notably *Masters of the Maze* and *Clash of the Star-Kings* (the latter retitled by Don Wollheim in a valiant but futile attempt to shunt it further downmarket)—and two pseudonymous detective novels, but he then reverted to more peculiar devices that were entirely and essentially his own.

Most of the long works Davidson published after despairing of his ability to adapt himself to popular tastes fell into a number of distinct series, each of which extended in a spirit of cavalier optimism with little sense of direction and no end in view. The Vergil

Magus series, the Peregrine Primus series, and the series begun with *The Island Under the Earth* all showed gaudy flashes of brilliance, but all of them became becalmed, left rudderless in some mysterious Sargasso of the Davidsonian imagination, where they were eventually given up for lost. Even his short fiction began to fall vaguely into step, much of it slotting into the potentially-infinite and unrepentantly various Dr. Esterhazy series. This seemingly-chronic inability to formulate clear aims or reach definite conclusions was not, alas, reflected in the author's life, which reached its inevitable terminus in 1993.

Among the works Davidson still reckoned to be in progress at that time, proliferating madly without any prospect of final shape or sensible closure, was a long novel based on a nightmarish dream of an unusual and distinctive apparition. In the hope of getting some medium-term reward out of the project, Michael Swanwick informs us, Davidson attempted to draw an encapsulated novella out of the mass, while his former wife and some-time collaborator Grania Davis attempted to design some kind of commercially- and aesthetically-viable frame into which the enterprise might ultimately be fitted. The eventual product of this labor, here made available for the literary connoisseur, is a version of Davidson's rough-hewn novella, carefully re-shaped to fit Davis's narrative frame.

The Boss in the Wall is, in essence, an academic fantasy somewhat reminiscent of Umberto Eco's *Foucault's Pendulum* and the more *recherché* works of R. A. Lafferty and James Blaylock. It describes the manner in which various scholars compete with paranoid fervent and collaborate with uneasy reluctance in tracking the distribution and progress of a peculiar item of American folklore. It appears that the notion in question originated with old soldiers who, obedient to the legend that insisted that they should never die, have elected instead to fade away to such thinness that they may hide in the margins between walls and wallpaper. From such refuges they occasionally emerge, via convenient cracks, to feed vampirically on those inhabitants of their dwellings who are ignorant of the elementary precautions required to keep them at bay. Because each inquisitive scholar jealously guards his intellectual territory, direly anxious to protect his opportunities for accredited discovery, Vlad Smith—the head of a family which actually encounters one of these demonic creatures—meets considerable resistance when he attempts to find out what precisely has happened to his beloved child and what might usefully be done about it.

Although Bella Smith's traumatic encounter is cleverly deployed as a narrative frame—providing the reader with a healthy charge of melodrama, an emotional hook and (eventually) the sense of an ending—the fascination of the novella lies in its multi-layered depiction of the communication, refraction and embellishment of the folktale. As in Eco's novel, the point is not so much to winkle out the truth underlying the myth as to marvel at the complex processes of myth-manufacture and myth-propagation. Due homage is paid to the irony of the fact that scrupulous attempts to investigate and demystify myths may actually serve to provide them with further cloaks of recomplication and further impetus to evolution.

This is, of course, a timely enterprise; the remaking of all manner of modern myths has recently gone into overdrive, shattering the sense-barrier and breaking through into a weird intellectual hyperspace where all conceivable conspiracies, cryptozoological specimens, angels, demons. *X-Files*, Millennial fantasies, popular delusions and ancient mysteries are wrapped up in a single multidimensional Gordian knot. The choice of *The Boss in the Wall* as the key description of the "paper men" is interesting, because it refers to one of the more obviously fictitious embellishments of the allegedly-actual phenomenon: a macabre moral fable about rebellious villagers who sealed their overlord within his protective tower, and would never have seen him again had he not grown so thin that he could extend his arms through the exceedingly thin window-slits to signal his desperation. This has no obvious relevance to the nature or behavior of the monsters in the story, but it can be construed as an allegory of the academic enterprise displayed in the plot, whereby the conscientious paranoia that attempts to exercise permanent control over oppressive knowledge inevitably leaves seams from which troublesome appearances will emerge.

The academic enterprise of the last two hundred years, which promised to banish superstition and put wisdom upon a secure footing, has had exactly this effect; those who have queued up to crush delusion have actually succeeded in making it more slippery. Come to think of it, that's what this kind of book review tends to do for this kind of book—all one really needs to say or know about *The Boss in the Wall* is that it is buoyantly witty, conscientiously odd, inventively bizarre, archetypal Avram Davidson. I hope it will prove to be the first of many posthumous works to slither through the cracks of his tomb.

Stardust by Neil Gaiman, Avon Spike, February 1999

The strident publicity material accompanying *Stardust* reveals that the *Dictionary of Literary Biography* places Neil Gaiman alongside Thomas Pynchon and William Burroughs as one of the "Top Ten Post Modern Writers in America". In Britain, of course—where Gaiman actually hails from—we do not have any "Post Modern" writers. I am not even certain that we have any Modern ones yet, unless nineteenth century standards of modernity are still in force hereabouts, but I know that, if we did, they would not be writing books like *Stardust*, which sets out carefully and conscientiously to be mock-archaic.

The acknowledgements appended to the text of *Stardust* express an "enormous debt" to four writers who "show[ed the author] that fairy stories were for adults too". Two of them are only marginally relevant to the present text (James Branch Cabell, who wrote no fairy stories, and C. S. Lewis, who wrote none for adults) but the other two—Hope Mirrlees and Lord Dunsany—are much more obviously influential. The plot of *Stardust* is loosely modeled on that of Mirrlees' *Lud-in-the-Mist* (1926), while several of its story-elements are echoes of the Dunsany classics *The King of Elfland's Daughter* (1924) and *The Charwoman's Shadow* (1926). Although Gaiman presumably encountered these works in modern paperback reprintings (they were all re-released in the Ballantine "Adult Fantasy" series while Gaiman was a boy) their original editions were products of a brief boom in "modern" English fairy tales for adults, whose other key works include Gerald Bullett's *Mr Godly Beside Himself* (1924) and Margaret Irwin's *These Mortals* (1925).

Although it is difficult now to ascertain the extent to which the authors of these works influenced one another, we can be reasonably sure that the existence of the earlier volumes helped to persuade the publishers of the later ones that adult fairy tales might be marketable—an opinion that they soon recanted, re-establishing for the next half-century the conventional wisdom that such stuff as dreams are made on is strictly for kids. Oddly enough, although the success of the early paperback editions of *The Lord of the Rings* weakened that assumption for a while, their eventual effect was to institute a new kind of fundamentalism (especially evident in the narrow and bigoted backwater that is UK publishing, where all genre editors are nowadays weighted down by the authority of stone tablets hewn by that uniquely Modern incarnation of God, the Sales Department) whose central dogma is that the only True Fantasy is the logorrhoeic

Holy Trinity. One presumes that Gaiman was encouraged into his heresy by the example of the excellent series of anthologies of contemporary fairy tales edited by Ellen Datlow and Terri Windling, and that access to the precious pulpit of publicity was conceded because his last book—the novelization of the TV series *Neverwhere*—became (again I quote the publicity material) "*the*...underground bestseller of 1997".

As a lifelong fan of heresy I naturally approve wholeheartedly of the fact that *Stardust* has been published and enthusiastically promoted, and I hope that the heresy in question spreads like wildfire, at least until it begins to hypostasize as a new item of received wisdom. There must be a slim chance of this happening, because *Stardust* is very well-written, reasonably heartfelt and absolutely inoffensive.

The story begins in a mid-nineteenth-century English village named Wall, so-called because of the closely-guarded wall which separates it from the lands of Faerie. Once in every nine years the fairy folk bring a fair to the meadow beyond the wall so that a certain limited trade can take place between the world of the imagination and the World As It Is. Given the way things are in the world of the imagination it would hardly be surprising if there were a considerable traffic in genes, but fairy stories tend to be a bit coy about that sort of thing, so the hero born of miscegenation, Tristran Thorn, is represented within the plot as a rare freak of circumstance.

Raised in Wall until he is in his eighteenth year, Tristran naturally takes the opportunity offered by the fair's return to go into Faerie in search of a fallen star, which the girl with whom he is infatuated has demanded as a token of his love. The star in question turns out to be a lovely girl, who has been knocked off her heavenly perch by a well-aimed shot of which various others are in quest, and her heart is a precious resource to those equipped with magic that can derive immortality from its consumption. For these reasons, Tristran is by no means alone in wanting to locate his prize, and once he has found her he has a tough time holding on to her—but in the end, the two of them guide one another to a better destiny than they could ever have attained on the quotidian side of the wall. The inhabitants of Wall, meanwhile, remain conspicuously unenriched by the whole endeavor.

It is perhaps unsurprising that a writer who made his reputation scripting comics (and is undoubtedly one of the finest modern writers for that medium) should come down so heavily in favor of the world beyond the wall, but it is worth noting that none of the four writers he cites as cardinal influences—and very few others who worked similar ground—felt able to be so uncompromising. Mirrlees, like Bullett, was attempting tentatively to regenerate an allegedly-lost détente between the World As It Is and the world of the imagination. What her questing humans learn in Faerie would have been a poor reward had something of its wealth not filtered back downstream to the Mist-beleaguered sons of Lud. The whole point of Dunsany's romances in this vein is that the real and the ideal are frankly contradictory, but that no matter how much work must be done before they may be sensibly amalgamated, their resolution is highly desirable. Of the main contributors to the 1920s boom, only Margaret Irwin—who operated her allegory in reverse, bringing her questing heroine out of Faerie into an analogue of the World As It Is—concluded her novel (it was her first) with an uncompromising retreat from sick reality, but she had already publicly recanted that conclusion in *Still She Wished for Company* (1924)—which was written after *These Mortals*—and never wrote another book-length fantasy. C. S. Lewis required seven volumes, an imaginatively-crippling religious conversion and a determined retreat into crabby old age before he could bring the Narnia series to a similar conclusion.

It is significant, of course, that Gaiman anchors his Faerie lands to the 1840s rather than the 1990s, or even the 1920s. This moves his story back to an innocent time before the "modern" British fairy tale had been pioneered by George MacDonald—who also embraced, however reluctantly, a keen awareness of the fact that if Faerie has lessons to teach, it was in the World As It Is that they will have to be applied. The careful disconnection of Gaiman's story not merely from its own era but from the entire lifespan of the "modern" British fairy tale is a tacit confession of the fact that this is purely an exercise in literary pastiche, devoid of any claim to contemporary relevance.

That was not the case with the works produced in the 1920s boom, which owed their inspiration to a particular moment in British history: the end of the Great War—which, because it had been a greater carnival of destruction than its promoters had been able to imagine, contrived as its aftermath the most ruthless exercise in Disenchantment ever to sweep up a nation. (Anyone who doubts this interpretation need only consult the first-published of these imaginative exercises, Stella Benson's *Living Alone*, 1919, which clearly maps the source of the relevant creative wellspring.) For this reason, no matter how well-executed *Stardust* is, it is a work without a shadow, whose heart beats less purposefully than it might, and which is, at the end of the day, only one order of magnitude better than the spiritless and sapless soap-operatic "epic fantasies" that will presumably surround it on the bookshop shelves. We may hope, however, that it might turn out to be merely the gentle *avant garde* of a bolder and bloodier-minded legion.

Northern Stars edited by David G. Hartwell & Glenn Grant, Tor, August 1998

Many years ago there was a brief fad in Britain for wearing T-shirts bearing the legend ACAB, which was so widely understood to stand for "All Coppers Are Bastards" that one unlucky youth on a picket line was actually charged with incitement to riot by virtue of the fact that he was displaying one in a provocative manner. Unfortunately for him, he chose to defend himself by stating that he had always understood the acronym to stand for "All Canadians Are Bastards", a contention so manifestly unbelievable that he was promptly found guilty. It remains true even to this day that the only safe response that an individual caught in possession of a transatlantic accent in the rougher kind of English pub can make to the question "Oi—you American?" is "No, Canadian." I have no idea why this is, but the knowledge could not help but color the temper in which I approached this anthology, expecting to encounter suave urbanity, deft wit, thoughtful intelligence and a modest touch of class. I am happy to report that its contents did not dispel my illusions, even though there is an understandable (but mercifully slight) hint of brashness about those contributions supplied by Americans in exile.

Unlike Britain and Australia, which are divided from the Americas by wide oceans, or Mexico, which, although joined to its huge neighbor by an extremely long border, is distanced by a comprehensive language barrier, Canada's relationship with the USA is interestingly complicated by its own internal divisions. No Canadian resident with one eye on the future and the other on the 49th parallel can entirely ignore the fact that he or she is living in a nation that might soon be fractured sideways as its French speakers make a bid for political and cultural independence. Nor can any be unaffected by disputes as to whether division would be progressive or retrogressive, or whether the price of compromise might be exacted by the march of history even from those reluctant to pay it. Perhaps inevitably, such concerns shadow the greater number of the stories in this collection, although it is arguable that the more interesting among them are those which remove the politics of necessary division and awkward alliance to wholly hypothetical situations. (On the other hand, the temptation to fillet the stories in the service of an obsessive hunt for "Canadian-ness" might be a mere foxfire; after all, the pragmatist philosopher John Dewey has argued that the root of all aesthetic experience is the observation and analysis of processes of combination, breakage and recombination.)

In "A Niche" by Peter Watts, a two-person team of divers under extreme stress is rudely sundered, the better-adapted of the two being re-equipped with the survivor of another broken couple. In "Mother Lode" by Phyllis Gottlieb, a catalyst sent to heal the breach between a team of humans and their alien host actually hastens the breakdown of the relationship before diagnosing the cause of the trouble. In "Home by the Sea" by Elisabeth Vonarburg, an unusual daughter goes in search of her estranged mother, woefully uncertain as to what kind of relationship can and might be rebuilt between them. In "Under Another Moon" by Dave Duncan, a petty warlord who has succeeded so well in the service of the realm as to have become an apparent threat must figure out how to save his family and fief from unjust eradication. In "Remember, the Dead Say" by Jean-Louis Trudel, Quebecois separatists must pay the price of unsuccessful rebellion. And so on (these are the first five stories in the collection and the list might become tedious were I to extend it to cover all twenty-eight).

Fast-forwarding, therefore, my personal favorites in the collection are: "The Loneliness of the Long Distance Writer" by Lesley Choyce, a buoyantly satirical description of the post-literate era; "Ballads in 3/4 Time" by Robert Charles Wilson, which, although not translated from the French, firmly presses home the moral that *plus ça change, plus c'est la même chose*; and Candas Jane Dorsey's "(Learning About) Machine Sex", whose unadulterated misanthropy is magnificently splenetic. I did not much like the stories by Andrew Weiner and Robert J. Sawyer, one of which seemed to me to be utterly feeble and the other overly contrived, but *chacun à son goût*. The majority of those items translated from the French display the virtue of manifest strangeness, which is not to be underestimated in a science fiction showcase; I would not have been averse, bearing that in mind, to find a contribution by the great Canadian sf pioneer A. E. van Vogt, even though that would have required excavating somewhat deeper than the 1973 date of the Gottlieb story (apart from which the earliest are both from 1983—the collection, incidentally, dates from 1994, this being a slightly belated trade paperback reissue). Canada's second-most-famous sf-communitarian-in-exile, John Clute, is also unincluded, though not entirely uncited.

Canadian sf is now well-established as an artistic niche, if not a viable marketplace. It has its own awards and its leading English-language small press magazine, *On Spec*, has shown steady improvement throughout its lifetime. (I am, alas, not qualified to comment on the progress of its French equivalent.) Whether the colonizers of the niche will continue to thrive will inevitably depend on the sweeping changes which seem likely to overtake the entire literary ecosphere, which will be too disruptive to permit easy anticipation of their side-effects. Like Canada itself, whose natural wealth has long been blighted by an unreasonably ferocious climate, Canadian sf writers will presumably continue to suffer an economic chill far worse than that affecting their southern neighbors and distant cousins, but they might conceivably be so hardened by adversity that a greater proportion of their population will contrive to preserve a certain literary and futurological integrity against the ravages and temptations of apocalyptic despair.

Stinger by Nancy Kress, Forge, October 1998

Stinger is advertised on the front flap as a "biomedical thriller", which description places it within the same literary subspecies as most of Robin Cook's novels and some of Michael Crichton's (the species of which it is a subdivision being the "technothriller" sector of the thriller genre). The fact that technothrillers are defined by their use of innovative technological motifs brings them close to the edge of the science fiction genre, overlapping the activities of sf writers who borrow elements of the narrative structure of the thriller in order to capitalize on the dramatic suspense innate within the relevant generic formula.

The thriller formula is not very far removed from the standard "law enforcement" formula that dominates the various kinds of crime fiction and the various kinds of TV series drama. It requires that the plot's central motif—a technological innovation in the technothriller variant—should be presented to the virtuous characters as a puzzle and a threat. Although the heroes of thrillers are often policemen, secret agents or civil servants, the conventional thinking of contemporary plot-strategy frequently place them in the junior ranks of the relevant hierarchies. This facilitates a "double jeopardy" tactic whereby their attempts to meet the challenges presented to them can be frustrated or blocked by their superiors, often to the extent that they suffer exclusion and isolation. In many modern thrillers, therefore, the bureaucratic apparatus of supposedly-virtuous organizations is mobilized against their own heroic operatives, thus amplifying the insidiousness and apparent irresistibility of the threats that provide the suspense element of the plot. The thriller formula demands, however, that the puzzle must eventually be solved, the threat neutralized and the challenge overcome; normalizing endings are compulsory.

The application of this formula to hypothetical technologies requires that the relevant innovations should serve a sinister function within the story. They have to be deployed as instruments of menace, and in the conclusion of each story they must be carefully tidied away. Although some popular writers within the genre (*e.g.* Michael Crichton) really do seem to think that all technology is inherently sinister and that most scientists are dangerous morons who neither know nor care what they do, those with more than half a brain recognize that, because knowledge itself is morally neutral, the invocation as a plot device of technologies designed to serve malign ends requires the further invention of malign manufacturers, who must serve as the overt or covert villains of the piece.

In the first phase of the technothriller's evolution—which extended from the espionage and world-blackmail stories of the 1920s to the 1970s—international politics laid on a ready supply of villains for English-language writers. Throughout this period there were incipiently hostile nations with evident technological clout, and anxieties about the implicit xenophobia of the genre were relatively muted. Writers who felt that Germans and Russians were inherently dull could always invent international crime syndicates to serve in their stead. For good or ill, the entire mythos of that kind of thriller fiction died with the end of the Cold War—by which time organizations like SMERSH and SPECTRE had been retired to comic books, where they had always belonged.

Modern thriller-writers have to work much harder to find serviceable villains than their forebears, and technothriller writers have to work even harder than the rest. The evident technical superiority of the USA, coupled with the awesome success of cultural coca-colonization, has forced the American thriller writer in search of suitable villains to look much closer to home. Unfortunately, making villains of the CIA, Big Business and insurance companies tends to impart a political spin to thrillers, which can easily prejudice popularity, and hence profitability. The result of this uneasy situation is that the notion of a "Secret Government", operating independently of formal democratic, corporate and military structures, has inevitably been elevated, if only for a while, to the status of Champion Cliché, maintaining a comfortable lead over the silver medal-winning Psycho Terrorist-cum-Mad Genius. (The fact that the bronze medal position is still securely held by the Nazis is ample testimony to the poverty of real competition.) Any writer wishing to avoid or ameliorate these clichés has his or her work cut out.

Stinger tells the story of an outbreak of a genetic engineered version of the malarial parasite in the southern states of the USA. Unlike the natural version, which cannot invade "sickled" blood cells—an incapacity that gave individuals heterozygous for the sickle-cell genre a selective advantage in malaria-infested countries for thousands of years—the engineered *Plasmodium* actually selects out sickled cells for attack, and does so with such alacrity as to produce stroke-inducing clots. The story's two protagonists are minor operatives in the FBI and the World Health Organisation, both of whom are turfed out of the official investigation because they will not meet the standards of diplomacy required by their careful superiors—standards made ticklish by the fact that the vast majority of American residents carrying the sickle-cell gene are of African descent, most of the remainder being from the Indian subcontinent.

The trail followed by these two renegade investigators, as they doggedly pursue the evidence of the aborted plague's origins that their superiors seem determined to discount, leads them inexorably towards Fort Detrick and the CIA, although the WHO also seems to be implicated. This process might have been a little more suspenseful and disquieting had the reader not been afforded—by courtesy of the initial "teaser" chapter with which all thrillers nowadays come equipped—the privilege of knowing that the initial release of infected mosquitoes in Maryland was accidental, and cannot therefore be a calculated attempt at what is nowadays called "ethnic cleansing" (although Kress refuses to use that particular euphemism, presumably on the grounds that it is disgustingly hypocritical). In consequence, the "surprise" that reveals the actual guilty party inevitably falls a bit flat.

If it is considered as a whole, the technothriller subgenre cannot help but give the impression that all technological innovations are bad, if only because most of the people interested in their deployment are malevolent. It nourishes and sustains the paranoid delusion that the world is chock-full of conscienceless scientists engaged in the manufacture of malevolent technology on behalf of evil masters. The problem for technothriller writers who want to retain some semblance of political sanity, faith in the possibility of progress and narrative plausibility is that this tacit technophobia makes it terribly difficult to discover an adequate lever with which to move a plot and provide it with a satisfactory conclusion. Kress does try, but cannot succeed.

It would be unfair to give away the crucial plot-twist of *Stinger*, even though it is a mere face-saving device rather than an authentically ingenious solution to the hypothetical mystery, but I have to admit that I thought it frankly preposterous as well as inept. Perhaps this is an unimportant criticism, given that I have never read a technothriller whose ultimate revelation seemed anything but preposterous and inept, but I shall cling stubbornly to my conviction that this sort of fault is worth mentioning, even if it has no apparent effect on the enjoyment that readers who like this sort of thing obtain from it. To complain that, in spite of its attempts to put on a dutiful show of political correctness, the implicit technophobia of the subgenre is here supplemented, just as it is in most other examples, by a tacit xenophobia, would probably be equally redundant—after all, nine out of every ten movies in this subgenre are carefully equipped with villains played by European actors, in order to avoid blackening the image and reputation of American ham.

If science fiction has any merits as a genre (*i.e.*, over and above idiosyncratic literary merits which individual examples might display) they must surely include the fact that science fiction, seen as a collective entity, cannot help but insist that the future is a limitless spectrum of competing possibilities, whose Utopian potential must at least take account of technological progress, and might in fact be entirely dependent on technological progress. Science fiction that serves the cause of the genre as a whole is fundamentally technophilic and xenophilic even when it is cautionary or alarmist, and that fundamental technophilia and xenophilia is the genre's main claim to social usefulness. If, however, recent patterns in British publishing are to be duplicated in America the cause in question may well be on the brink of being lost, and it may well be that those sf writers who feel that they must live (an imperative that Voltaire would not necessarily have recognized) might be wise to take up writing technothrillers instead. They may do so in the secure confidence that no red-blooded, red-necked and red-hating American would ever dream of accusing them of intellectual treason.

As Nancy Kress and everyone else in the world knows perfectly well, mosquitoes are not equipped with stings—but if a title sounds okay, who the hell cares what's true and what's not?

***Starfarers* by Poul Anderson, Tor, November 1998**
***Operation Luna* by Poul Anderson, Tor, August 1999**

The French sociologist of literature Robert Escarpit once published two graphs showing the ages at which famous writers had written the books hailed by critics as their best work. There had to be two because the curve of dead writers looked quite different from the curve of living writers. The former was very nearly a "normal" curve (i.e. a bell curve) whose mode, median and mean were all very close to 40; the latter peaked in the same place but then trailed off far more slowly, shifting the median and the mean fiftywards. Escarpit's explanation for this phenomenon was that critics always tend to be a lot kinder to writers who are still alive and kicking, politely waiting until they are dead before relegating the work they produced in their dotage to negligibility.

We have seen this phenomenon at work in the sf field in recent years, in the interminably tedious but sometimes stoutly-defended late works of such one-time paragons of virtue as Robert Heinlein and Isaac Asimov, but we have also seen some quite remarkable—and quite unprecedented—examples of authentically-sustained creativity. One (the amazing Jack Williamson is the most obvious) might have been written off as a statistical freak, but enough examples are now accumulating to make one suspect that the habit of sciencefictional speculation, if acquired sufficiently early and applied with sufficient assiduity, might well help to maintain mental and artistic flexibility. Poul Anderson is now in his seventies, but his ability as a writer—and, more significantly, his enterprise—has not so far shown the slightest sign of diminution.

Starfarers is one of the best hard sf novels written in recent years, and *Operation Luna* is a fine example of the logically-fortified kind of fantasy that was pioneered in *Unknown* while John Campbell was also busy laying the foundations of modern magazine sf. Both novels carry forward themes and ideas with which Anderson has been occupied for decades, but they do carry them forward, confidently, cleverly and skillfully. People like me, who have been reading Poul Anderson since we were thirteen (nearly forty years in my case) will probably have favorites that made a deep impression while our own minds were not yet case-hardened, but no matter how fondly we remember "We Have Fed Our Sea" (1958; aka *The Enemy Stars* 1959) or "Operation Afreet" (1956) and its sequels, we could not plausibly argue that *Starfarers* or *Operation Luna* are in any way inferior—and might, indeed, be forced to concede the opposite. We NYRSF diehards should all be delighted by this discovery, because it offers us the hope that if we can only stick to our speculative guns, we too might still be firing with this degree of accuracy and penetration when we are in our seventies, our eighties and....well, who knows how many more books the Williamsons and

Andersons will produce before they finally declare the record well and truly set?

Chapter XXI of *Starfarers* first saw the light as "Ghetto" in 1954: a brief idea-as-hero story in which the "kith"—starfarers whose lives are extended relative to those of Earth-dwellers by virtue of Einsteinian time-dilatation—find themselves becoming progressively more alienated from the settled cultures of their native planet. The idea was to crop up several times more in Anderson's continuing work, but it remained marginal while he was prepared to assume, as most of his contemporaries did, that there might be a way around the constrictions of relativity, whose employment would permit the development of a galaxy-wide civilization. Much of his endeavor from the '50s to the '70s was devoted to the extrapolation of a loosely-knit future history that included Nicholas van Rijn's Polesotechnic League and Dominic Flandry's Terran Empire. Times have now moved on, though, and sf writers have become increasingly preoccupied by the so-called Fermi paradox ("If we are not alone, where the hell are they?"). *Starfarers* attempts to resolve this problem by suggesting that cultures which take up starfaring usually do so for a relatively sort span of time, because their "kith" gradually but inexorably lose the support of their increasingly distant worldbound kin.

The story told by *Starfarers* is mostly that of the starship *Envoy*, dispatched on a sixty-thousand-light-year journey to make contact with the only other starfaring culture to have been glimpsed by the radio telescopes of Earth's slowly-growing interstellar culture. Although *Envoy* can make the journey in a few years, the effects of time-dilatation are such that more than a hundred thousand years will pass on Earth before she can return—enough to ensure that the crew will be comprehensively distanced even from the kith whose voyages are much more limited. To complicate matters further, they discover on their outward voyage that the culture they are going to meet will have given up starfaring by the time they actually make contact. *Envoy*'s eventual arrival causes awkward tensions to develop in the post-starfaring culture, which are reflected in the diverging priorities of her own crew members. The contact is difficult, but it produces a great deal of new knowledge and an unexpected opportunity to make further discoveries by investigating a black hole. (It is here that the plot begins to echo and reassess the concerns of "We Have Fed Our Sea", which has always seemed to me to be the most heartfelt as well as the most effective of Anderson's early novels.)

Like all the most grandiose endeavors in hard science fiction, *Starfarers* has little in the way of a plot and might perhaps be a better book, from a purely aesthetic point of view, if it had even less, but Anderson has always been conscious of the fact that—as he once put it—all genre writers are competing for people's beer-money. There is, therefore, a token madman's mutiny to get through before the story returns to its philosophical subject-matter: the implications of the discovery, as *Envoy* finally heads home, that humans too have passed through their starfaring phase, and are likely to greet the returning ship with even less enthusiasm than the aliens (who had the useful option of refusing to recognize the visitors as any kith or kin of theirs).

Starfarers is as seriously-intended as it is earnest, and there is much in it that is worth taking seriously. It attempts to provide us with an up-to-date image of the cosmos in which we exist, and an accurate assessment of our place therein, and it deserves every respect for the honesty of that endeavor. *Operation Luna* is, by contrast, written for fun. In place of the cosmos we have discovered it presents an alternative world in which all the ancient mythologies of Earth have been redeemed and re-energized, carefully relocated within a metaphysical framework that forces them into consistency. The roots of this novel also extend back to the 1950s, to "Operation Afreet" (1956), "Operation Salamander" (1957) and "Operation Incubus" (1959)—which became the elements of the mosaic novel *Operation Chaos* (1971). Like the serial version of Anderson's other novel in the *Unknown* vein, *Three Hearts and Three Lions* (1953; in book form 1961), and, for that matter, "Ghetto", these tales appeared in *The Magazine of Fantasy & Science Fiction*, but they are similar in spirit to Randall Garrett's Lord Darcy series (which ran in *Analog*) in that they bring magic under the umbrella of science, as a series of law-governed phenomena, which—when properly understood—can give rise to continuous technological innovation.

Although *Starfarers* is about space travel, it is tonally and thematically redolent with the deep sense of hope betrayed that has affected many sf writers since the actual space program stalled. *Operation Luna* is set in a world that has still to initiate its space program, and the story begins with the sabotage of the alternative world's equivalent of an Apollo launch. It quickly becomes obvious that there are forces at work that will stop at nothing to prevent the dawn of the Space Age, and that their efforts involve the most awful conspiracy ever imagined—not, as briefly seems to be the case, between the scum of demonkind and the evil Oriental mastermind Fu Ch'ing, but between the scum of demonkind and the IRS (which stands, in this world, for something subtly different, but is essentially the same institution all that Americans in every imaginable world must love to hate).

The extrapolation of the imaginary world of *Operation Luna* is entirely playful, never more earnest than the requirements of good melodrama demand, but the whole point of the game is to imagine a world where all the hopes that were once incarnate in 1950s future histories like Anderson's are still alive. There is a brazen absurdity about the broomstick-ride into outer space that ultimately has to be taken by the eldest child of the hero and heroine, but there is an element of unashamed fever in its absurdity that makes it authentically heroic and affectively powerful. Although *Operation Luna* is a fantasy novel it is far closer kith, if not actually kin, to *Starfarers* than may appear to be the case to readers who do not bother to read both. Most fantasy novels are content to be straitjacketed by their fundamental assumption that magic works, bound by that limitation to suppose that evil demons are the worst thing imaginable. *Operation Chaos* accepts the necessity of accommodating vicious demons—and a literal Hell—but the underlying import of its story, especially when juxtaposed with that of *Starfarers*, is that the world would be a much more hospitable place than it actually is if all we had to overcome were demons. The indifference of the actual cosmos is, in the final analysis, far more ominous than any amount of imagined malevolence.

At the climax of *Operation Chaos*, as at the climax of any fantasy novel, there is a battle in which the forces of good line up against the forces of evil. They win, as they always do (that is what fiction means, as Miss Prism pointed out) but the result matters less than the taking part. In the world of *Operation Luna*, unlike ours, everyone really can do his or her bit for the Great Cause. The battle in *Starfarers* is only there as a sop to readers who wouldn't feel that they'd got their beer-money's worth if there wasn't one, and it cannot possibly provide a climax because it cannot be a battle between good and evil. The best that can be laid on in a serious novel of any kind is a tiff between reasonableness and unreasonableness (*aka* madness), and such squabbles can only provide a series of inconsequential preludes to the climactic confrontation between human ambition and cosmic implacability—a confrontation that cannot be won, even in meaningful fiction, but which nevertheless demands a unique kind of heroism from its exemplary representatives of humanity.

It is presumably because the climax of *Starfarers* demands this much more challenging and much more difficult kind of heroism that Anderson felt the need to follow it up with the easy-going *Operation Luna*, and it is because *Operation Luna* is not a flight from the reason and commitment of *Starfarers*, but merely an interval of rest and recuperation, that I have every confidence that Anderson will be able to follow it up with something equally admirable, equally forward-looking, and well worth taking seriously.

Foreign Bodies by Stephen Dedman, Tor, December 1999

I have been a lifelong consumer of good advice on the hows and wherefores of science fiction writing, and have always tried to maintain a sharp theoretical awareness of the relevance of items of practical advice to the peculiar aesthetics of science fiction. One such hazard of prescription that has stuck in my mind for twenty years, maintaining a quiet everpresence when I write, is a brace of deceptively simple observations by Samuel R. Delany. I can no longer remember their exact source, and might therefore be misquoting ever so slightly, but if memory serves me right he inserted into a series of partly-disjointed notes the dictum that "Everything in a science fiction story should be mentioned twice", supplemented a few pages later by the necessary modifier: "Everything in a science fiction story should be mentioned twice, except perhaps science fiction".

Because I am addressing myself to an audience of sophisticated professionals I need not go into elaborate detail here as to the many and subtle reasons why everything in a science fiction story needs to be mentioned twice, but I hope I might be forgiven for giving some additional attention to the possible exception. There, I fear, lurks an awkward trap into which even the wary sometimes fall.

On page 16 of Stephen Dedman's *Foreign Bodies* a character who subsequently turns out to be a stranded time traveler interrogates the hero as to the contemporary limits attained by science fiction stories about time travel. Having been assured that some basic variants are so hoary that they have even been used in *Star Trek*, the hapless castaway is put off a few subtler twists by the citation of precedents by Isaac Asimov and Arthur C. Clarke. Only then is she/he able to settle on the particular version of her/his own experience that will earn her/him the cash necessary to build the gizmo that will allow her/him to switch bodies with the hero (who thus, of course, becomes the hero/heroine). Nor is this the last time that the hero/heroine, when faced with a tough decision or the need to improvise, remembers science fiction stories he/she has loved or hated. It does not take much imagination to picture the author doing exactly the same thing as he tried to massage his plot along—and one of the reasons why repeatedly mentioning science fiction in a science fiction story is not a good idea is that such reflexive backward steps are not conducive to immersion in the narrative.

There is a sense, of course, in which Dedman is merely being realistic. If I were ever unfortunate enough to be bounced out of my body and into somebody else's by a stranded time-traveler desperate to trade up (fat chance!) I would doubtless find it impossibly difficult to avoid likening my predicament to that of characters in sf stories I had read and loved, and that legacy of imaginative experience would probably be my primary resource in trying to figure out how to cope with my predicament. Then again, any writer setting out to write a time travel story in this day and age is well advised to be careful not to merely to duplicate in his/her plot twists any spiffing wheezes that have already been milked for all they were worth by the likes of Isaac Asimov and Arthur C. Clarke. Alas, a science fiction story as heavily laden with overt and covert references to other science fiction stories and the sciencefictional enterprise in general is bound to call attention not merely to its own artifice but to its unfortunate circumscription by a historically-limited set of alternatives. However paradoxical it may seem, those time paradox stories which work best are probably those which are set, at least tacitly—for how could it be explicit?—in worlds devoid of time paradox stories.

Although Stephen Dedman is an Australian, he is sufficiently familiar with the narrow world of science fiction to know that the only market that offers any significant commercial rewards is the USA, most of whose citizens have never even contemplated applying for a passport. *Foreign Bodies* is, therefore, set in a near-future USA. In the world of the story, technological progress has succeeded in eliminating much of the social progress for which it was formerly responsible. As anticipated in Ignatius Donnelly's celebrated ideological reply to Edward Bellamy, *Caesar's Column*, contrary to the appearances of 1887—or, as things actually turned out, 1987—the eventual outcome of science guided by Capitalism has been the creation of a world in which the gap between the technology-rich and the technology-poor is widening rapidly, leading inexorably (unless heroic measures can be taken) to a situation in which the technologically-poor will have no alternative but to revolt, and be slaughtered in vast numbers by the technology-rich.

Having invented time travel, the people of the civilization that has emerged, *Iron Heel*-style, from the aftermath of the unsuccessful revolution, have naturally given some thought as to the kind of heroic measures that might, had they been taken, have produced a more Bellamyesque timeline. As good post-modern time travelers, they are not much given to reading Ignatius Donnelly or Jack London, and they are certainly no fans of Robert A. Heinlein or *The Turner Diaries*, but passing familiarity with the latter examples at least allows them to work out who their worst enemies are. The shape of their hypothetical crusade is thus beset by luscious temptation. All they have to do, they figure, is gather all the fascist bastards in America in one place, at a mutually convenient time, and blow the lot of them to smithereens. It is a solution of which L. Ron Hubbard might have been proud, had he not had other orgs to save from squirreling.

This cabalistic plot does not, of course, run smoothly, as evidenced by the fact that the unlucky castaway has to resort to such extremes of logic-twisting to produce a sciencefictional plot that almost looks, but for a moment's thought, as if it might actually make a convoluted sort of sense. Those readers who have already been moved to take a backward step, however, so as to look at the text as an artifact, will already have engaged the awareness that the art and craft of literary plotting is mostly a matter of establishing obstacle-courses that make it damnably difficult for heroes/heroines and other cabalistic plotters to get from square one to the big climactic bang, so they are likely to be less surprised by the fact that things continually go wrong as they might have been had they been more securely gripped. And once having been forced to adopt that kind of binocular vision, they are far less likely to be persuaded that the higgledy-piggledy mess that is eventually presented to them as an ordnance survey map of the sense that the plot is supposed to make, when all its implausibilities and paradoxes have been ironed out, is anything other than the higgledy-piggledy mess it looks like and actually is.

Which is a pity, in a way, because Stephen Dedman really does work bloody hard to keep his story whizzing along, with fashionably noirish slickness and style and a generous seasoning of right-on sexual politics. He is, as the supplementary advertising suggests, a writer "capable of depth as well as engaging entertainment"; unfortunately, his attempts to do justice to both aims have landed him in the kind of abyssal blur that always tends to lurk between two stools.

Delany's dictum about not mentioning science fiction twice does not, of course, apply to reviews as well as to stories. Quite the reverse, in fact.

Rings by Charles L. Harness, NESFA Press, 1999

NESFA Press is one of the most prolific and most enterprising of the current generation of small presses specializing in science fiction. Such presses have made a highly significant contribution to science fiction publishing since the pioneering days of Gnome Press, Fantasy Press and the ill-fated Shasta, and their importance is increasing again as mass market publishers concentrate their efforts on the relatively narrow bands of the vast spectrum of imaginative fiction that reliably generate massive sales. Science fiction has always been a broad church—far broader, virtually by definition, than any other popular genre—and it will always play host to a considerable range of esoteric literary sects. One of the reasons why science fiction magazines have stubbornly resisted the ill wind that has virtually scoured the planet clean of fiction magazines is that they can combine materials with general popular appeal with items that serve a wide range of minority interests, and one of the reasons why the science fiction and weird fiction pulps were far more interesting than the general run of pulp magazines is that the nooks and crannies of their bedrock of formularistic action-adventure costume-drama provided rooting opportunities for a host of fascinating writers who were doing things that no one had ever done before, or had ever considered possible. Arkham House provided the paradigm example of a specialist press serving as a bridge by means of which deserving writers could extend their presence from such transient literary backwaters to secure tenure in the literary marketplace, thus enriching the lives of a small but steadfast population of aficionados.

Rings, an omnibus of four novels, is the second book by Charles L. Harness to be issued by NESFA Press, following the previous year's collection of shorter pieces *An Ornament to His Profession*. I must confess that I have never understood why Charles Harness is not considered in his native land to be a great sf writer, but the plain fact is that he is not, and that his work does stand in need of the kind of service that organizations like NESFA Press provide. I am, therefore, as glad to obtain *Rings* as I was to acquire its predecessor, and heartily recommend it as an item that ought to have a permanent place on the shelves of every true sf fan. I hope that NESFA Press will see their way clear to continuing this series with at least one more collection combining classic and previously-unseen work—and, for that matter, that Charles Harness, even at the age of eighty-four, is capable of taking enough encouragement from its existence to persevere with his creative endeavors.

Given that Harness's merits as a writer have been obvious to several of my countrymen whose critical acumen is beyond reproach, it is all the more puzzling that he seems to be a prophet without honor in his own country. It is presumably no coincidence that American attitudes to Harness's most obvious literary model, A. E. van Vogt, have also been ambivalent, and that several other highly accomplished writers who have attempted to work in a vanVogtian vein—most notably James Blish, Barrington J. Bayley, and "Ian Wallace" (John W. Pritchard)—have had much of their work consigned to the same paperback original ghetto to which most of Harness's works have been condemned. The only writer in that vein who conclusively broke out of the paperback ghetto to win wider acceptance was Philip K. Dick, but it was not until Dick had taken his work to his own particular extreme that he began to attract attention, and not until he died that the avalanche of critical acclaim picked up speed (so to speak). Ironically, the award named after Dick, for books issued as paperback originals, has never been given to a novel of this particular stripe.

Harness' reputation might be more considerable had he been more prolific during the first phase of his career as a science fiction writer, but it was always a sideline to his work as a patent attorney and it soon petered out. That phase was launched in the pages of John Campbell's *Astounding* in 1948 with "Time Trap", and scored its most significant success in the following year with the novel *Flight into Yesterday*, a revised version of which is reprinted in *Rings* under its alternative title *The Paradox Men*. The sole comment Harness offers on his writing in the space reserved for autobiographical statements in *The St. James Guide to Science Fiction Writers* is "I did it for money", and he has observed elsewhere that he was initially motivated by the need to pay off some medical bills, but this retrospective cynicism may reflect the fact that the most aesthetically ambitious of his early stories, the novella "The Rose", failed to sell to the US magazines and ended up in the conspicuously third-rate British magazine *Authentic* in 1953, constituting a peak of achievement that the periodical in question never looked like matching in subsequent years. If it was the failure of that story which discouraged Harness from further efforts, it is a great shame that it failed to find a better home.

Although Bouregy and Curl reissued *Flight into Yesterday* in hardcover in 1953 (it was initially published in *Startling Stories* and became the *The Paradox Men* when reprinted as half of an Ace double in 1955) Harness published no more sf for thirteen years thereafter, although he did appear occasionally in the pages of *Astound-*

ing under the pseudonym Leonard Lockhard, in which capacity he assisted Theodore L. Thomas with some of the items in a series of peculiar satires exploring possible—if rather improbable—technological challenges to patent law. (Alas, these clever satires failed to anticipate the field in which patent law really would eventually be thrown into a spectacular tangle by the definition-bending challenge of a new technology, although Harness made belated compensation under his own name with the *Analog* article "The Bug, the Mouse and Chapter 24" in 1994).

Harness's return to sf writing in 1966 may well have been encouraged by the continued interest his work had attracted in Britain. Brian Aldiss contributed an introduction to a Faber & Faber edition of *The Paradox Men* (1964)—coining the term "widescreen baroque" to describe it—and Michael Moorcock reprinted a number of his pulp stories in *New Worlds*. Moorcock also prompted *New Worlds'* publisher, Roberts & Vinter, to issue a collection of three Harness stories, headed by *The Rose* (1965). His enthusiasm for Harness's work was strongly supported by his close friend Barrington J. Bayley, who was always wont to describe "Time Trap" as "the best science fiction story ever written". Although the first few of the many stories Harness was subsequently to contribute to *Analog*—including the title story of *An Ornament to his Profession*)—made clever use of his experience as a patent lawyer, he soon reverted to a broader canvas in the novel *The Ring of Ritornel* (1968), which is also featured in *Rings*.

Since retiring from his primary profession Harness appears to have kept up a steady production of science fiction novels and stories, maintaining a clarity of mind and a fertility of imagination comparable to that of the eternally-youthful Jack Williamson. His published work has all been engaging and intellectually enterprising—which makes it all the more remarkable that when I contacted him in 1992, in connection with the article on his work I was updating for the second edition of *The Encyclopedia of Science Fiction* (1993), he told me that he had several completed novels for which he had been unable to find a publisher. His presence in the US marketplace always seems to have been rather marginal; although *The Ring of Ritornel* appeared in hardcover in Britain, and *The Rose* was actually reprinted in a UK hardcover edition following it paperback appearance, both works were published in the US as original paperbacks and virtually all his subsequent works have been consigned to the same fate. Only *Krono* (1988) achieved first publication as a hardcover, although *Firebird* (1981)—the third item in *Rings*—was reprinted by the SF Book Club. The most interesting aspect of *Rings* for long-time admirers of his work—especially those who, like me, already have hardcover versions of the three reprinted items—is that it concludes with the previously unpublished *Drunkard's Endgame*. Like its predecessors, this is a relatively short novel by today's standards, and it is possible that one of the reasons Harness has had difficulty selling his recent produce is that fashions have moved on to such an extent that commercial publishers now seem to regard anything under 90,000 words as unmarketable.

George Zebrowski's introduction to *Rings* quotes Harness on the subject of van Vogt's influence, explaining that he had been "awed" by such works as *Slan* and *The World of Null-A* because they were "all overflowing with action, mystery, suspense and superhumanity" and "his worlds unfolded before us with multidimensional clarity". Harness adds to these observations the confession that "I tried to figure out how he did it. Fifty years later I'm still trying." A. E. van Vogt has, of course, explained at length exactly how he did it, blithely giving away the secret of the 800-word scene and the unique quality of the "fictional sentences" typical of genre sf (they all refer to something left carefully unspecified), but, as everyone who has ever tried to apply these rules knows perfectly well, the real essence of the man's art lies far beyond the scope of such eccentric craftsmanship. There is an authentically challenging paradox in the fact that, although van Vogt deliberately aimed for obfuscation rather than clarity, and constructed plots which—as Damon Knight conclusively proved in the most brilliant and most brutal of his critical essays—never came remotely close to making sense, he really did give an impression of "multidimensional clarity". Like Blish, Wallace and Bayley, Charles Harness has amply demonstrated that it is not actually necessary for a van Vogtian plot to be nonsensical, and that the strategy of obfuscation can be kept under much tighter restraint, while still retaining the essential virtues of the subgenre.

The four novels in *Rings* are, as the title implies, linked by a common narrative strategy, which achieves closure by folding the plots back upon themselves ouroboros-fashion. This is certainly a common vanVogtian ploy, but it is not a definitive feature of vanVogtian fiction and its frequent recurrence in Harness's work (other striking examples can be found in *An Ornament to His Profession* and in novels not collected here) is as much a matter of personal fascination as the recapitulation of a subgeneric archetype. The real collective heart of these enterprises is not the knotting together of their beginnings and ends but the flamboyant and far-reaching fashion in which the resultant loops are cast. Their power derives from the way in the way each loop becomes a noose capturing and entangling big ideas of disparate provenance. One of the central problems of science fiction has always been to discover ways of embedding the more grandiose and esoteric aspects of scientific vision within plots possessed of human interest: of hybridizing the cosmic and the personal, the abstract and the everyday. No other pulp sf writer did that work of chimerization with as much flair and panache as A. E. van Vogt, and it was this bold insouciance that recommended him to his fans and such progressive followers as Harness.

Time-loop stories were ten a penny by 1949, but *Flight into Yesterday* was the only one that dared to combine Arnold Toynbee's theories of history with the cavalier spirit of *The Mark of Zorro* and a whole series of ideative innovations, ranging from the casually preposterous (illusions cast by reversing the photonic flow of sight) to the defiantly magnificent (the sun-stations). *The Ring of Ritornel* and *Firebird* use the same basic methodology to dramatize theories of cosmology. The former might be held to have backed the wrong horse in choosing to celebrate the Hoyle/Gold/Bondi steady state theory, which subsequently lost out catastrophically to the Big Bang, but the extrapolation of that theory to produce the image of the Deep—the womb from which matter is born at the birth-canal of the Node, thus maintaining its density as the universe expands—is an imaginative *tour de force*. In *The Ring of Ritornel* the birth-pangs of matter cause quakes in fabric of space, whose energy fuels a marvelously strange ecosystem. These disturbances of the implicate order are mirrored in a long-running dispute between the worshippers of Ritornel, the personification of destiny and design, and the followers of Alea, the personification of randomness and spontaneity, who disagree as to whether the life-cycle of the cosmos involves eternal repetition or infinite variation. *Firebird* takes up in like manner what is now the more familiar dispute as to whether the universe is fated to expand forever or to collapse in a Big Crunch—which might, of course, be the prelude to another Big Bang. The way in which Harness contrives to entwine this issue, intimately and constructively, with a plot that replays the oft-told tale of Tristan and Isolde, is another masterpiece of ingeniously-calculated mock-naivety.

The most obvious literary precursor of these attempts to make human endeavors relevant to cosmological matters is van Vogt's "Seesaw" (subsequently integrated into *The Weapon Shops of Isher*) but it may be worth noting that the first writer to address a similar problem was Edgar Poe, whose "prose-poem" Eureka (1848) provided the first literary image of the Big Crunch (and, in the process, produced the first coherent solution of Olbers' so-called paradox, which had troubled the minds of astronomers for generations). Critics sometimes suggest that the only reason A. E. van Vogt is so highly esteemed in France is that *The World of Null-A* was translated by Boris Vian, but this argument is a straightforward reflection of the one which holds that Poe's European reputation is entirely due to the heroic efforts of Charles Baudelaire. I suspect that this is nonsense, and that there really is something in van Vogt, as there is in Poe, that commends itself more readily to European appreciation than to American appreciation—and that it is precisely this determination to find a literary voice, however quirky, for cosmological representation that is the crux of the matter. America has, of course, produced Freeman Dyson and Frank Tipler to balance out—and perhaps to surpass—the imaginative endeavors of Fred Hoyle, David Bohm, James Lovelock, Ilya Prigogine, and Isabelle Stengers, but it is at least arguable that their ideas do not sit so comfortably within a more general cultural context in which the display of cosmological speculations is not seen as a significant literary problem even by the great majority of American science fiction writers.

By this, as by any other, criterion *Drunkard's Endgame* is the least of the four novels in Rings. As its title implies, its plot is built around the slightly surprising mathematics of the so-called drunkard's walk (a random progression of moves), which has previously intrigued such writers as Frederik Pohl and Martin Gardner. Admittedly, this lacks the intrinsic sublimity of the Deep or the Big Crunch, but the heart of the novel is the bizarre civilization that has evolved on the fugitive starship whose course has been plotted as a drunkard's walk. My principal complaint against the story is, in fact, that this fascinating cultural artifact is so summarily dismissed in order to set up a conclusion that sacrifices moral as well as narrative propriety upon the altar of ouroborosian neatness.

I suppose that it is not entirely beyond comprehension that some readers will be less forgiving than I am of such small atrocities as this one, but it seems to me that the occasional dodgy side-effect is a price worth paying for the inventiveness, audacity and sheer vivid entertainment that a writer like Harness provides. No matter what he might say, Charles Harness did it for love as well as for money, and he produced books that are deserving of love as well as the price of purchase. He should have received more thanks long ago, but it's not too late. Buy *Rings*.

Prophets for the End of Time by Marcos Donnelly, Baen; November 1998

I am not entirely certain why a review copy of a book published in November 1998 should have arrived on my doormat in March 2000. Perhaps it was lost in a time warp. Indeed, according to the meager research I have been able to carry out with the aid of my limited resources, the text in question appears to have been lost in a time warp for quite some time. When Marcos Donnelly published his second story, "Tracking the Random Variable", in *Full Spectrum 3* (1991), the accompanying note stated that he was working on his first novel, *An Improper Apocalypse*. When he published his fifth story, "Bloodletting", in *The Magazine of Fantasy & Science Fiction*'s June 1994 issue, the accompanying note said that he had recently completed his first novel, *Prophets of the End Time*. It is probably safe to assume, therefore, that what eventually appeared as *Prophets for the End of Time* had been bouncing around the marketplace for a fair few years before ending up at Baen, which is unlikely to have been the author's first choice of publisher for a work so long in the making. It is probably safe to assume, too, that the text was done and dusted some while before its author had had a chance to read James Morrow's *Towing Jehovah* (1994), let alone either of its sequels.

Given that Donnelly's sixth-published story, "El Hijo de Hernez" (1995), is set in a Roman Catholic school not dissimilar to the one that Clayton Pinkes attends in *Prophets for the End of Time*, and that some items of background detail recur in both stories, one is rather tempted to infer (although my meager researches have failed to turn up any further evidence) that Marcos Donnelly attended a Roman Catholic school of a similarly devout stripe in the days when he was still known as Mark Patrick Donnelly. One is further tempted to infer that the experience left an indelible mark upon his inner life, considerably affecting the tenor and temper of his imagination when he eventually joined the slim but ever-expanding ranks of lapsed Catholic writers of heretical fantasy.

Given that Donnelly does not appear to have published any stories in 1996, 1997 or 1998 (the last year covered in the CD-ROM version of the *Locus* index) one is also somewhat tempted to infer that the difficulties he experienced in finding a publisher for *Prophets for the End of Time* were sufficiently disappointing to dissuade him from further literary endeavors of this or any other kind (given that his third-published story, "The Resurrection of Alonso Quijana", 1992, is a Quixotic fantasy in the purest possible sense, he must already have been aware of the hazards of tilting at wordmills). It is not at all improbable, however, that Donnelly's divorce in 1994—from fellow writer Nancy Kress, after six years of marriage—also had a slightly crushing effect on his spirit and ambition, and one is irresistibly tempted to infer that events leading up to that divorce had an even-more-crushing impact on the work he did in bringing his novel to its brilliantly peculiar conclusion.

The fact that Nancy Kress was a copywriter in Rochester, New York when she married Donnelly—also a copywriter, according to the note in *Full Spectrum 3*—lends some slight further credence to the suspicion that Clayton Pinkes' school in the Rochester suburb of Brighton is based on one that Donnelly actually attended, and that the characterization of Clayton involves substantial aspects of spiritual autobiography. This may, of course, be only marginally relevant to the inspiration and development of the story, but I strongly suspect otherwise. Lapsed Catholic fantasy writers—among whom the late Brian Moore is perhaps the most famous—are notoriously prone to dramatizing their own idiosyncratic crises of faith in a flamboyantly fervent and bitterly sarcastic fashion, and all the best heretical fantasy is deeply heartfelt. *Prophets for the End of Time* may not quite be a match for James Morrow's heartfelt heretical fantasies in terms of analytical flair and panache, but it is definitely in the same ballpark when it comes to flamboyant fervor and bitter sarcasm.

Like the Morrow trilogy concluded in *The Eternal Footman*, *Prophets for the End of Time* addresses the fundamental problem of a Deus Absconditus: a God who has absented himself from any evident involvement with His Creation. Instead of re-revealing Himself as a corpse and leaving his angels to molt and die of grief, however, Donnelly's God has simply gone AWOL, leaving the archangel Michael in charge. Michael, enthusiastic to repair this breach, decides that the only way to force God to resume normal service is to initiate the program for destruction outlined in the Old and New Testaments, fulfilling the pattern of prophecies whose scheduled climax is the return of God to Earth. This requires the fulfillment of several specific criteria, including the union of Urim (knowledge) and Thummim (perfection)—which are, for the sake of convenience, incorporated in two bones. one situated in the left arm of Henri Elobert and the other in the right arm of Clayton Pinkes, both of whom are born thirty-three years before the Millennium.

Henri Elobert is a precocious supergenius raised in isolation on a remote island in the Kerguélen peninsula by a company of European scientists—including his father, who is presumably the Henri

Elobert quoted at the outset of the horrific metaphysical fantasy "Bloodletting". These experimentalists have presumably borrowed their methodology from M. P. Shiel's classic account of *The Isle of Lies*, but they have failed to take due note of Shiel's assessment of what is likely to occur when such a powerful personality realizes what has been done to him and decides to make his own way in the world. Easily outdoing Shiel's sociopathic anti-hero, the murderously amoral and ruthlessly efficient Henri—having renamed himself Henry Albert—becomes the ultimate Management Consultant, in charge of a crack team of suicidally-inclined geniuses. In this capacity he lends himself so enthusiastically to Michael's plan for world devastation that he eventually takes it over and sets out to make further improvements in its destructive potential. The devil, we are assured throughout the text, is merely an imaginary scapegoat, but the likes of Henry Albert are frightening precisely because they have no need for scapegoats.

Clayton, by contrast, is all too human in his frailty—and if that were not handicap enough, he is unlucky enough to have Raphael, alias Paolo Diosana, assigned as his managing angel. Raphael is the only angel able to make actual contact with the world of matter, which gives him the useful ability to heal, but also makes him corruptible. Having revealed himself to Clayton in 1976, Raphael follows God's example in going AWOL, greatly increasing the poor boy's confusion. Clayton grows up to be a charismatic preacher, who will be empowered to bring about the apocalypse, in collaboration with Henry Albert, as soon as his faithful following consists of 2.76% of the human race. He is assisted in the later stages of his work by Elizabeth Goddard, who graduates from being the world's only moral comedienne to being Clayton's warm-up act (having already served that function, in a slightly different sense, in high school). Clayton also gets some useful late input from a disarmingly perverse pope, who bears very little resemblance to John Paul II.

Clayton never seems happy in his allotted role—or, indeed, in any wise whatsoever—but he eventually comes into his own when, having lost both Elizabeth and his right arm to his partner and rival, he is summoned by Lucifer (who is not the devil, although his cunning is definitely of the low sort) to take a key role in the trial of his long-lost managing angel, on a charge of dereliction of duty. In the course of that trial, which is his, Michael's and God's as much as Raphael's, Clayton finally finds a way to exert himself against the oppressive forces of prophecy and destiny, winning a truly remarkable, if distressingly limited, victory.

Few readers will be inclined to deem the ending of *Prophets for the End of Time* wholeheartedly upbeat, but it does offer a triumph of sorts, along with the dogged assurance—the only assurance possible to a lapsed Catholic atheist—that no better prize could possibly have been wrung from the toils of a God-abandoned Creation. I found it very powerful—but then, I would, wouldn't I? I also found the entire text utterly gripping, very funny and very clever—but I am often told that many Americans don't find esoteric exercises in fantastic theodicy especially gripping and don't find bitter sarcasm funny or clever, no matter how deftly-executed it is, so I might be in a minority there too.

I do feel, strongly, that this is a book that deserved far better than to appear in a bottom-end-of-the market paperback line—but by the same token, I also feel that the Baen editor who bought it deserves considerable congratulation for making sure that it did get published, albeit in strange company. It would have been nice to have been able to give it a plug way back in 1998, but I remain glad to have had the opportunity to give it a plug at all. Go forth and find this book, no matter how difficult a task it might be. Read it, laugh and weep—and remember that thine own day of judgment is not only at hand but always shall be, no matter how far or fast thou hast lapsed, nor from what faith. Amen.

Alexandre Humboldt-Fonteyne: La Collection interdite by Michel de Spiegeleire, Éditions Labor 2000

This excellent book is one of two guides to the exhibition of the Alexandre Humboldt-Fonteyne "Forbidden Collection", which has been displayed at various venues in Brussels, including (in connection with the festival of fantastic literature centered there in March-April 2000) the Maison du Livre in the Rue Rome. The other guide is a video-tape lasting about 20 minutes, which is far less detailed but does have the advantage of some exceedingly rare footage of the great man's epoch-making expeditions and a few glimpses of the indefatigable Michel de Spiegeleire, the man who has worked hard and long to give his countrymen the opportunity to see the cream of this remarkable collection. After a preface by Henri Vernes, the book offers a brief biography of Humboldt-Fonteyne and a history of the collection from its foundation in 1935 to its rediscovery in 1995 before offering a detailed account of the expeditions in which Humboldt-Fonteyne collected his specimens. The story told in these chapters is as follows:

Alexandre Humboldt-Fonteyne was born in 1883 in Paris. His mother was French and his father Prussian; both were of aristocratic descent. His early years were divided between his parents' two homes: the Maison Alfort and the Schloss Langweil in Berlin. His determination to be an explorer was formed at an early age, partly under the influence of his uncle, Charles Fonteyne, the curator of the "museum" attached to the Alfort Veterinary School (which included some exceptionally fine 18th century anatomical specimens). After a brilliant career at the University of Berlin, where he studied zoology, botany and paleontology, Humboldt-Fonteyne obtained a commission from the Academy of Sciences in St. Petersburg to venture into Siberia to collect specimens of mammoths preserved in the glacial ice. He remained in Russia until 1907, when he returned to Paris, but in 1909 he was invited to accompany Wilhelm Branca, director of the Museum of Paleontology in Berlin, on an expedition to eastern Africa.

During the next eight years Branca and Humboldt-Fonteyne were able to return from sites in what is now Tanzania some 500 batches of specimens, totaling some 185 tonnes, but the dutiful Humboldt-Fonteyne eventually returned to war-torn Europe in order to play his part in the conflict. It was during his military service (on the German side) on the Balkan Front during 1917 that he found the relatively recent and controversial anatomical specimens that formed the nucleus of the "forbidden collection" (so-called because the museums that had been only too glad to display his earlier discoveries refused to accommodate them). Thus began his long alienation from the scientific establishment; almost as soon as he was declared unorthodox he began, defiantly, to direct his studies towards the most controversial fringes of his subject, thus establishing a vicious circle that made his reputation increasingly equivocal.

Humboldt-Fonteyne established a new home with his similarly-surnamed cousin Monica in Naples, at the Villa Hermosa, but almost immediately set out with Roy Chapman Andrews for Peking. His subsequent voyages in the good ship *Albatros* took him, by stages, around the world. In 1924 he was in the Himalayas, in 1928 in Timor; in 1931 he rejoined Andrews in Australia, and in 1934 he reached the Americas. By 1939 he had sent back thousands of specimens from his various ports of call—which Monica had carefully stored at the Villa Hermosa but had never made public—and he was only persuaded to think of returning to Europe when Monica made a personal pilgrimage to inform him about approaches made to her by the Ahnenerbe: the scientific section of the SS, created by Himmler in 1935. The Ahnenerbe had begun to take an interest in Humboldt-

Fonteyne's work soon after its inception 1935, but it appears that he flatly refused their offers of financial support.

Although their exact fate remains stubbornly mysterious, it seems that the Humboldt-Fonteynes never made it back to Europe. It is similarly unclear exactly what authority the Ahnenerbe had to take over the material stored at the Villa Hermosa, or where they installed it for further study. What is known, however, is that it was captured by the Red Army in 1945, boxed up and shipped with vast quantities of other loot to the Hermitage Museum, before being transferred to the University of Krazgoyarks in 1953. There it rested, apparently unexamined, until its rediscovery by Dr. Gerassimov in 1995.

The contents of the current exhibition are, of course, only a sample, but they deserve to be reckoned the highlights of the collection, including as they do the remnants of the last survivor of the species that gave rise to the Chinese mythology of dragons, an entire skeleton of the gigantic ape that was remembered in the Himalayas as the yeti (plus a yeti costume still used in the 1930s by Nepalese tribesmen in arcane rituals), numerous fascinating teratological specimens, including those which seem to have given rise to vampire mythology, and—perhaps most remarkably of all—the mummified remains of the Martians who landed in what is now the southern USA in the days when the Anasazi still flourished.

Having had the privilege of seeing the collection at the Maison du Livre I can testify that it is a truly wonderful assembly. It is an unprecedentedly rich mixture of paleontological and zoological specimens and related cultural artifacts, with a good deal of supportive illustrative material and apparatus from Humboldt-Fonteyne's exploratory armory (including his pioneering bathysphere). It would not be an exaggeration to say that the display is capable of changing the way one looks at the world; it builds bridges between the worlds of the familiar and the fantastic of a kind that has rarely been attempted, and never so successfully executed.

Unlike the exhibition or the fascinating video-tape, the guidebook has a sealed section, which offers suggestions for an alternative "methodological approach" to the Humboldt-Fonteyne collection. Naturally, I have not opened this section, because to do so would detract from the value of an eminently collectible volume, but there are certain hints in the remainder of the text which—if my uncertain knowledge of French has not betrayed me—offer useful clues as to what might be contained there. These "forbidden pages" (if you will forgive the pun) might well contain a detailed but inevitably speculative account of an international conspiracy that has contrived to cover up not merely the extent and import of Humboldt-Fonteyne's discoveries, but almost to obliterate all knowledge of the very existence of the great man. The members of this conspiracy are ruthless in their promotion of the theory that all these specimens and artifacts are, in fact, works of art, and that Michel de Spiegeleire ought to be assessed a sculptor rather than a historian.

I can confidently respond to this suggestion, even in ignorance of the exact contents of the sealed pages, by saying that, if it is so, then Spiegeleire must be an artist of exceedingly rare talent and prodigious thoroughness: an artist whose masterpiece—for this exhibition and its associated documents must surely qualify as his masterpiece, even though he looks astonishingly young on video—is far more convincing, as well as more bizarre, than anything I have seen in any British or American exhibition of fantastic art. I would, however, be failing in my duty as a reviewer if I did not give this thesis full and proper consideration.

During the last hundred and fifty years there has grown up a strict distinction between the typical formats of "fiction" and "non-fiction" that stands in some contrast to earlier norms. For instance, dialogue, which was once the principal vehicle of philosophical reportage—unhesitatingly employed by Galileo in extrapolating his astronomical observations into the realm of cosmology—is nowadays entirely confined to "fiction". The modern distinction between "fiction" and "non-fiction" is, of course, very different from that between "fantasy" and "truth"; literary sophisticates insist that the very best fiction is the most naturalistic, which most faithfully reproduces the fabric of social and psychological reality. For this reason, speculative thought of all kinds finds as much difficulty in adapting itself to the formal demands of "fiction" as to those of "non-fiction". This difficulty was glaringly obvious to all the early writers of science-based speculative fantasy, who frequently felt forced to return to old or obsolete story-forms in order to dramatize their speculations (Francis Bacon formatted *New Atlantis* as a traveler's tale, while Kepler shaped his account of the Copernican solar system as observed from the moon as a dream-story and Voltaire had to reinvent the moral fable as the *conte philosophique* in "Micromegas".)

Edgar Poe, the first person to produce science-based speculative fantasy on a wholesale basis, experimented with numerous obsolete formats, including the dialogue ("The Conversation of Eiros and Charmion") and the meditation (*Eureka*) but his borrowing of the contemporary innovation of the newspaper hoax ("The Balloon Hoax") has tempted too many subsequent critics—most conspicuously Patrick Parrinder—to lump all his unstorylike enterprises together as "hoaxes". This does grave disservice not merely to the underrated *Eureka* but to the item usually known as "The Facts in the Case of M. Valdemar", which is an early attempt to present a speculative fantasy in what was then a fledgling format, but which eventually evolved into the modern "scientific paper".

Items of this last kind have been a perennial feature of modern "science fiction", but no one has ever quite decided what they ought to be called. Various editors of *Analog*, in playing host to reportage of the hypermercurial properties of thiotimoline, have sometimes referred to "non-fact articles", while the invented items that newspapers and scientific periodicals traditionally sneak into their April 1st issues are often known as "spoofs", but many such items are not in the least comedic, and a considerable grey area—flanked on either side by the vast wildernesses of intended and unintended scholarly fantasy—extends from whimsical intellectual confections to entirely respectable scientific "thought experiments".

The simple fact is that there are some kinds of fantasy that benefit greatly from presentation in "non-fictional" formats, even—perhaps especially—when there is no intent to deceive or generate a precious hesitation between belief and non-belief. There are some kinds of pretence that cannot readily be accommodated to the modern formats of "fiction", or to the particular contracts that "fiction" employs to bind a reader's "willing suspension of disbelief", and which therefore work better by appropriating "non-fictional" formats. Consider, for instance, R. A. Lafferty's reports on the society of the Camiroi, Ursula le Guin's extracts from the *Journal of the Association of Therolinguistics*, Stanislaw Lem's volumes of reviews of non-existent books (perhaps, in case a few of my readers are too clever for their own peace of mind, I should re-emphasize at this point that this really is a review of an actual book) or Jeff VanderMeer's redaction of Duncan Shriek's history of Ambergris. None of these qualifies, as a "hoax" or a "spoof", and none deserves the casual dismissal implied by such terms. The notion of "non-fictional fantasy" is actually no more—and no less—oxymoronic than the notion of "science fiction".

Whether any of this has any relevance to the exhibition to which this book is a guide—or, for that matter to the entire Humboldt-Fonteyne collection—must, of course, be left unsettled, at least until the sealed section of the book is opened by a more daring reader. Perhaps, one day, American audiences will be lucky enough to have the chance of seeing and evaluating this cabinet of marvels for themselves. What can be said, though, is that if the entire edifice comprised by the book, the video and the exhibits is merely the apparatus of an illusion, it is a brilliant conjuring trick. Perhaps there never were dragons in China, or yetis in the Himalayas, or vampires in the Balkans; perhaps there never was a monstrous birth whose rumor grew into a tenacious superstition; perhaps Alexandre Humboldt-Fonteyne never actually observed the development of the larva of the "Peula-Peula" (*Eucerna thanatos*) or the predations of the Haitian *papaloi*; and perhaps the mummified aliens found in the Anasazi ruins of New Mexico didn't actually come from Mars at all but from some more fanciful location—but if so, we owe a great debt to Michel de Spiegeleire, firstly for going to such extraordinary lengths to demonstrate that the world might be a little richer and stranger than it probably is, and secondly for his conscientious modesty. What, after all, might a less painstaking and vainer man—Erich von Däniken, for instance—have made of evidence like this?

Oceanspace by Allen Steele, Ace, February 2000

Science fiction stories dealing with the exploration of the ocean depths have been thin on the ground in the twentieth century, although there was a period in the late nineteenth century when the precedent established by Jules Verne's *Twenty Thousand Leagues Under the Sea* spawned an entire mini-genre of adventures featuring sea-monsters and relics of Atlantis. In reclaiming the theme for modern hard sf, Arthur C. Clarke's *The Deep Range* (1957) and Isaac Asimov's "Waterclap" (1970) both made much of the vastness and mysteriousness of the world beyond the continental shelves, and of the intriguing parallels that could be drawn between the technological imperatives governing its exploration, but the fact that the deep-ocean wilderness seemed to be almost as barren as outer space did not recommend it as a useful medium for spiffing tales of derring-do. Within the last few years, however, the discovery of exotic ecosystems surrounding hot vents in the ocean floor and the possibility of "mining" the metal-rich nodules scattered thereon have helped to reawaken a scientific and pragmatic interest that has spawned several new literary endeavors, of which Peter Watts' psychodrama *Starfish* (1999) is perhaps the most impressive.

Allen Steele's *Oceanspace* attempts to import all the elements of fashionable thinking about the exploration and exploitation of the ocean into the standardized format of the near-future technothriller. Because he is an accomplished and conscientious hard sf writer, Steele performs this task as well as could possibly be expected, but he runs into exactly the same difficulty as anyone else would: that the technothriller formula is essentially stupid, utterly ill-fitted for the talents of writers who cannot set aside their intelligence and rational appreciation of probability.

Because he is an honest man, unwilling to welcome the frankly ridiculous into what is supposedly a realistic representation of actual possibilities, Steele is content to use the thriller formula merely as a disguise, like a plastic party-mask with the features of Frankenstein's monster or the wolf-man. He is earnest—and successful—in his initial attempts to deceive, but he cannot and will not drive deception to absurd lengths, so his final chapters are much less robust than his openings. When the party-mask comes off to reveal the plain and straight-dealing face beneath, Steele simply discards some of the expectations he set up, on the grounds that they are incapable of further development, while he fulfils the others in a manner so casual and superficial as to seem almost insulting. This is a strategy with which I can sympathize—and even admire, a little—but it is one that will presumably disappoint a lot of the readers at which Ace's sales department and the chain-store booksellers will aim the book. Given that there is no audience for intelligent hard sf that refuses to employ the methods and apparatus of modern pulp melodrama, there is no commercially-viable alternative to the production of books like this, but the fact remains that they are all curate's eggs: in spite of their good bits, they exhale a distinct whiff of literary hydrogen sulphide.

Following the standard technothriller recipe, *Oceanspace* introduces three separate plot threads, which become intriguingly intertwined: a sea monster that trashes a submarine collecting cargo from mining robots; a brand new hot vent opening up in mid-Atlantic; and an exercise in industrial espionage carefully recomplicated by a bogus kidnap attempt that goes awry. The expedition mounted to settle all three issues is seasoned by various spices taken from the standard cliché-rack: a husband and wife whose personal relationship is subjected to undue stress by their professional obsessions and ambitions; a magazine reporter whose substandard journalistic ethics are mirrored in her sexual mores; and a cute kid whose adolescence is troubled by a representative sample of what TV shrinkspeak terms "issues". When the failure of these elements to cut the melodramatic mustard becomes painfully obvious—because the close encounters with the sea monster and the hot vent remain conscientiously slight—a psychopathic assassin is hurriedly introduced into the plot in the desperate hope that he might make up the shortfall, but Steele cannot muster nearly enough conviction to make a bogey-man of that sort anything more than an arbitrary cartoon.

The not-inconsiderable virtues of *Oceanspace* are all in its didactic elements: in the wealth of technical and practical detail, and in the carefully measured popularization of all the information scrupulously gleaned from the sources listed in the two-page bibliography. Readers who can find fascination enough in that, and can simply ignore the lame elements of the plot, will find the book rewarding; those who are avid for a page-turner in the great tradition of Alistair MacLean will, alas, think it weak. However crippling their weaknesses may be, however, I believe that it is important that books of this kind should continue to be written and marketed, because if hard sf writers were not ready, willing and able to make this kind of compromise, the entire technothriller subgenre would be composed of Frankensteinian fables in which quasi-scientific discourse is used merely as a supporter of hideous threats to human life and sanity. I do not know whether that kind of teratological pornography is actively dangerous, in the sense that it helps to promote, sustain and disseminate the imbecilic hostility to science that has become so commonplace in contemporary society, but I do know that, in rational and aesthetic terms, it stinks to high heaven. It is a pity that we live in a world in which honest men must wear cartoonish disguises in order to publish their work, but rather that than a world in which every writer who put on a monstrous mask did so merely to conceal a monstrous face.

Kingdom of the Grail by Judith Tarr, Roc, September 2000

The oldest extant manuscript of *La Chanson de Roland*, I am assured by *The New Oxford Companion to Literature in French*, is an Anglo-Norman copy made in the mid-twelfth century, currently held in the Bodleian library. The legend contained in the poem refers back to a battle lost by Charlemagne's forces in 778 while they were crossing the Pyrenees on their way home, after a long and mostly unsuccessful campaign against the Saracens of Spain. The poem relates how the Saracens had sued for peace, and the Franks—having been seven years away from home—had been grateful to accept. The lone dissenting voice among them was Charlemagne's nephew Roland. Roland nominated his stepfather Ganelon as chief negotiator in the peace settlement: a dangerous position that Ganelon did not relish, but which provided him with an opportunity to turn traitor. Ganelon arranged to have Charlemagne's army ambushed at the most vulnerable point of its homeward trek: the pass of Rencesvals.

The poem goes on to tell how Ganelon succeeded in placing Roland in command the rearguard, which bore the brunt of the attack. When all his close companions—including his great friend Olivier and the warrior priest Turpin—had been slain, the sorely wounded Roland blew his horn to summon Charlemagne, but the exertion was too much for him and God sent the Archangel Gabriel and Saint Michael to bring his soul to Heaven. Charlemagne went on to wreak extravagant vengeance against the Saracens, while Ganelon was tried as a traitor and executed. Other versions of the story vary considerably, many later manuscripts amplifying the part played by Roland's grief-stricken bride-to-be Aude.

Opinions differ as to whether there ever was a written "original" of *La Chanson de Roland* or whether all the written versions are distillates and expansions of oral performance-pieces. Either way, the tale became public property, and its many Medieval and Renaissance re-tellers felt free to reshape it to suit their own exhortatory purposes, while retaining the fundamental sequence of events and its implicit allegory. For its French tellers, the tale was a central myth of the foundation and identification of the French nation, and for other Europeans it remained a significant guiding myth of the long historical contest between Christianity and Islam. This process of revision is still ongoing—and the revisions inevitably reflect the priorities of the world in which we now live: a world in which the national identity of every nation except one is being gradually pounded into dust by the relentless appetite for globalization manifested in the exception, and in which all the great religions are subject to a similar but subtler process of syncretization by means of a liberal Holy War, whose central cause is to establish the primacy of a generalized "spirituality" allegedly underlying all particular creeds and dogmas.

In Judith Tarr's *Kingdom of the Grail*, Roland is neither Charlemagne's nephew, nor Ganelon's stepson, nor Aude's intended husband. He is, instead, the direct descendant of Merlin and Nimue; indeed, Merlin's immortality—albeit within an unorthodox prison—allows the great enchanter to play the role of Roland's effective father, training him to follow in his footsteps as a magician and shape-shifter. In this version, Ganelon is also an immortal, and his treachery is no trivial matter of striking bargains with Saracens; he is, in fact, the same powerful sorcerer who brought about the doom of Camelot, although his grander plan went awry when Merlin—his intended instrument—turned against him, forcing him to settle for Medraut rather than Arthur as the key instrument of his scheme to hijack the Holy Grail from its resting-place in the castle of Carbonek, in the kingdom of Montsalvat. In Tarr's version, the ambush in the Pyrenees is the next phase of that same plan: a second strike at the Grail.

Parsifal, having defeated Medraut and Ganelon in becoming Grail King in Montsalvat, is dying, and the Grail must choose a new champion. Both Ganelon and the Grail's emissary, Sarissa, expect that champion to be Charlemagne, but the magic sword Durandal, which Sarissa brings from Carbonek to find its proper owner, picks Roland instead. In this version, Roland is not borne away to Heaven after the crucial rearguard action but to the parallel world inhabited by the Grail and its female custodians, which has been continually refreshed by immigrants from the human world: its King, its fairy knights, and such luminaries as Huon of Bordeaux (who serve as barons holding the feofs of Montsalvat).

Sarissa is one of nine supernatural women appointed to guard and serve the Grail. They are an ill-assorted company, representing by their various origins the syncretic nature of the Grail itself. Although it is indeed the cup from which Christ drank at the Last Supper, it is much older than that, and it symbolizes the essential unity of the Christian faith and its masculine God with previous pagan traditions worshipping various aspects of a Mother Goddess. The other guardians include Morgan (le Fay), Freya (wife of Odin) and Innana (the Babylonian mother goddess), although—if my count can be trusted—a couple are left carefully unnamed, in order to signify that even the pagan traditions we know are a mere sample. (I must confess that I have no idea who Sarissa is supposed to be, nor can I find a convincing original of Nieve, although the name is probably an anglicization of the Irish name Niamh, meaning "brightness".)

The all-purpose deity served by this motley crew and symbolized by the radiant Grail is opposed by an equally protean dark adversary, whose nature includes all the attributes of the Christian Devil, although its limits, origins and ambitions are carefully unspecified. It is manifest only while it lends magical assistance to Ganelon, whose own nature and origins are equally vague. Because Merlin's intermediate position, as a one-time servant of the dark who turned his coat, is implicitly ambiguous, so is Roland's.

Because Sarissa is suspicious of Roland's "blood" she will not tell him the truth about the scheme that has embroiled him—a reluctance that lends heroic service to the greatest narrative cause of all: that of unfolding the plot by slow and awkward degrees of enlightenment. The same concealment gives its protagonist a reason of sorts to manifest extreme reluctance in accepting the inevitable burden of heroism, thus setting a moat of dramatic suspense about a conclusion that is never really in the slightest doubt. In the end, though, Ganelon misses his objective as much by virtue of his failure to control the royal instrument who must serve as intermediary between him and the Grail: Charlemagne's hunchbacked son Pepin.

Pepin is the most peculiar character in the text. His role activates two of the hoariest clichés in the book: the notion of the Divine Right of Kings (which enables him to touch the grail no matter how nasty he might be), and the notion that disabled and unprepossessing individuals are ever ripe for conversion to the cause of evil. It seems to me that the former notion is not easy to reconcile with the syncretic dissolution of masculine God-Kings into a sexless and more democratically-inclined figure, and I also find it slightly surprising to find the latter notion being so casually endorsed by a writer who is herself slightly challenged (albeit in a purely auditory fashion). Tarr is, of course, perfectly ready to defy tradition in numerous other matters; for instance, her Grail ladies are by no means committed to virginity.

La Chanson de Roland is by no means an unproblematic work, but its fundamental allegory is fairly clear. Like almost every other legend produced in Western Christendom while the art of authorship took its first few hesitant steps, it is a tale of heroic martyrdom and of the good example that a martyr may set. The effect of the slaughter of Roland and his companions is to renew Charlemagne's appetite and zeal for the war against Islam. Some of the variant versions take leave to point out that dead heroes leave a legacy of grief as well as righteous indignation, but that is not out of keeping with the more fundamental message; Christian faith is supposed to supply wards against grief as well as the energy to fight holy wars.

There is much in Tarr's account of the defense of the Kingdom of the Grail that is similarly transparent, but there are some key places in which the glass clouds over, in spite of the blinding light emitted by the item in question whenever a bolt of benevolent lightning is required by the logic of melodramatic hype. The novel has considerable narrative force—much more so, in fact, than *La Chanson de Roland*, thanks to all the progress we have made in the science of narratology and its associated technics since the 12th century—but it is not entirely clear to me to what end that force is being directed, or why. Perhaps this is my fault; I have never quite been able to get to grips with the logic of Macdonald's and Disneyland either, although most Americans seem to have no problem with them.

The Christian God who lurks in the background of *La Chanson de Roland* is, thanks to the Bible, a fairly clear-cut character. We know not only what He is for (the ten commandments) and what He is against (the seven deadly sins) but who He is for (Christians) and who He is against (everybody else). The Roland of tradition had no particular difficulty, therefore, in figuring out how he ought to conduct himself in his quotidian existence, who he was bound to defend, and who he was supposed to kill, the sixth commandment notwithstanding. It is easy to see—or at least to accept the poet's assurance—that he is both a good man and a clear-sighted one, although sending forth the Archbishop Gabriel and St. Michael to collect him from the battlefield does seem a trifle over the top.

The God/dess of *The Kingdom of the Grail* is, by contrast, a much more shadowy figure. Given that He/She/It is an amalgam of many images. He/She/It obviously does not endorse the first two commandments, and it is anyone's guess which of the remaining eight are approved and to what extent. Although the seven deadly sins still seem to be subject to a certain disapproval, that disapproval is by no means uniform or unmodified. Lust is perfectly okay (Roland is far from monogamous, or even serially monogamous, and every woman who claps eyes on him is haplessly delivered into its grip). Covetousness fuels the contest to win Durandal. Pride is fairly okay, as is anger, and even poor oft-neglected sloth is treated with a fair degree of tolerance. On the whole, only envy and avarice get a uniformly bad press here. These issues pale into insignificance, however, by comparison with the questions of *who* Tarr's God/dess is for and against. Because the possibility of heresy is ruled out *a priori*, He/She/It's champions have no ready-made enemies to pursue. This deficiency can only be compensated by inventing an antithetical anti-God/dess and hypothetical worshippers thereof—but Tarr is too honest a writer to suppose very readily that there are many people in the world willing and able to conceive of themselves as evil. Her anti-God/dess seems, in fact, to have only a single human fan, whose armies are gathered more by trickery than bribery and still require their numbers to be swelled by demons and monsters, whose own nature and ambitions have to be left irremediably vague. The distinction between Good and Evil is here made not by reference to any explicit moral philosophy but by means of the conventional evasive analogy that unites God with (white) light and Evil with darkness, implying a simplicity and obviousness that are blatantly deceptive.

Given this mock-theological background, Tarr's Roland can hardly help being a much more ambiguous figure than his model. Even if it were not for the "taint" carried in his "blood" by virtue of his descent from and education by a problematic ancestor, it would surely be as difficult for his readers to measure his virtue accurately as it is for him to figure out exactly how he should behave. The immediate context in which he operates is equally problematic—here, Charlemagne enters Spain to help the Moors and their Caliph against rival Islamic invaders, although he does not tell his army that, and his campaign fails largely because the Christians of Spain see him as an invader too. In a world whose politics are as confused as this, the parallel world of Faerie/Montsalvat can hardly help but seem reassuringly straightforward.

Being a hero, Tarr's Roland has, of course, to be good—in fact, he has to be very, very good indeed—but such is the confusion of the world-within-the-text that he seems to owe his virtue entirely to the fact that he has been picked by the Grail to play on Good's team. Even though they know this, other players on Good's team remain anxious that he might not really be good, on the rather paradoxical grounds that one of his forebears, having been picked to play on Evil's team, had actually played on Good's, thus giving Good a crucial but unfair advantage. Given that Roland has been picked to play on Good's team, however, it does seem a trifle unsporting of him to throw such awful tantrums about it, even to the extent of going out of his mind—although one can sympathize with the dilemma he finds himself in after recovering his sanity, when he is required to cement his position as Good's team captain by killing the previous captain.

All of this seems to me to raise certain questions that are conveniently unasked by the text and difficult to answer satisfactorily.

Why does the Grail—allegedly the very essence of Good—require Roland to carry out the seemingly Evil act of executing (or "sacrificing") Parsifal? [Well, because it just does, okay?]

Why does Roland not turn round—as Abraham surely should have done when required by a similar tyrant to kill Isaac—and tell the Grail to fuck off and do its own executions? [Tarr may know (although, frankly, I doubt it) but I don't.]

Why does Roland, having recovered his sanity to discover that the paradisal Kingdom of the Grail is a feudal society no more egalitarian than the one he left behind, not get behind the cause of progress—whether seen in terms of the Communist manifesto, *Atlas Shrugged*, the Omega Point or any other euchronian credo—instead of meekly accepting all the ideological garbage that goes with the idea of Divinely-sanctioned Royalty, including the idea of Bad Blood? [Actually, I think I can probably figure that one out—which is not to say that I approve of the probable answer.]

Finally (and crucially), why, when all the fancy dueling on dragonback is done, does the question of who gets the Grail actually come down to the matter of Pepin's petty selfishness, so that the ultimate victory of Good is not sealed by the champion of virtue at all, but by the two unchallenged petty evils—envy and avarice—working away within the twisted soul that seems, in this world-within-a-text, to be the natural accompaniment of a crooked back? [Why indeed?]

The one thing of which we may be certain, of course, is that if there is a heartfelt allegory in this—and Tarr is a writer of sufficient artistry and intelligence to lend us confidence that there must be—then it has to be an allegory of contemporary America's image of itself, and of its purpose in what was once the greater world but is now just a mere cultural annexe. Perhaps, because I am not an American, I cannot be expected to read that allegory accurately, but there must be at least a possibility that cultural distance can impart a measure of objectivity, so I shall feel free to do my best.

In my hopefully-inspired reading of the allegory of *The Kingdom of the Grail* the eponymous Kingdom is presumably yet another Disneyland writ large, and what the Grail—an adman's dream if ever there was one—actually holds instead of Christ's blood is presumably Coca Cola. Roland is presumably the spiritual father of Ronald Macdonald, and the fact that Ganelon doesn't seem to be anybody at all is presumably a reflection of the desperation with which a military superpower looks around for enemies once its last actual enemy has called it quits and embraced the magic of Starbucks. As for Pepin (or Pepsi, as his friends would presumably address him, if he had any)—well, presumably he must be there to remind us that, in spite of every strident whine of protest that rises out of the Bible Belt, it's avarice and envy and the logic of the competitive marketplace that make the world go round, and always have and always will, no matter how many heroes kill and die in whatever holy causes they may choose. And also, I suppose, that as long as Hollywood and Advertising rule the world, the links between beauty and virtue and between ugliness and malice will be sealed tight in the human imagination....for ever and ever, amen.

That, as the saying goes, is entertainment. It's as authentic as the proverbial nine-bob note, but it *is* entertainment. That's why the all-consuming, all-encompassing, all-singing-and-dancing syncretic mishmash of genre fantasy is thriving, not merely in the USA but everywhere else that mass-produced entertainment holds sway.

The Essential Hal Clement, Volume 2: Music of Many Spheres, NESFA Press, May 2000

The second volume of the *The Essential Hal Clement* follows an omnibus edition of the novels *Needle, Iceworld*, and *Close to Critical*. This book reprints seventeen shorter pieces, including five novellas, whose original publication dates range from 1942 (his first and second stories) to 1987.

Four of the stories here, "Uncommon Sense" (1945), "The Logical Life" (1974), "Stuck With It" (1976), and "Status Symbol" (1987)—which form a series featuring interplanetary explorer Laird Cunningham—were previously collected in a collection that NESFA Press produced in 1987 in less ambitious days, when it used to publish booklets of work by the guests at the organization's SF conventions. Two, "Impediment" (1942) and "Technical Error" (1944), were included in Clement's first collection, *Natives of Space* (1965). Four more, "Halo" (1952), "Sun Spot" (1960), "Raindrop" (1965), and "The Mechanic" (1966), were in his second, *Small Changes* (1969). Seven of these eleven previously-reprinted stories were also to re-reprinted in *The Best of Hal Clement* (1979), along with one other to be found in these pages, "Bulge" (1968). Of the six previously-uncollected pieces, one is a squib from the long-running *Astounding Stories* feature "Probability Zero"; the others are "Proof" (1942), "Attitude" (1943) "Cold Front" (1946), "Planetfall" (1957), and "Longline" (1976).

Although I might have missed a few items published in not-very-obvious places, I reckon there are five Clement stories that have never been collected, and seven that are in the earlier collections but not here—perhaps enough to add up to a reasonably-sized second volume, if NESFA Press happened to take the view that there is nothing in the Clement canon that is really inessential. On the other hand, the fact that the author is still alive and active—*Half Life*, a mosaic novel whose individual parts were published in the small press magazine *Absolute Magnitude*, was published by Tor in 1999—it is unlikely that NESFA will be able to acquire the rights to everything that the author has ever done, so we shall have to wait and see how many more volumes this particular series will produce.

Hal Clement is the hardest of hard sf writers, so perfect in his embodiment of one of the several standards by which that subgenre is routinely measured that he sometimes seems more monument than man. He is a purist writer, the magnitude of whose achievement can only be properly assessed by purist readers. His work will always be an acquired taste, and the world contains millions of habitual and sophisticated readers who would find this book impossible to read, but he is a writer who does what he does with such relentless ambition, awesome imagination and ferocious discipline that he holds a unique place in the annals of twentieth century literature. There are, I suppose, a few shriveled and puerile souls in the world who would deem it a place not worth holding, but they are fools whose opinion is worth no more than the noise of thorns crackling under a pot. Hal Clement ought to be in print, and NESFA are doing a valuable service to literature by making his work available. I would be lying if I said that *Music of Many Spheres* is an easy read, even for someone like me, who has read most of the stories before and is used to their manner and method; it is very tough meat and it takes a hell of a lot of chewing, but it is authentically nutritious, and it boats some exotic taste sensations whose like cannot be found elsewhere.

The stories herein provide graphic illustrations of all the crucial problems of hard sf writing. They are mostly long, because they are obliged to carry an enormous burden of exposition and explanation; they stretch the art and science of info-dumping to its limits. Several of them are narrated entirely from the viewpoint of alien beings whose unhumanity is very radical indeed, making efficient communication with the reader so extraordinarily difficult that few other writers would have ever dared to tackle their substance. The puzzles they present to the reader—and they are all, without exception, puzzle stories—are mostly based in such abstruse items of scientific theory as to seem utterly arcane to non-specialists. Precisely for that reason, however, they have a strange majesty that no common-or-garden mystery story could ever possess. No one but Hal Clement has ever shown us the world from such bizarre but utterly authentic angles as those possessed by the aliens in "Proof" (his first-published story), "Planetfall", and "Longline".

As if these unavoidable problems were not enough, almost all the stories here embody and promote, with a politeness that conceals a certain evangelical verve, a highly distinctive moral order. This fact is fascinating in itself, all the more so by virtue of the rarity of the moral precepts in question. Clement steadfastly refuses to manufacture cheap narrative energy by setting up villains whose function is to be blown away in morally-satisfying climaxes. Although "Uncommon Sense" does feature treacherous space pirates, they are only peripherally relevant to the ecological puzzle that powers the main plot-line. Similarly, the aliens who kidnap and imprison a human starship crew (along with several non-human starship crews) in "Attitude" are not stigmatized in the end as an enemy to be opposed, but accepted as possessors of a polite and scrupulous curiosity, who deserve respect, admiration and charity. Even the manifestly piratical and treacherous alien in the author's second-published story, "Impediment", is deemed to be pitiable, and is subjected to no violent retribution, even though its trespasses are not entirely forgiven. As Clement has observed, the universe of his stories—which is the universe revealed to us by our scientific analyses—is sufficiently hostile to human life without populating it with imaginary monsters. In Clement's work, the first priority is always to establish communication with the alien, and the second to offer assistance in the shared cause of progress. This, I assume, is the basis on which he selected his pseudonym.

Given all this, it is little short of astonishing that Hal Clement managed to publish his early work at all, let alone in a pulp magazine; he could not have done so without the presence in the pulp marketplace of the highly idiosyncratic John W. Campbell Jr.—but let no one think that the alliance between Clement and Campbell was a marriage made in Heaven. Campbell, a human chauvinist and oddball social Darwinist, was nowhere near in tune with Clement's moral standpoint—and that is why so much of Clement's post-1950 work went to other editors. His was a literary career built in hostile circumstances, and was a triumph of persistence. His finest works are novels—the best of them all being *Mission of Gravity* (1954) and *Cycle of Fire* (1957)—but there is no book that offers a wider perspective on Clement's unique talents than this one, and it is to be treasured on that account.

Having said all that, I wish that I could approve of the book wholeheartedly, and I do feel rather mean in criticizing NESFA Press for being slightly less than perfect, when it would be very difficult indeed to think of anyone who does such good work half as well. I do, however, regret the lack of any useful supportive material in this book. The introduction by Ben Bova is simply a puff; the volume does not provide anything to help the reader place the works in context, except for a standard list of dates and places of original publication. If one compares this book with the collections of stories by Theodore Sturgeon that are currently being issued on an annual basis by a rival small press one can immediately see the opportunities that have been lost. The Sturgeon series presents the stories in chronological order, with notes clarifying—as far as is possible—the dates and circumstances of their composition. Paul Williams' biographical and critical notes are a model not merely of clarity but of helpfulness; without the least trace of academic bluster, they allow the reader to see how Sturgeon's individual works fit into an overall pattern of endeavor, and how they constitute a highly-problematic but wonderfully worthwhile project. The Sturgeon series is a magnificent example of what is achievable, and sets a standard at which all similar projects ought to be aimed. Perhaps it is unfair to blame NESFA Press for not even trying to do anything similar, but I cannot help feeling that they could have done a much greater service to the author and his readers had they (and perhaps he) been prepared to make the effort.

One example of an instance where more information would have been useful is "Planetfall". The acknowledgements page states that this was published as "Planet for Plunder" in the February 1957 issue of *Satellite Science Fiction* but "Planet for Plunder" was actually a hybrid work billed as a collaboration between Clement and Sam Merwin Jr., the latter having attempted to make the story more reader-friendly by adding a human-viewpoint narrative to complement the alien-viewpoint narrative. Although Leo Margulies' editorial in the relevant issue claims that this was done solely in order to make the story a more appropriate length, I strongly suspect that the original only ended up being submitted to *Satellite* because it had been rejected everywhere else, on the grounds that it is too difficult for a merely human reader to grasp what is happening solely on the basis of the alien's often-mistaken deductions. The present version—it first saw publication in a paperback anthology—cannot have been taken from Clement's original manuscript because it still contains several editorial intrusions by Merwin, which refer to his additions; some of them are quite meaningless in this context and even those that are not are a trifle awkward. Given that this text has obviously been derived simply by chopping the human-viewpoint passages out of the *Satellite* version, it must be regarded as corrupt—and even the purist reader who flatly refuses to endorse the view (for which I have a guilty sympathy) that "Planet for Plunder" is a considerably better story than "Planetfall" surely has cause to regret the lack of information about the story's peculiar history.

It is those jobs that are genuinely worth doing that are worth doing as well as is humanly possible. This book might easily be reckoned ninety-five percent perfect, but I cannot help feeling the lack of that other five percent.

Summers at Castle Auburn by Sharon Shinn

The issue of the NYRSF (#154) that reached me while I was in the middle of reading *Summers at Castle Auburn* contains a letter from Ginjer Buchanan complaining, on behalf of Sharon Shinn and Allen Steele, that two NYRSF reviewers—including me, as reviewer of the Steele book—had accused them of "somehow cutting their authorial cloth for marketing purposes". Our noble editor responded by immediately conceding the point, apologizing, and promising that any such comments would be excised in the future. I suppose I ought to do my best to fall in with this exciting new strategy, lest I be cast into the outer darkness. I have, therefore, taken due note of Ms Buchanan's comment that "Sharon, in particular, would be amused" by any assumption that the notion of a "marketing strategy" had ever entered her head—and given that Ms. Shinn has certainly not amused me, I surely ought to do my utmost to return the compliment.

Having said all that, I must admit that I am not quite sure what purpose I am supposed to be serving now that all my old assumptions about the nature and function of book reviews—and, indeed, of books—have been torpedoed. I must, it seems, assume that there is no marketing going on here, and hence no commodity that is being offered to the readers of this piece. There is no product for sale, nor any entrepreneurial scheme that is in any way responsible for the object I held in my hands while the substance of Ms. Shinn's entirely spontaneous fantasy somehow made its way (fleetingly) into my consciousness. I am not at all sure how this transference could have happened, unless at some stage—purely by a random accident of happenstance, of course—that fantasy fell into the form of a double-spaced typescript, which was delivered to Ms. Buchanan by some altogether miraculous agency (perhaps the stork that also delivers babies)....but let us not continue to sully our thoughts with such essentially tasteless matters, lest the wellsprings of our own inspiration be irreparably corrupted.

I shall improvise as best I can.

Summers at Castle Auburn dreams of Coriel (Corie to her friends), a young girl whose illegitimate birth has left her in a marginal position with respect to the court of the petty kingdom where she lives. The kingdom seems to have no borders with other earthly lands, but Alora—the realm of the fairies, who are here called aliora—is just the other side of the river. This is convenient for the fairy-hunters who exploit the fairies' allergy to heavy metals in shackling them as slaves, and even more convenient for those lucky mortals who realize that fairyland (where all are welcome) is so super-duper that no sane person would ever want to return therefrom.

Corie has been brought up in relative poverty—which conveniently prevents her from having the least trace of vanity, although she is a wilful and spirited gel and is in training to be the kind of witch-cum-herbalist whose bag of tricks includes cures for absolutely all ills—but she is allowed to spend her summers at court once she becomes a teenager. As she grows older she discovers that this is less of a privilege than it once seemed, and realizes to her horror that she is political marriage-fodder, just like all her better-born friends.

Corie's beloved legitimate half-sister Elisandra is destined to be married to Bryan, the heir to the throne—a fate much worse than death, given that he is a thoroughly rotten egg. Corie is, however, far too goody-goody to get around to the serious business of poisoning the (metaphorical) bastard herself. Instead, she limits herself to the more nakedly heroic task of freeing the kingdom's fairy slaves (although she has to wait until they have conveniently been gathered together in one room in order for the task to become manageable at a stroke). Had Corie ever read Karl Marx or Martin Luther King, of course, she might have had a very different idea about the nature and methodology of liberation, but it seems that the only reading matter available in the kingdom (presumably in manuscript form, given the apparent absence of printing presses) consists of improbably accurate herbals and trashy romances. In any case, although Corie is not above inflicting the occasional bruise, she is definitely not one for upsetting whole apple-carts. Who can blame her, given that what passes for a happy ending in this kind of dream is marrying the good egg who—thanks to the mercy of happenstance—is next in line to the throne once the bad egg has been murdered?

(Actually, even the kind of reader who finds this sort of thing amusing, were the mercy of happenstance ever to allow one access to the fantasy, *might* wonder why Corie bothers to hang around even for the dubious privilege of being queen, since an infinitely more spiffing alternative is available just across the river—and, for that matter, why Auburn is not the deserted village it ought to be—but this is not the kind of dream that goes in for overmuch explanatory commentary.)

Being the kind of reader who remains quite unamused by this sort of thing, I am really quite glad of the opportunity to be able to treat it as a dream rather than a commercial product, because that approach to it raises all kinds of interesting questions about the interpretation of dreams. Sigmund Freud would probably think that *Summers at Castle Auburn* and similar fantasies are all about sex—and so they are, on a superficial level—but I think we ought to be prepared to try to cut a little deeper than mere symptoms, in the hope that we might one day be able to understand the profound moral and existential malaise that underlies them.

The kingdom of this dream is one whose sociopolitical system is rotten through and through, and it is obvious even to the meanest intellect that its essential rottenness cannot be "cured" by the application of palliative herbs to miscellaneous wounds, occasional judicious regicide, or the temporary manumission of currently-enslaved aliora. It is a kingdom without any history to explain its inner tensions, nor any external enemies to explain why its internal coherency matters, but more important than either of these facts is the fact that it has no future. Everything in the world-within-the-text is the way it is because there is no scope within it for meaningful change. Although defection to fairyland is a mysteriously unheeded option, the world is utterly devoid of any real progressive element, whether technological or political, all such potential having been ruled out *a priori* by authorial diktat.

We may infer from participation in this particular adventure that the personnel of the world-within-the-text will continue to come and go—good kings and bad ones, nice girls and not-so-nice ones, virile guardsmen capable of generous deeds and decrepit noblemen committed to ungenerous ones—but the fundamental state of being seems to be set in stone. Petty evils will crop up, to be defeated or not, but no closure will ever be available to any story that is told of this world except that the *status quo* is recovered—with one or two of the more obvious blots effaced from its eternal landscape, but with the underlying picture quite unmodified.

What kind of imagination is it that spontaneously bursts forth in fruits of this dire and bitter kind? What depths of pessimism are required to model existence in these dark and meager terms, not merely as a prison but as an *oubliette*? What kind of mind is it that can occupy itself so relentlessly with the ridiculous trivia of erotic relationships, insisting all the while that *every* human emotion—not merely love, of which it is almost believable, but really serious matters like hope and clarity of vision—is a mere illusion of chemistry, always obtainable and sustainable, if you only know someone who knows the trick of it, by chewing on a plant with a silly name?

The point should not need laboring, but all fantasy is not like this. There are some fantasies that are prepared to insist, ingeniously and with some creative authority, that we do *not* live in an unchangeable world, and that even those of us who *are* the helpless victims of whatever psychotropic drugs we happen to have in our luggage might have some cause for genuine hope and some capacity for authentic ambition.

We are, of course, powerless and cowardly creatures, far too stupid to hold the complexity of the world in our minds or to comprehend its dynamics—but we are not compelled by these real failings to employ the gift of imagination in the ridiculous and repulsive task of making worlds that reflect our pusillanimity, and where the characters' capacity for thought and virtue is correspondingly restricted. Whatever else is lost to us, we are surely free to imagine worlds-within-texts in which meaningful questions might be raised and addressed by intelligent beings: worlds that are more than just tatty patchworks of worn-out ideas that were utterly useless even when briefly alive. What reason, then—and what excuse—can there possibly be for refusing to do that, even in a world where there is no market for it?

The Space Opera Renaissance edited by David G. Hartwell and Kathryn Cramer, Tor, 2006

The compilation of a showcase anthology of space opera is, as David Hartwell and Kathryn Cramer (hereafter referred to, for economy's sake, as "H/C") point out in their introduction, a project dogged by two awkward difficulties. One is that space opera, however defined, is not a short story genre; it mostly consists of novels and novellas, thus ensuring that any showcase anthology is likely to be improbably big even at its most distortively selective. The other is that the history of the term is somewhat confused, thus ensuring that any such anthology is likely to generate differences of opinion as to whether all of its contents really are space operas, or whether it should also have cast its net in waters that the editors let well alone.

In practical terms, H/C's solution to the first problem has been to accept the necessity of producing a very big book, the bulk of whose contents consists of novellas—a move that has the virtue of making their book good value on a words-per-dollar basis. They claim that their solution to the second was to try to provide examples representative of all the variant definitions, and to explain how those variants came about. This move might have worked better if their account of the history of the term's usage and implications had not been so resolutely and idiosyncratically revisionist, couched as an occasionally-intemperate attack on previous definers of the term. (Declaration of interest: although H/C do not cite yours truly's article in the Clute/Nicholls *Encyclopedia*, that article is a cardinal example of the kind of account they attempt to write off as fundamentally misconceived.)

Like other reference-book definers, H/C note the coinage of the term by Wilson Tucker in 1941, in an outflow of condemnatory bile. They differ from other definers, however, in insisting that the term was intended simply as a shorthand term for bad sf, not as an identification of a particular subgenre. They assert that it was used purely and simply as a term of contempt until the end of the 1960s; the first citation they give of the term being used as a near-value-neutral subgeneric description is from 1970. They go to some trouble to "emphasize" that the term was used before that date to refer to "all bad sf hackwork...[not confined] to the future, or off-Earth settings," although they associate the first significant shift in its implications with an ad that appeared on the back cover of the first (October 1950) issue of *Galaxy*. The ad quoted the opening paragraphs of two hypothetical stories featuring one Bat Durston, one of them a bad Western and the other a sciencefictional transfiguration of the bad Western, together with the proud boast "You'll Never See it in *Galaxy*". H/C suggest that this ad "helped to spark a popular redefinition of space opera as any hackneyed SF filled with stereotypes borrowed from Westerns."

In the 1960s, H/C contend, the term "began to be regularly confused with fondness for outworn, clunky, old-fashioned SF, guilty pleasures" and suggest that it was only in this period that it began to be associated specifically with space fiction. "We don't know the first time anyone used the term in reference to Doc Smith, or the early work of John W. Campbell Jr.," they admit, "but by sometime before the middle of the 1960s, but sometimes as early as 1950 it was so used, though not universally." (I am working from a proof copy, so it is conceivable that this sentence might be adjusted slightly in the final version.)

The pejorative connotations of the term were, H/C allege, renewed by British New Wave antipathy to space fiction, which proclaimed that space opera was both obsolete and dead—as illustrated by Brian Aldiss's "two-volume anthology *Space Opera* and *Galactic Empires*". (Judging from appearances, it seems highly probable that Brian Aldiss did intend to issue his showcase in two volumes as *Space Opera* and *Galactic Empires*; if so, however, both volumes were considered overlong by their US publishers and subdivided, the former into *Space Opera* and *Space Odysseys*, the second into *Galactic Empires Volume I* and *Galactic Empires Volume II*.)

H/C claim that the New Wave-originated criticisms and the Aldiss showcase generated a backlash in the USA, which resulted in the term being used, allegedly for the first time, as a defiant term of praise. They cite Leigh Brackett's introduction to a 1976 anthology of stories from *Planet Stories* as a cardinal example of such defiance, and that anthology's publisher, Judy-Lynn del Rey—along with her husband Lester—as the key propagandists responsible for the championship of space opera as a virtuous subgenre. "Thus," they observe, "the term 'space opera' reentered the serious discourse of sf in the 1980s with a completely altered meaning; henceforth, 'space opera' meant, and still generally means, colorful, dramatic, large-scale science fiction adventure, competently and sometimes beautifully written, usually focused on a sympathetic, heroic central character and plot action...and usually set in the relatively distant future and on other worlds, characteristically optimistic in tone."

This, in a nutshell, is the narrative that the H/C showcase sets out to embody and illustrate. It is balderdash. The "orthodox narrative" from which H/C are dissenting is, in fact, much closer to the truth—a contention easily provable by means of the most cursory examination of the usage of the term. H/C will hopefully not mind my attempting to carry out such an examination and report its findings, given that I was asked by David Hartwell to review the book—for publication in his own magazine—in spite of the fact that I gave up reviewing some years ago, and in the full knowledge that I would undoubtedly dissent from its introductory thesis.

* * * * * * *

Like H/C, I have no idea when "space opera" was first used to refer to the kind of fiction that E. E. "Doc" Smith wrote, but Doc Smith did it himself in 1947, in an essay on how to write "The Epic of Space" in Lloyd Arthur Eshbach's symposium *Of Worlds Beyond: The Science of Science Fiction Writing* (p. 82). Space opera was not Smith's preferred term for "epics of space", but he clearly recognised it as a term used by others to refer to the type of story he wrote. It was widely used in that fashion as soon as sf magazines began to publish review columns—a move mostivated by the establishment of specialist small presses to reprint pulp sf. The existence of such columns forced their reviewers to devise a primitive generic taxonomy and critical terminology, which was mostly based on terminology invented in fanzines.

The first review column to appear in *Thrilling Wonder Stories*, in the October 1947 issue, was devoted to Jack Williamson's *The*

Legion of Space, and its judgment began: "This is space opera with a vengeance—with passably good characterization and dialogue." (p. 111). The review's author (identified as "The Editor"—*i.e.*, Sam Merwin, Jr.) clearly expects his readers to know what a space opera is, and is obviously using it to designate a particular subgenre. In subsequent reviews Merwin mapped out the field implicit in his use of the term, identifying John W. Campbell Jr.'s *The Mightiest Machine* as "space opera in its ultimate or E. E. Smithian form" (*Startling Stories* March 1950, p. 162), saying of George O. Smith's *Nomad* that "if you like your space opera, this is your dish" (*Startling* July 1950, p. 161) and describing Jack Williamson's pseudonymous *Seetee Shock* as "good swift space opera" (*Startling* November 1950, p. 158). In no case that I can find did he use the phrase as a term of abuse.

Other pioneering reviewers followed a broadly similar policy. In *Astounding* P. Schuyler Miller, reviewing E. E. Smith's *Triplanetary*, stated that "Dr. Smith should never take offense when he is called the father of space-opera" (October 1948 p. 141) and goes on to defend both the author and the subgenre. When he reviewed *Skylark Three* in the September 1949 issue Miller observed that, in the Skylark series, "space-opera, previously monopolized by the world-saver school of Edmond Hamilton, took on a new freedom and stature" (p. 152).

In *Super Science Stories*, Frederik Pohl, reviewing George O. Smith's novel, says: "if you want tingling action, colossal space-struggles and a whole new arsenal of super-scientific weapons, by all means invest in a copy of *Nomad*; you'll wait a long time for a better space opera than this" (July 1950, p. 70). In *Galaxy*, Groff Conklin, reviewing *The Skylark of Space*, said "this ancient item...was the first venture of the greatest of all the old-time space opera boys" (June 1951, p. 54). Pohl and Conklin both make clear their personal distaste for space opera, but both concede that there is a considerable audience that does like it, and both take pains to allow that there is nothing wrong with that aesthetic choice.

This practice continued when sf criticism first made the giant leap to book publication, in Reginald Bretnor's *Modern Science Fiction: Its Meaning and its Future* (1953). Isaac Asimov's essay on "Social Science Fiction" is perfectly prepared to admit that "space opera within the limitations of its own field can reach a high level of excellence"—an assertion followed by the observation that "Edward E. Smith and John W. Campbell brought this type of story to its heights" (p. 170).

There is a certain defensiveness in many of these uses of the term, which implies that it did carry contemptuous implications against which it needed to be defended. Fan critics were especially likely to be wary of using the term. Sam Moskowitz did not employ it in his profiles of Doc Smith, John W. Campbell or Edmond Hamilton, although—after citing a newspaper review of *Seetee Shock* that had employed the term—he was unapologetic in recording that "*The Legion of Space* had many of the epic qualities that had made the space operas of E. Smith [*sic*] or John Campbell so popular" in his profile of Jack Williamson (*Amazing Stories* October 1964, p. 89). Donald A. Wollheim was similarly discreet, although he was perfectly happy in *The Universe Makers* to describe John W. Campbell Jr. as "one of the best writers of space opera of the thirties" (p. 74) and to say of A. Bertram Chandler that he "has been turning out good space opera for perhaps thirty years" (p. 93). Moskowitz and Wollheim were more likely than any of the other users here cited to have been keenly aware of Wilson Tucker's coinage of the term, but in their case, as well as the others, it is likely that their wariness resulted from the manner in which the term was routinely used by critics outside the genre looking in.

I do not have access to the article on the science fiction market written by Margaret St. Clair for the June and August 1947 issues of *Writer's Digest*, but Forrest J. Ackerman's review of that article in the August-September 1947 issue of *Fantasy Review* alleges that the gist of her argument is contained in the quoted words "Currently the present trend is dead away from the aptly-named 'space opera'" (p. 1). This is an interesting observation, partly because it illustrates that even in 1947—let alone 1974—space opera was being touted as something obsolete and on the verge of extinction, but also because it reflects an opinion commonly held by observers outside the pulp genre that, although Earth-based science fiction set in the future might have something to recommend it, space fiction was essentially worthless.

A clear statement of this position can be found in the introduction to Phil Stong's *The Other Worlds* (1941), the first hardcover anthology of "supernatural fiction" to include a considerable amount of pulp sf. Stong—writing before Tucker coined the term "space opera"—takes pains to explain his exclusion of all "interplanetary fiction" by putting the boot in good and hard. "In the magazines available," he says, "there are not a dozen such stories with even mild originality or amusement value. They fall into several common classes" (p. 14). He goes on to list three key examples of such classes: the "world-saver" formula in which invaders from "Mars or

Sirius" are frustrated; the plot-formula of the kind of interplanetary fantasy popularized by Edgar Rice Burroughs; and "the youngest lieutenant in the Interplanetary Police has trouble with pirates" (p. 14).

Given that this was a common view from outside the genre, it is not surprising that Margaret St. Clair should take the trouble to insist that these sorts of things were being put away by the genre's trend-setters. Some magazines outside the pulp genre did their best to encourage that demise; J. T. McIntosh, complaining in a guest editorial in *Science Fantasy* no. 9 (1954) that space opera was unwanted by many editors, cites the market guidelines published by *Collier's*, which emphasized the magazine's openness to sf submissions while adding the qualification that: "We're not interested in standard space opera or propaganda stories disguised as science fiction" (p. 2).

* * * * * * *

Although US reviewers were mostly disposed to defend space opera against this kind of external contempt by disputing the attackers' parameters as well as their evaluations, British reviewers seemed more inclined to accept the external judgment of what space opera was. A review-article in *Science-Fantasy* no. 2 (Winter 1950) by John K. Aiken—a member of the famous literary family—entitled "The Charms of Space Opera" offered illustrative slices of two hypothetical texts eerily similar to *Galaxy*'s Bat Durston ad (which Aiken could not possible have seen before writing the article). This exemplar of space operatic transfiguration was followed by a comment-cum-definition: "By the Cosmos out of horse opera. An adventure story, in fact, in which the horse has been replaced by the spaceship and the terrestrial by a galactic setting; in which the plot—as in the best opera—is naive, the atmosphere fantastic, and the characters pure 'hack'" (p. 75) The description continues in a similarly sarcastic tone, but gladly concedes that space opera can be very entertaining. Considering contemporary exemplars, Aiken finds much to admire in Nelson Bond's *Lancelot Biggs, Spaceman* and L. Ron Hubbard's *The Kingslayer*, but less in George O. Smith's *Nomad* and *Pattern for Conquest*. Almost as an afterthought, he tacks on a sympathetic account of Otis Adelbert Kline's *The Port of Peril*, hailing its literary model, Edgar Rice Burroughs, as "one of the pioneers of space opera in its original, unsophisticated, form" (p. 76).

Aiken's piece is interesting for its endorsement the notion of space opera as transfigurative Western fiction, quite independently of the *Galaxy* ad, and also because it conflates what American genre reviewers normally considered to be space opera with the kind of fiction that is nowadays described—thanks to John Clute's popularization of the term in the *Encyclopedia*—as "planetary romance". Phil Stong had done likewise, and several other British critics followed suit, although, in the course of my cursory research, I could not find any example of an American genre critic doing likewise until Leigh Brackett wrote her response to Brian Aldiss' showcase anthology.

The most comprehensive early account of the meaning of "space opera", contained in Kingsley Amis' *New Maps of Hell* (pp. 44-45), is so similar to Aiken's that Amis must surely have used it as a source, although Amis scrupulously reports that it was H. Rider Haggard that stood at the head of the great tradition of Burroughsian romance. It is hardly surprisingly that Aldiss's account of space opera in his showcase anthologies follows the same groove, although he did not use the term at all in his history of sf, *Billion Year Spree* (1973). On the other hand, British reviewers whose critical horizons were more closely confined to the genre echoed US usage. In *New Worlds* no. 32 (1955), Leslie Flood's recently-instituted review column proclaimed that the British editions of Doc Smith's Lensman series were "good news for lovers of space-opera" and proceeded to give a eulogistic account of Smith's work.

* * * * * * *

According to H/C, "to say it flatly, before the mid-1970s, no one in the history of science fiction ever consciously and intentionally set out to write space opera". They swiftly add two supposedly-partial exceptions—Jack Vance and Samuel R. Delany—but the Vance example they quote is *Space Opera*, by virtue of its punning title. Personally, I find it extremely hard to believe that Vance was not consciously and intentionally writing space opera when he penned *The Five Gold Bands* (1950)—for a magazine whose editor was using the term freely in reviews—and am quite certain that he was doing that when he wrote *The Star King* (1963).

Although it is true that the editors of such magazines as the second incarnation of *Science Fiction Adventures* did not advertise their specialism as space opera, it is surely impossible to believe that Robert Silverberg—the author of one-and-a-half of the three items in the first issue of the reborn magazine—was not consciously and intentionally writing space opera. Even if he had somehow overlooked the fact, his readers did not; in the first letter in the magazine's first letter column (February 1957, p. 125), Billy Meyers characterized the magazine's contents as "not just space opera but *well-written* space opera" before proceeding to a lengthy defence of such fiction. When the magazine's British edition survived its parent's demise, the novellas written for it by such writers as Kenneth Bulmer and E. C. Tubb—not to mention Michael Moorcock—look very much like conscious and intentional exercises in space opera, as do the many novellas that Edmond Hamilton and others contributed to *Imagination* and *Imaginative Tales*.

Even if one sets these conjectural examples aside, however, there is at least one absolutely safe contradiction to H/C's cavalier allegation. In his article on "The Science in Science Fiction" in the November 1951 issue of *Science Fiction Quarterly*, James Blish identifies one of his own stories ("The Bore", 1950) as "just space opera", having earlier observed of astronomy-based sf stories that "such a story can also be unabashed space opera, if you're in the mood to write that kind of thing" (p. 113).

This observation is doubly interesting because Blish—along with Damon Knight—was one of the first genre reviewers to attempt a revision and refinement of the genre's critical terminology, and one of the terms he attempted to revise and redefine, in the interests of sharpening up the critical vocabulary and making it more useful, was "space opera". His first use of the term in the "William Atheling Jr." collection *The Issue at Hand* occurs in the context of a discussion—originally published in 1952—as to whether C. M. Kornbluth's "The Goodly Creatures" properly qualifies as sf. He contends that the story "epitomizes *F&SF*" and is "wonderfully written" but concludes that "in short, what Messrs. Kornbluth, Boucher, and McComas have here is a space opera" (p. 29). Blish went on to use "space opera" on several more occasions as a term for any sf story whose plot could have been relocated to any kind of non-sf setting.

Blish explained this idiosyncratic redefinition more fully in the penultimate essay reprinted in *More Issues at Hand*, "Science-Fantasy and Translations" (based on material initially published in 1960-63), where he cites the infamous *Galaxy* ad as a classic instance of "translation". His discussion of "science-fantasy" is also an attempt to give that term—previously used in several different ways by various commentators—a new and more specific definition, in order to give it a specific function within the critical discourse he and Knight were attempting to develop. (This process is observed but somewhat misrepresented by H/C, who claim that "Knight used the term 'science-fantasy' as a neutral term describing Brackett's work".) Having cited the *Galaxy* ad, Blish's essay goes on to say that H. L. Gold did not keep his promise, and that *Galaxy* did, in fact, play host to numerous "translations". He also claims that such "translations" were part of the staple fare of *F&SF*, although *F&SF* stories were more likely to "translate" soap operas than Westerns; it was in this context that he had earlier felt free to refer to "The Goodly Creatures" as a "space opera".

It is not surprising that Blish and Knight should have been unusually sensitive to the issue of sf stories that were what they called "translations" and I call "transfigurations". They would, in any case, have been easily able to observe that a great many pulp sf stories were "futuristic costume dramas" in which the plot-formulas of other genres or the plots of classic texts from those genres, were simply retold in sciencefictional settings—but they had both had their noses rubbed in that fact by working for the Scott Meredith Literary Agency, which offered critical appraisals of work submitted to the agency on the basis that there was a standard "plot skeleton" that magazine fiction in all genres ought to embody. Both men undoubtedly used that plot-skeleton, consciously and intentionally, in some of their early work, and presumably made sure that their fellow Futurians, as well as other clients of the agency, knew exactly what they were doing when they wrote calculated "space operas".

Blish and Knight were rebelling against the tacit assumption of the Meredith skeleton in their critical work, the fundamental thrust of which was that sf writers ought to try as hard as they could to make sf—including space fiction—into something distinctive and unique, irreducible to any kind of endlessly-transfigurable formula. "Space opera" briefly became Blish's shorthand term for all sciencefictional "translations", but he was the only person to use it in that way and it was not a straightforward term of abuse; it did not refer to sf that was intrinsically bad, but sf that imagined happenings in futuristic and alien settings as mere reiterations of established patterns. (Coming from the man who based his most famous future history explicitly and methodically on Oswald Spengler's theory of cyclic history, this might seem a trifle disingenuous—but he was prepared to admit that he was himself a writer of space opera.)

Armed with their sensitivity to transfigured plot-skeletons, Blish and Knight would have had no trouble observing that numerous space operas by Nelson Bond and Fletcher Pratt were straightforward transfigurations of Classical myths, or that Edmond Hamilton's *The Star Kings* (1947) was a futuristic version of Anthony Hope's *The Prisoner of Zenda*. The example Blish cites of Gold's broken promise is a series of stories by Robert Sheckley, but by the time he integrated his original essay into *More Issues at Hand* he could, had he so wished, have called attention to the fact that two of the most prestigious works to be serialized in *Galaxy* during its early years, Alfred Bester's *The Demolished Man* and *The Stars my Destination*, were transfigurations of Fyodor Dostoyevsky's *Crime and Punishment* and Alexandre Dumas' *The Count of Monte Cristo*. He could also have observed that Robert A. Heinlein had been sufficiently inspired by such examples to write his own transfigurations of *The Prisoner of Zenda* (*Double Star*) and *The Count of Monte Cristo* (*The Door into Summer*).

There was, of course, a blatantly disingenuous aspect to the *Galaxy* ad and similar characterizations of bad space operas as transfigurations of bad Westerns. There is a sense in which, when it is viewed as a generic whole, American science fiction is a manifest transfiguration of the Western. American sf originated and evolved in the same media as the Western, in parallel with it; early American Edisonades like Edward S. Ellis's *The Steam-Man of the Prairies* actually were Westerns. The mythical future formulated and embraced by American sf as its guiding light and binding cement was one of pioneering, frontiersmanship, conquest and colonization, which simply took the mythical core of Western and applied it to extraterrestrial space—archetypally redefined, as the makers of *Star Trek* recognised and advertised, as "the final frontier". It was inevitable, therefore, that the genre should be exceedingly hospitable to transfigurations of Western stories, not just at the contemptuously crude level represented by such stories as Chester S. Geier's "Outlaw in the Sky" (1953, by-lined Guy Archette)—which was obviously written as a pulp Western novel and required only half a dozen changes of terminology to sell to *Amazing Stories*—but at every conceivable level of sophistication thereabove.

What Blish pointed out in his early critical writings was that the kind of sophistication being carried out by magazine editors like Gold and Boucher was not so much a matter of discovering a distinct and self-contained form of science fiction, but merely of finding a wider and more prestigious range of models for transfiguration. This view concurs with the British line of thinking elaborated by Aiken, Amis and Aldiss, which suggested that all transfigurations of the kinds of popular fiction that might be described as "adventure stories" or "heroic fantasies" could sensibly be defined and described as "space operas"—and that space operas were capable of possessing exactly the same kinds of virtues possessed by classics of those kinds of fiction. It seems highly likely, therefore, that a considerable number of writers in the 1950s knew perfectly well that they were writing space opera and were quite unashamed of the fact. Why should they not be unashamed, given that Joseph Campbell had assured them, in *The Hero With a Thousand Faces* (1949), that all heroic fantasies are merely variants of a fundamental (and fundamentally virtuous) "monomyth", no matter what subcultural decor they might choose to employ?

* * * * * * *

All of this may seem like nitpicking, and would be if H/C's imaginary history of space opera had not led them to miss out an entire phase of its development. The temptation to do so is understandable, because it allows them to leap from their first group of four exemplary texts (headed "Redefined Writers"—four texts from 1931-50) to interim groups of "Draftees" (three texts from 1955-72) and "Transitions/Redefiners" (four texts from 1986-99) before getting to their actual subject-matter, which is a supposed "renaissance" of space opera that allegedly began in the 1990s. It might have been simpler just to leave out the first and second groups altogether and to begin the story in the 1980s with the likes of Ian Banks and Lois McMaster Bujold. As things stand, though, their false history generates a seriously flawed account of the nature of that alleged "renaissance" and the reasons for its occurrence.

Given that H/C did decide to incorporate a historical dimension to their anthology, there is a certain undeniable propriety in including Edmond Hamilton's "The Star Stealers" and Jack Williamson's "The Prince of Space" as comparative exemplars—benchmark illustrations of the distance that modern space opera has travelled since sf writers first developed a casually dismissive attitude to light-years. The propriety of the other two early exemplars is, however, much more dubious.

In view of H/C's fingering of Leigh Brackett as a key apologist for space opera, and Brian Aldiss's dogged pursuit of British precedent in conflating space opera with planetary romance in his own series of showcase anthologies, there is obviously some justification for acknowledging the conflation, and it has the convenient side-effect of allowing them to include a number of modern planetary romances in the anthology without having to worry overmuch about matters of definition, but it does seem to me to have been a serious mis-step, and that it would have been wiser as well as tidier had they stuck to the characterization of space opera common in the early days of terminology-formation to Doc Smith, Sam Merwin, P. Schuyler Miller, Frederik Pohl, Groff Conklin, Isaac Asimov, Sam Moskowitz, and Donald A. Wollheim. That may not have been the original definition, and it was certainly not the only one to achieve a measure of currency, but it was—and is—the most useful.

There is nothing wrong with the selection of "The Enchantress of Venus" as a type-specimen of Leigh Brackett's work; it is a hugely enjoyable story for readers who can sympathize with its fundamental conceit. It is not, however, a good illustration of the fact that the kind of universe routinely imagined by space opera had, by 1949, become the tacit ideative framework of the planetary romance. It is, in fact, a deliberately old-fashioned exercise replete with nostalgia for the days when Edgar Rice Burroughs still had an ounce of originality and—more pertinently—C. L. Moore had cleverly combined his influence with that of A. Merritt in order to import a kind of ultimate Haggardesque adventure fiction into the specialist pulp *Weird Tales*. Brackett extrapolated the calculated decadence of Moore's imagery in a hyper-nostalgic vein that was unrepentantly backward-looking—but that was only one aspect of *Planet Stories*' standard fare. The space-set adventure stories published in the magazine followed a different trajectory; so, for that matter, did the contemporary work of Brackett's husband, Edmond Hamilton, exemplified by such novels as *The Star of Life* and *The Star Kings*.

Hamilton and such fellow late-1940s and early-1950s space opera writers as A. E. van Vogt, James Blish, Jack Vance and Poul Anderson were developing a more sweeping and far more elaborate kind of decadent imagery—of whose development I shall say more in due course. For this reason, Brackettesque planetary romance is something of a sideline by comparison with a more sophisticated planetary romance that was also being developed by Anderson and Vance, and many other writers besides. Space opera and planetary romance both evolved in this period to embrace a much "harder" version of their mutual conceptual frame, but Brackett was a stubborn, though glorious, exception to the pattern rather than an illustration of its thrust.

The strangest decision H/C make, by far, is their choice of Clive Jackson's brief item of fan fiction, "The Swordsmen of Vardis" (1950) as their fourth comparative exemplar. One can see why Fredric Brown liked it enough to reprint in his and Mack Reynolds' *Science Fiction Carnival*, because it is the kind of punch-line-bearing shaggy dog story he loved to write, but its central joke has been done to death, and it is not at all clear that a fannish parody of Brackettesque planetary romance serves any purpose in this kind of anthology. (Incidentally, H/C say that "nothing is known of what became of him" but Jackson did publish two more sf stories in 1958-9—both progressive space operas in the more orthodox definition—

and apparently sold at least one other that did not appear. He was a Scotsman, although he was resident in Cheltenham by 1958, and it is not surprising that he deployed the same amiable sarcasm as John Aiken.)

* * * * * * *

The three stories in H/C's second section include Cordwainer Smith's "The Game of Rat and Dragon" and Samuel R. Delany's *Empire Star*, both of which are representative of an important trend in the space opera subgenre, to which H/C pay scant attention, but the third is another off-hand parody, Robert Sheckley's "Zirn Left Unguarded, the Jenghik Palace in Flames, John Westerly Dead", which is the only overlap between this showcase and Brian Aldiss's. The story has never seemed to me to pack the devastating punch that Aldiss and H/C attribute to it, but the real reason for its presence in both showcases is to celebrate the alleged demise of space opera by dancing on its grave. Its presence thus attempts to excuse the fact that the H/C anthology then takes a mighty leap forward, further exaggerated by the fact that the next section opens with David Brin's "Temptation" (1999), which is by far the most recent of the four inclusions in terms of its publication date. The others, whose publication dates are intimately clustered in 1986-90, are David Drake's "Ranks of Bronze", Lois McMaster Bujold's "Weatherman" and "Iain M. Banks' "A Gift from the Culture".

This leap is a big one even if one accepts H/C's contention that the notion of space opera's obsolescence and imminent extinction—and the ideological backlash against that proposition—dates from the 1970s. In fact, that notion dated from the 1940s; space opera, as a subgenre, was imagined as obsolete before the descriptive term was co-opted by the genre's early reviewers, and this assumption profoundly affected the conscious and intentional development of space opera from the late 1940s onwards. That consciousness of obsolescence had a powerful effect on the early development and subsequent evolution of the space-operatic frame that became the primary container of sophisticated planetary romance: the galactic empire.

In the introduction to *Galactic Empires Volume II*, Brian Aldiss observes that "the galactic empire is a sort of crystallisation of space opera" (p. vi), and so it is. Much of the confusion surrounding the term "space opera" arises from the desire to distinguish sf that used "functional" crystals of this sort as a facilitating backcloth for earnest thought-experiments in world-building or *contes philosophi-*

ques—thus removing them from the field of adventure fiction—from the kind of space opera that used imperial cascades of rhinestones in a purely decorative sense. (In 1947, of course, space opera could not be excused total damnation by the evocation of such notions as kitsch and camp, but by 1974 a theory of sciencefictional kitsch was beginning to emerge, and Aldiss's showcase anthologies are appreciative of that fact.)

It is highly significant that—with the principal exception of early examples like "The Star-Stealers"—almost all fictional images of galaxy-spanning civilizations are deeply-tinted with the imagery of decadence. The primary model of the kind of galactic empire that became a standard backcloth for much genre sf—extravagantly and enthusiastically promoted as such by Don Wollheim, as editor at Ace and DAW, long before Judy-Lynn del Rey got in on the act—was Isaac Asimov's Foundation series: an explicit transfiguration of the history of the Roman Empire's decline and fall. This was the work that Asimov was trying to distinguish from run-of-the-mill space opera in his essay on "Social Science Fiction", precisely because he was acutely conscious of the fact that it was an attempt to sophisticate the standard background of space opera and make it fit for use as a venue for what Kingsley Amis was to characterise—by contrast with Haggard-descended adventure stories—as "idea-as-hero" stories.

The magazines of the 1950s that specialized in space opera—of which the second version of *Science Fiction Adventures* and its British continuation were the most telling examples—were fully conscious of the fact that they were dealing in nostalgia, and their writers found it very easy to translate that nostalgia into the imagery of cultural decadence. That kind of rescue move is blindingly obvious in the work that Robert Silverberg did as Calvin M. Knox for the US magazine and the work that Ken Bulmer did for the UK version; it is equally manifest in the contemporary work that Edmond Hamilton did for *Imagination* and Poul Anderson's similarly-inclined Dominic Flandry series. This kind of decadent ambience did not remain static. Indeed, it was carefully extrapolated to new extremes, stylistically as well as conceptually, by a number of writers, including three that H/C credit with laying key foundation stones for their space opera "renaissance": Jack Vance, Cordwainer Smith and Samuel R. Delany. Far from being eccentrics swimming against a tide of contempt, as H/C attempt to paint them, these writers were, in fact, the proud and sparkling tip of a vast iceberg.

H/C are not alone in trying to efface this phase of space opera's evolution from the fossil record. Their story introductions routinely include quotes from the sampled authors illuminating their views of space opera, and Colin Greenland's note accompanying his story in section IV, "The Well Wishers", includes an account that echoes (or is echoed by) H/C's estimation of the situation of British sf prior to the supposed reinvention of British space opera by Iain M. Banks. Space opera, Greenland claims was once "off-limits to British sf writers" and "held in deep scorn". He states that "'British space opera' was an archaism that described the less interesting work of John Brunner; or more specifically Ted Tubb, the absolute paradigm of reliable generic sf writers knocked flat by the tsunami of the New Wave. Though Brian Aldiss...delighted in the subgenre he identified as 'widescreen baroque', the rest of Michael Moorcock's motley crew had followed J. G. Ballard in pulling out of the Space Race."

This is complete and arrant nonsense. While the New Wave was at its height, and for some years after its near-total eclipse, the principal British writers of space opera were enjoying their most productive and profitable heyday. Ted Tubb and Ken Bulmer were producing it in vast quantities, and John Brunner never stopped, although his output was much more varied and interrupted by personal misfortune. John Phillifent (alias John Rackham) and James White—the great pioneer of pacifist space opera—were also very active. They were, however, mostly publishing in the USA, with such stalwart supporters of the genre as Don Wollheim and Judy-Lynn del Rey. Because of the traditionalist stance of those editors, much of the work they sponsored was unapologetically old-fashioned, and Greenland may therefore have felt entitled to regard it as irrelevant, but he has no conceivable excuse for ignoring the most adventurous of all British writers of space opera—who was, incidentally, one of the inner circle of Michael Moorcock's "motley crew" and who published a great deal of work in *New Worlds*: Barrington J. Bayley.

As with the US writers cited above, Bayley consciously and intentionally took the decadent imagery of space opera to blithely exotic extremes in such novels as *The Garments of Caean*, *Star Winds* and *The Zen Gun*, in the last of which galatic-imperial humankind reaches the cosmic limit of *ennui* and hands the whole enterprise over to the pigs. Had Greenland taken Bayley as his exemplar rather than M. John Harrison's leaden satire *The Centauri Device*, his own space opera, including "The Well Wishers", might not have been so conspicuously effete; the latter seems feeble by comparison with Peter F. Hamilton's "Escape Route" and the exuberant American inclusions in its section:, Dan Simmons' "Orphans of the Helix", David Weber's "Ms. Midshipwoman Harrington", Catherine

Asaro's "Aurora in Four Voices", R. Garcia y Robertson's "Ring Rats" and Allen Steele's "The Death of Captain Future".

* * * * * * *

It was the profusion of decadent imagery in space opera—at every level of the sf marketplace—that paved the way for the new phase of sophistication wrought by the writers sampled in sections III and IV of H/C's anthology. They were not redefining anything, nor were they reviving anything; they were merely carrying the project forward. To some extent, the sophistication they wrought was simply the natural result of a post-Vietnam cynicism regarding military organization, and a certain spirited response to that cynicism. Bujold was such an important writer not merely because she imported a mischievously subversive female sensibility into what had previously been the most conspicuously male-dominated of sf's subgenres, but because she deftly combined a conspicuously light-hearted version of contemporary cynicism with an even-lighter-hearted narrative antidote compounded out of romance and Romance—a chimerical combination carried forward very successfully by Catherine Asaro, although David Weber's explicit space-operatic transfigurations of C. S. Forester's Hornblower novels lack conviction in more ways than one.

There are, of course, numerous other more-or-less explicit transfigurations among the stories selected by H/C, the most blatant being "Ranks of Bronze". There is a flagrant incestuousness about two of those that explicitly transfigure earlier fantasy stories, although "The Death of Captain Future" is much more scrupulous in advertising its own cynicism than Michael Moorcock's Leigh Brackett pastiche "The Lost Sorceress of the Silent Citadel" in section V. The most interesting of all the transfigurations is, perhaps, Dan Simmons' "Orphans of the Helix", because it provides a beautiful illustration of the other chief axis of sophistication that has given rise to contemporary space opera.

If one extracts the plot from "Orphans of the Helix" it is not so very different from that of "The Star-Stealers"—but that observation should by no means be taken as an insult. In his introduction to *Galactic Empires Volume I* Brian Aldiss dissents from C. S. Lewis's view that sf transfigurations are intrinsically "tasteless" by observing that such objections miss the point. "We read the love-story, the spy-story, or whatever," Aldiss says, "*because* it takes place on a fifty-kilometre long spaceship, *because* it is set on a planet where the sun goes into eclipse every hour on the hour, *because* it happens in the capital city of the greatest empire the universe has ever known. Our sensibilities are affected by these settings" (p. xi). The importance of this point—largely overlooked by James Blish (and, for that matter, Joseph Campbell)—is thrown into sharp relief by Simmons' story, which is a triumphant demonstration of the fact that in much science fiction, including the great majority of space operas, plot is quite irrelevant: what really provides the heart and soul, not merely of the subgenre but of the genre, is the decor.

When sciencefictional transfiguration is a mere matter of changing costumes and swapping six-guns for blasters, as in the old *Galaxy* ad, then the result is likely to be unconvincing, but when the trick is performed masterfully—as it is in "Orphans of the Helix"—the outcome is very different. Indeed, in Simmons' story the essential familiarity of the plot is what enables the reader to get a grip on, and follow the development of, a sequence of events that would otherwise be almost entirely alien, and whose near-entire alienness is the whole point of the story.

* * * * * * *

Within the context of this anthology, "Orphans of the Helix" is a key anticipator of the scrupulous method and divine madness of the better pieces that constitute the final two sections. Section V is conspicuously weaker than sections IV and VI, even though it includes Gregory Benford's "A Worm in the Well", Ursula K, le Guin's "The Shobies' Story" and Stephen Baxter's "The Great Game", all of which are excellent stories testing the boundaries of "new" space opera. Donald Kingsbury's "The Survivor" is much more central to the subgenre, but as the longest story in the book—more than 60,000 words—it takes up more space than it warrants. Sarah Zettel's "Fool's Errand" scrupulously adds another female author to the contents page, but has little else to recommend it, and neither Robert Reed not Paul J. McAuley is at his best, or his most relevant, in "Remoras" and "Recording Angel". Michael Kandel's "Space Opera" is as irritating as its jokey predecessors.

Having got past the boundary-testing section, however, the five pieces that conclude the anthology—the representatives of the "next wave" that is carrying space opera into the twenty-first century in such robust condition—bring the subgenre back into much clearer focus. The thematic movement from Dan Simmons's subgeneric work to the authors represented in this last section underlines in no uncertain terms the extent to which space opera was forced to inherit the mantle and take over the task of another kind of space fiction that became redundant in the period when the Vietnam war was changing common perceptions of military endeavour and the politics of coca-colonization.

It was in that era of post 1960s disillusionment, when the Apollo programme limped to its ignominious end, that "realistic" space fiction found itself in a dead end—because the first flight to the moon was not, after all, the first step on a ladder that would lead all the way to the stars. The myth of the Space Age, in the particular version advertised by such generically-central writers as Arthur C. Clarke and Robert A. Heinlein, died when its first step proved, very obviously, to be headed into nowhere. As Clarke had shrewdly observed, in spite of his own intentions, in *Childhood's End*, it was proven beyond any reasonable doubt that the stars were not for man. The kind of galactic empire envisaged by Isaac Asimov—the human-monopolized galactic empire of "social science fiction"—was a dead duck (or, at least, to judge by the extent to which its most ardent supporters continued to flog it, a dead horse).

Far from devastating space opera, however, this realization paved the way for the new phase in its sophistication and imparted valuable new impetus to its development. Given that the galactic empire was already irredeemably decadent—and always had been—there was no need at all for any surprise or major tactical rethink. The crucial shift of perspective was that, henceforth, the stars would belong to a potentially infinite array of post-human species that were bound to replace a human form that was already obsolete and human habits that were already senescent. The stars—as sf writers like James Blish had always known but had never permitted themselves to assert too loudly—were actually only potentially available to our intensively genetically-engineered and cyborgized descendants (including, of course, the pigs and other similarly "uplifted" species).

"Orphans of the Helix", and its subsequent analogues within this anthology, are Edmond Hamilton with post-humans, an extra dash of decadent imagery, and a healthy injection of cynicism—but what a difference that kind of seasoning makes to the reading experience! The point about stories of this kind is not that they use the same plots that Anthony Hope once used, or the same rambling plot-replacements that H. Rider Haggard once used, but that they develop backcloths infinitely richer and stranger than Ruritania or the imagined dark heat of Africa. They insist, more powerfully and more eloquently than any other kind of contemporary fiction, that if there is to be a future for our descendants, it cannot and will not be anything as simple as a renaissance, but must in fact be a transfiguration—in every sense of the term.

It is for this reason that the authors sampled in the final section of H/C's anthology—Tony Daniel, Scott Westerfeld, Alastair Reynolds, Charles Stross and John C. Wright—are absolutely the right selections, in spite of the fact that Daniel and Westerfeld have to be represented by "Grist" and "The Movements of her Eyes"—which are the preludes to much longer works—while the other three are exemplified by thin slices of extraordinary life abstracted from sprawling series projects. Reynolds is represented by "Spirey and the Queen", Stross by "Bear Trap" and Wright by "Guest Law"; the stories are very good, but in each case they give only the merest glimpse of what the authors have to offer in visions that span whole multivolume series.

Whatever the deficiencies of these particular samples, though, the authors represented in this last section—along with such previously-sampled writers as Simmons, Reed and Baxter—represent not merely the cream of contemporary space opera but a considerable arc of the cutting edge of modern science fiction. None of them confines himself to writing space opera, but it is in their space operas that the ambition and coherency of their vision is most strikingly manifest. Their authentic diamonds are set within complex structures made of gems that are semi-precious at best, but there is nothing wrong with such contrivance, and never has been—and what dazzling displays they make!

REFERENCES

Aldiss, Brian W., ed. *Galactic Empires, Volume I*. New York: St. Martin's Press, 1976.

-------. *Galactic Empires, Volume II*. New York: St. Martin's Press, 1976.

-------. *Space Odysseys*. New York: Doubleday, 1976.

-------. *Space Opera*. New York: Doubleday, 1974.

Amis, Kingsley, *New Maps of Hell*. London: Gollancz, 1960

Atheling, William, Jr. [James Blish]. *The Issue at Hand*. Chicago: Advent, 1964.

-------, *More Issues at Hand*. Chicago: Advent, 1970.

Eshbach, Lloyd Arthur, ed. *Of Worlds Beyond: The Science of Science Fiction Writing*. Reading, Penn.: Fantasy Press, 1947.

Bretnor, Reginald, ed. *Modern Science Fiction: Its Meaning and its Future*. New York: Copward-McCann, 1953.

Wollheim, Donald A. *The Universe Makers*. London: Gollancz, 1972.

Stong, Phil, ed. *The Other Worlds*. New York: Funk, 1941.

PART TWO

Reviews from *Interzone*

The Death Guard by Philip George Chadwick, Roc, 1992

We have long become used to a world in which apocalyptic anxieties have been specifically tied to the idea of nuclear war, and it is difficult to remember or understand that, even before the advent of the atom bomb, the fear was commonplace—in Britain at least—that a second world war would bring about the end of civilization. Throughout the period between the two world wars, British scientific romance was dominated by anxious fantasies of future war, which became steadily more extreme in the 1930s as the shadows cast across Europe by the Fascist regimes in Spain, Italy and Germany grew gradually darker.

Anxiety about the apocalyptic potential of a new world war was by no means restricted to prophetic voices crying unheard in the wilderness; indeed, such anxiety was politically sanctioned and supported in a way that more recent anxieties about nuclear war have never been. In 1924 Winston Churchill published an article called "Shall We Commit Suicide?" in the *Pall Mall Gazette*, in which he argued that, had hostilities not been suspended in November 1918, the Great War would have entered a new and even more hideous phase in which "poison gases of incredible malignity" would have been released upon armies and non-combatant civilians alike. In 1932 Stanley Baldwin addressed the House of Commons in similar terms, insisting that the man in the street must be made to realize that there was "no power of earth that can protect him from being bombed". In 1935 the Home Office issued *Air Raid Precautions Handbook no. 2*, which contained detailed and bloodcurdling details of the various kinds of poison gas that might be deployed, and what their effects would be—a document contrasting very strongly with *Protect and Survive*, the last Conservative government's uplifting essay on how to cope with the advent of nuclear war with the aid of upturned tables and whitewash.

In this climate of fear it is hardly surprising that the late thirties produced a clutch of novels describing, in icily sensational terms, the annihilation of whole nations by poisonous blitzkrieg. Among the most horrific were Joseph O'Neill's *Day of Wrath* (1936) and S. Fowler Wright's *Four Days War* (1936) and *Megiddo's Ridge* (1937), but even these failed to match the awesome repulsiveness of Philip George Chadwick's *The Death Guard* (1939), which featured the development of an entirely new weapon: monstrous android soldiers made out of artificial flesh. All of these novels are now extremely rare; it is possible that this is because the stocks that remained when the blitz actually started were destroyed by incendiary bombs, or because they were pulped in response to paper rationing, but one is tempted to observe that, once the government had switched into morale-building mode, there was a considerable incentive for alarmist texts of this kind to be quietly condemned to oblivion. Whatever the reason, though, *The Death Guard* has long been legendary for its rarity, and I was unable to obtain access to a copy while researching my not-quite-definitive study of *Scientific Romance in Britain, 1890-1950*. I am glad now to be able to repair the gap in my knowledge, although there will presumably never be a chance to correct the sad error of omission.

Viking Penguin were apparently persuaded to reissue *The Death Guard* under the Roc imprint by their sf advisor, Nick Austin; it is abundantly clear from the packaging that they had not the slightest idea what market to aim for. The book comes in a wraparound cover that mimics the worst excesses of blurry pulp sf art, but the text is internally ennobled by an introduction by Brian Aldiss, which describes the story (entirely appropriately) as a "prodromic nightmare". Hopefully those with a connoisseur interest in the history of the scientific imagination will not be put off, while those in search of vivid thrills will not be disappointed. By contemporary standards the book is slow-moving, and its treatment of politics is a trifle cartoonish, but it certainly has more than its fair share of violent action. The most difficult aspect of the text for a modern reader to accommodate is the author's crude racism, which goes beyond the unthinking commonplace prejudices of the day to reveal a particularly nasty and bizarre contempt for black people. Given, however, that this is a book intend to appal rather than to appease, the racist commentary might perhaps be regarded as one more element of the unfolding nightmare.

Until the moment of its spectacular closure, and the ugly revelation of what had happened in the Nazi death camps, World War II was a much gentler affair than anyone had anticipated. The Geneva Convention banning the use of poison gas remained almost inviolate, if only because of the fear of reprisal. Nothing like the "Flesh Guard" was ever contemplated, let alone deployed (although some of the other weapons used against Britain in the course of Chadwick's plot are reminiscent of real-world developments, including the V-1 rocket-bomb) and the biological theories recruited by Chadwick to explain the origin and evolution of artificial flesh can hardly help but seem naive in a modern era to which the biochemistry of DNA has been so comprehensively revealed. For these reasons, the novel is easier to read as an allegory than an alternative history, with the secret development of the Flesh Guard symbolizing that ideology of "defense" that has maintained covert research in chemical and biological warfare during the last fifty years and will presumably continue to do so. The repulsive passages that describe what happens to their artificial flesh after the members of the Guard are "destroyed" by enemy fire thus become a savagely satirical reminder of the potential that biological weapons have to be recklessly promiscuous in affairs of destruction.

Anyone interested in the evolution of imaginative fiction should buy and read *The Death Guard*; it is a useful antidote to the notion that the history of such fictions can be conveniently abridged into a marvel-ridden account of the early development of American pulp science fiction and its eventual coca-colonization of the rest of the world. There was a time when the foreseeable future looked very different, and very much bleaker, when seen from a European perspective. Although it was the Americans who have always had their feet in the gutter and their eyes fixed on the stars, it is not at all obvious, even today, that they were or are the ones gifted with clearer vision.

The Wrong Tree?

Nearly fifty years have passed since Groff Conklin's *The Best of Science Fiction* (1946) provided genre sf with its first representative anthology. Much has changed in the interim as sf has expanded out of its pulp ghetto to become a book-based genre rubbing shoulders with fantasy, horror, techno-thrillers and "magic realism". Its motifs have been plundered by these neighboring genres to the extent that purists have been forced to designate a special category of "hard science fiction" to distinguish the sf that aims for some kind of extrapolative rigor from that which simply uses the imagery of sf as window-dressing. The recent 864-page *Norton Book of Science Fiction* edited by Ursula le Guin and Brian Attebery offered a representative collection of North American sf from 1960-1990 that was conspicuously short on the harder kinds of sf, favoring dilute forms of literary fantasy that play with speculative ideas in deft and delicate fashion; now, ostensibly by way of compensation, David Hartwell and Kathryn Cramer offer as a 1004-page rival *The Ascent of Wonder: The Evolution of Hard Science Fiction* (Tor, 1994).

Like Conklin's *Best of SF*, *The Ascent of Wonder* has two sententious introductions, and it is similarly careful to extrapolate the tradition it wishes to define backwards in time to take in such significant precursors as Poe and Wells. Only two stories are common to both anthologies, Hartwell and Cramer being content to take a few scattered samples from the pulps, while reprinting the bulk of their material from the same period as the Norton anthology (with which it also has two stories in common), but there is a definite continuity of enterprise.

Unfortunately, the manifesto for hard sf laid down by Gregory Benford in *The Ascent of Wonder*—which makes much of "play[ing the game] with the net of scientific fact up and strung as tight as the story allows"—is no better borne out by the contents of the book than the manifesto provided for Conklin by John W. Campbell Jr. himself. Nathaniel Hawthorne's "Rappaccini's Daughter" is here presented as an important proto-hard sf story, while J. G. Ballard, Gene Wolfe and John M. Ford all become hard sf writers of such significance that they warrant double inclusion (unlike the singly-represented Hal Clement, Larry Niven and Poul Anderson or the unrepresented Charles Sheffield). Anne McCaffrey's "Weyr Search" is included on the grounds that "intentions count"—in frank defiance of the philosophy of science, which opines that what really counts is how things check out—while Katherine MacLean's "The Snowball Effect" is included on the grounds that it allegedly treats sociology "as if" it were a hard science.

The mere passing mention of mathematical or philosophical notions is sufficient, in these editors' eyes, to qualify a story as hard sf, so we find Richard Grant's "Drode's Equations" and Alfred Bester's "The Pi Man" here alongside Ian Watson's "The Very Slow Time Machine" and Ford's "Chromatic Aberrations". Jokes at the expense of science, or even at the expense of sf, also qualify, so we also find Philip K. Dick's "The Indefatigable Frog" and Arthur C. Clarke's "The Longest Science Fiction Story Ever Written" (whose text has not been corrected—in this proof copy, at least—even though Arthur C. Clarke is now well aware of the fact that it was Morley Roberts, and not H. G. Wells, who wrote "The Anticipator").

It is, of course, true that the notion of hard sf is problematic and constitutes, at best, a "fuzzy set" with many marginal cases. Even writers who are interested in the careful extrapolation of specific scientific premises tend to use facilitating devices like faster-than-light starships, dimensional gateways and time machines to transport their characters to the appropriate fictional spaces. *Astounding/Analog*, the magazine that supposedly set the standard for "real" science fiction, was prepared to admit all manner of fantastic follies into its pages even before John Campbell became sufficiently undiscriminating to play host to L. Ron Hubbard's Dianetics and the psi-boom of the 1950s. There is, however, a world of difference between admitting a few problematic stories to test the limits of a definition and filling half a book with stories that manifestly violate the logical limitations and typical attributes of hard sf, on the grounds that they are somehow "engaged in a dialog" with it.

The simple truth is that intentions *don't* count; the fact that a man sincerely believes in fairies (or magic, or Jungian archetypes, or flying saucers, or flying dragons, or the God of his choice, or Evil Incarnate, or the power of chain letters to make fortunes) cannot be adequate grounds for elevating his fairy stories to the status of realistic fiction. It is precisely because it is so very easy for writers to introduce arbitrary miracles into their fiction that works which refuse such facile options are worthy of particular attention. The kinds of soft-centered sf that merely replay fairy tales in futuristic guise have always been more popular than the kinds of sf that aspire to some measure of intellectual rigor, and perhaps they always will be, but it does no service to the cause of intellectual rigor to pretend that a glossy surface provides adequate cover for a hollow core. Lovers of hard sf are likely to feel that this anthology does grave disservice to their cause; readers who feel that any kind of fidelity to science or reason is a disposable irrelevance (and there are many who believe this of life as well as their favorite fictions) will find little to dent their confidence here.

Hartwell and Cramer are two of the editors of *The New York Review of Science Fiction*, which has played host since its inception some seventy-odd issues ago to a long-running debate on the nature and merits of hard sf; this anthology might well bring that debate to an inglorious end. As of now the term "hard sf" seems to be as stubbornly devoid of any coherent meaning as the term "science fiction"—not so much an ascent of wonder as a case of barking up the wrong tree.

The Seductions of Undeath

It can hardly have escaped anyone's notice that literary vampires have enjoyed an astonishing explosion of popularity in the last twenty years, with the result that vampire fiction has virtually become a genre in its own right. We are still a couple of years away from the centenary of Bram Stoker's *Dracula* (1897), which provided the definitive model of the literary vampire, but the evolution that the model has undergone in the meantime has suddenly entered a divergent phase unparalleled in the history of imaginative fiction. The literary vampire is no longer a straightforward and slightly ludicrous figure of menace but a fascinating case-study in existential and erotic confusion: a problematic character, whose distinctive metahuman angst has somehow come to seem far more meaningful than the common-or-garden varieties that formed the focal point of Colin Wilson's ground-breaking scholarly fantasy *The Outsider*.

The great pioneer of revisionist vampire existentialism was Anne Rice, but some of those following in her footsteps have set out to explore differently reconfigured images of the vampire in such a way as to heighten even further the existential predicament and perverse sexuality of the undead. No one else has done so with such intensity, inventiveness and clarity of mind as Freda Warrington, whose pioneering work in *A Taste of Blood Wine* is now carried forward by the first of a projected series of sequels. *A Dance in Blood Velvet* (Macmillan, 1994). This is not the kind of sequel that simply recombines established materials; the new novel carefully and conscientiously extrapolates the notion of the "Crystal Ring", exploring metaphysical corollaries of the concept while deftly employing its potential for the design of wonderfully melodramatic plots. The story neatly and scrupulously takes up the most important loose ends left dangling by the earlier volume, and moves with measured vigor towards a hectically extended climax, building a remarkable crescendo of action and emotion. Although the author is careful not to overdo the philosophical speculation (unlike at least one person not a million miles away from where I sit) she remains well aware that she is conducting an exploration of unknown imaginative territory, and is careful to register the benchmarks around which future maps might be constructed. *A Dance in Blood Velvet* amply fulfils the promise of its predecessor, and there is no doubt that the series will become one of the literary monuments of the nascent genre to which it belongs.

It is hardly surprising, given the intensity of her concentration on the ethics, etiquette and erotic possibilities of undeath, that Freda Warrington has become one of the two native heroines of British vampire fandom. The other is, of course, Storm Constantine—an inevitable appointment, given the remarkable extent to which vampire fandom is fused with the "Gothic" subculture that emerged as an offshoot of punk but comfortably outlasted its parent. Although the figures that provided Goths with their initial stylistic cues (Siouxsie of Siouxsie and the Banshees, Robert Smith of The Cure and Andrew Eldritch of The Sisters of Mercy) made no particular use of fantastic motifs in their songs, many of the bands which came after them have taken aboard vampiric imagery in a big way, to the extent that Thee Vampire Guild have issued an eclectic compilation album, *"What Sweet Music They Make...."* featuring bands from Germany, France, Finland and the USA as well as the UK. The music is varied but always extraordinarily vivid, taking aboard all kinds of suggestive sound-imagery—including emotion-enhancing cinematic music and the deep solemnities of reverent Church music—to enhance its cavorting dance-beats. The lyrics encapsulate both the menacing and erotic aspects of vampire mythology, separately and in combination. The House of Dracula offers a double cassette, *Gotisch* featuring a wider range of bands and subject-matter.

While some of the bands who have used vampire imagery to shape their on-stage appearance, the content of their songs and the tenor of their publicity might be regarded simply as genre fellow-travelers there is no doubt that the kind of ideological identification with the undead facilitated by books like Anne Rice's and Freda Warrington's is nourishing a considerable creative force. One of the German bands featured on *"What Sweet Music They Make..."*, Sopor Aeternus and the Ensemble of Shadows, has released the seven-track *Sopor Aeternus*, which is a remarkable exploration of exotic musical atmospherics, ranging from the insistently anguished to the hauntingly mournful.

The literary productions of vampire/Goth fandom are numerous, featuring in such fanzines as Thee Vampire Guild's *Crimson*, The House of Dracula's *Bats and Red Velvet*, the Vampyre Society's *For the Blood is the Life*, the Gothic Society's *Grimoire* and *The Penny Dreadfull*. The most extensive by a wide margin is Jackie Askew's novel *SunDown SunRise* (NightShade, 1994), in which a Lugosi-esque aristocratic vampire cuts a broad swathe through the Goth community, converting a host of darkly enthusiastic acolytes before the inevitable *deus ex machina* cuts short his career (but leaves a record number of loose ends splayed in every direction). It is a work with far more zest than sophistication, but is certainly more deserving of attention than some of the books produced by commercial publishers hoping to cash in on the vampire boom. A particularly horrid example of this kind of exploitation is *Vampire: The Complete Guide to the World of the Undead* (Aurum, 1994), which claims to have been written by one Manuela Dunn Mascetti although the bulk of its text has been untimely ripped—more or less verbatim—from Paul Barber's excellent *Vampires, Burial and Death: Folklore and Reality* (1988), of which it is a calculatedly moronic trivialization. Credit to the original is given in the small print at the end but many readers may feel that licensed plagiarism is still plagiarism and that the (mostly silly and irrelevant) illustrations serve only to add an inopportune element of travesty.

Those readers who thought that the vampire boom was a mere editorial whim, whose fashionability would quickly wane, have undoubtedly underestimated the extent and complexity of the matter in hand. There is more than mere faddishness involved in this orgiastic feast of blood, and it seems likely that the boom will become much louder before its echoes and reverberations begin to die—but, just for this once, I shall refrain from concluding with any of the thousand excruciating puns to which commentary on this phenomenon usually falls prey.

Monsters of the Twentieth Century

Much has been written about the manner in which twentieth-century writers have repeatedly made use of the nineteenth century's favorite monsters, Frankenstein and Dracula. The promiscuous fashion in which such figures have extended themselves across the media landscape—becoming household names in the process—has been as extensively documented as the processes of serial metamorphosis simultaneously forced on them by changing mores, new ironic insights and the desperate search for novelty-within-familiarity.

The monsters of the twentieth century are one step behind their august predecessors, but they too are being continually repackaged and reprocessed—and with each new phase of their reiteration the depth of analysis which readers and critics must bring to bear on new versions becomes more demanding. I have before me two new accounts of modern myth-figures, which cannot be fully appreciated without some awareness of the histories which lie behind them, and which might conceivably benefit from assessment in tandem;

Ataraxia's *Il Fantasma dell'Opera* (Avantgarde Music 1996) and David Britton's *Motherfuckers: The Auschwitz of OZ* (Savoy 1996).

The first manifestation of *The Phantom of the Opera* was a feuilleton in *Le Gaulois*, one of three such daily serials that the prolific Gaston Leroux produced during 1910. It relates the history of the Opera Ghost, a mysterious figure with a face like a death's head, whose career climaxes with events following his demand that a singer named Christine Daaé be promoted to leading roles. Christine's affection for Raoul, Vicomte de Chagny, results in the murder of Raoul's brother and her own abduction by the Ghost, who imprisons her in the catacombs beneath the Opera. There she discovers that her unseen singing tutor—who claimed to be the Angel of Music about which her father used to tell her stories when she was a child—is a maleficent stonemason named Erik, who wears a mask to conceal his hideously disfigured face.

Although a dozen of Leroux's novels were filmed in France during his lifetime *The Phantom of the Opera* was not reckoned among his best works and it was left to Hollywood to produce a movie version in 1925, as a vehicle for Lon Chaney. Making the most of three key scenes, in which the Opera chandelier crashes down on the audience, the phantom appears at a masked ball costumed as the Red Death, and Christine first snatches away the phantom's mask, the silent film became a classic. It was remade several times. The 1943 version—in which Claude Rains played the Phantom—was hijacked by Nelson Eddy, whose overblown singing performances leached the impetus from the plot, but the 1962 version starring Herbert Lom was routinely deferential to its Hollywood predecessors and the 1983 version starring Maximilian Schell was another carbon copy. The 1989 version starring Robert Englund introduced a diabolical pact, possibly under the influence of *The Phantom of the Paradise*, which was much the better of the two caricaturish *hommages* released in 1974 (the other was *The Phantom of Hollywood*). The 1990 TV mini-series starring Charles Dance was developed from a 1983 play by Arthur Kopit.

Other dramatists eventually realized that, if Nelson Eddy could use *The Phantom of the Opera* as a means of carrying forward his Hollywood career, a stage musical might be able to reclaim a little of Hollywood's glamour. Ken Hill's theatrical version employed authentic operatic set-pieces as a background to his rather tongue-in-cheek version of the story, but it only reached the stage on a wave of sympathy which accrued to the author when he claimed that Andrew Lloyd Webber's extremely popular musical—first staged in 1987—had plundered his idea.

The transfigurations that the Phantom's role underwent in the course of these adaptations were partly forced by the conventions of the new media. Whereas Leroux's Erik, deformed from birth, is frankly wicked, Hollywood preferred to represent the Phantom as a mild-mannered frustrated composer, who switches from Jekyll to Hyde after his disfigurement. In the Hollywood versions the Phantom's face is ruined by acid or fire after he concludes—correctly or not—that his masterpiece has been stolen. Only the 1989 version implies that the masterpiece in question was the result of a diabolical bargain.

When Lloyd Webber elected to provide his own quasi-operatic music it was entirely natural that he should retransfigure the plot as a tragic romance of the kind that lends itself so well to operatic melodrama (although the Kopit play had earlier moved in the same direction). Although this was represented as a reversion to the original plot there is all the difference in the world between Lloyd Webber's anguished Phantom and Leroux's malevolent one, the strong note of sympathy following the modern fashion for the ironic rehabilitation of the monsters of old. Ataraxia's version takes this trend to its logical conclusion; in the wake of Lloyd Webber's weak claim to have restored the original, it pretends to even greater authenticity—the sleeve notes are careful to specify to which chapter each of the twelve tracks refers—but in fact it carefully inverts Leroux's most basic assumptions, while parodying both the great tradition of Italian Opera and the sentimentalized bombast of Lloyd Webber's music.

The fact that modern technology permits four people—one of them peripheral—to reproduce the sound of an entire orchestra and a whole cast of singers, not to mention a battery of cinematic sound-effects, is both a miracle of engineering and an aspect of *Il Fantasma dell'Opera*'s parody. The quality of the joke is fully revealed by the shock with which the listener discovers that the song in which Christine is tutored by her unseen Angel of Music in preparation for her debut on the Opera stage—in the track entitled "La Nuova Margherita"—is in fact Kate Bush's "Wuthering Heights", here presented as it might have been had it been an aria in a Puccini opera. Some authentic opera-music (from Gounod's *Faust*)—is reprocessed in track 6, this being one of three lyrics sung in French (only one is in modern Italian, although two are in Latin; the climactic song preceding the instrumental finale is the second in English)

The sleeve notes provide further tongue-in-cheek commentary on the transformation that *Il Fantasma dell'Opera* has wrought, obligingly rendered into a language that is not the writer's first (and perhaps not his second):

"The Monster owns geniality [he means genius], the one that leads you towards the sublime creation from which it is not possible to come back alive; the powerful act of creating goes over the mental capacity of containing so high revelations....

"The Phantom leaves us with a deep acquired wisdom abandoning all the ingenious inventions and day-dreams; he dies with or without a mask (it doesn't matter) 'cos he's the faceless man, the erased essence who returns to earth disintegrating his psichic substance. 'Il Fantasma dell'Opera' is dedicated to all of you who feel the 'living-pain' like we do in a continuous up and down of absolute creativity and harsh tension to the end, departure, dessolution, evaporation, extinction...."

Like Dracula and Frankenstein's Monster before him, Leroux's musically-gifted but socially-ostracized Phantom is fully, if ironically, rehabilitated. Here, he really is an Angel of Music, offered for hearer-identification a purely tragic figure, the agonized victim of a loathing that is unreasoned, unreasonable and lethal. In making this point Vittorio Vandelli, Giovanni Pagliari, and Francesca Nicoli—the three permanent members of Ataraxia, here supported by Lorenzo Busi as the Phantom—are careful to challenge the aesthetic presumptions underlying all the previous usurpations of the story, while still producing music that is as beautiful as it is combative.

David Britton's *Motherfuckers* is combative in a far more aggressive fashion than *Il Fantasma dell'Opera*, and it makes no attempt at beauty. Quite the reverse, in fact: its sets out to be as ugly as possible. There will undoubtedly be many readers who cannot sympathize with this ambition, and who will consequently find the book disgusting, but its method is not without purpose, and that purpose has to do with certain monstrous idols of the twentieth century. Whereas Ataraxia's aim is to rehabilitate that which was unjustly judged monstrous, however, Britton's aim is to protest against the manner in which that which is truly monstrous has been covertly preserved and protected.

Unlike Ataraxia's Erik, whose ugliness prevented his being recognized as an Angel of Music, Britton's essentially elusive protagonist—the spirit of the Holocaust, variously and partially incarnate in Dr. Mengele, Lord Horror, and the separated Siamese twins Meng and Ecker—embodies an evil whose authentic ugliness has been sheltered and hidden, partly by virtue of a misguided sense of decency and partly to conceal and disguise its continuation into modern times and its residual infection of modern culture. Britton's purpose is to reveal the monstrousness of the ideas that brought about the Holocaust, as dramatically as he can.

As with Ataraxia's sleeve-notes, Britton takes care to make the theme of his novel explicit in several passages:

> "Every monster imagined by mankind had died and was reborn a hundred times more terrifying in the concentration camps of Bergen-Belsen and Dachau." (p. 65)

> "Killing Jews produced its own dynamic—and could ever be policed by 'good taste'. Down that path lay a recipe for further genocide. The killing grounds were elemental and contagious—and often outrageously funny, if selectively so...." (p. 86)

> "People might fear Dracula and Dr. Frankenstein's monster and the wayward impulses of the serial killer, but Mr. Auschwitz dwarfed them all with the sheer terror of its existence.
> "Lord Horror was Auschwitz made myth.
> "Natural selection had produced Lord Horror. He was prime cut. Primate man. Tabula Rasa. Mussolini and Jerry Lee Lewis. Elvis on the wire." (p. 223)

These explanatory passages provide the key to the decoding of the remainder of the text, although turning it within the lock is by no means unproblematic. Taken out of context, Chapter Three—in which Meng subjects a jaded audience to a torrent of racist jokes—might seem atrociously and irredeemably repulsive, but the point of the exercise is exactly that. Savoy is based in Manchester, where Bernard Manning holds court in his legendary club, still unable to see the unfunny side of his own jokes, in spite of the careful analysis provided by Trevor Griffiths' excellent dramatic study *The Comedians*.

It is, admittedly, difficult to judge what effect *Motherfuckers* is most likely to have on its readers. It is difficult to believe that anyone would find it pornographic in the sense that it could be used for titillation, but there is no doubt that it is a seriously discomfiting work. Readers enthusiastic to like the books they read will not find much in it to delight them; even those ready and willing to relate to texts in a more sophisticated fashion might find it hard going. That may qualify as a weakness in the commercial arena, but it is also a strength.

Motherfuckers is a sequel to *Lord Horror*, which was successfully annihilated by the Manchester police, in spite of the fact that their seizure of the stock under the Obscene Publications Act was successfully appealed in the Manchester Crown Court (only a handful of copies was returned). It is also a companion-piece to the Savoy comic books featuring Meng and Ecker, whose seizure was approved by the same court of appeal in 1992.

Savoy's legal representatives are continuing the fight to have this issue laid before a jury; the magistrates who have approved the seizures and sentenced the comic-books to extinction by fire remain absolutely firm in their resistance to that prospect. David Britton—who has already served two jail terms for selling books and magazines which are openly and legally on sale in every other city in the country—will presumably remain entangled in this very real game of "Spot the Monster" for the foreseeable future. According to the heirs of James Anderton, Britton is the Monster; in his view, their actions can only serve to blur the image of the one twentieth century Monster that is definitely no mere bogeyman, and of whose terrifying aspects we still need to be reminded.

"Ataraxia" is calmness of mind, the primary objective of Stoic philosophy; "Motherfuckers" hopefully requires no explanation.

Another Case of Conscience

The ever-problematic relationship between science and religion continues to generate fuss and bother; the features pages, review sections and letter columns of broadsheet newspapers continue to devote a good deal of space to disputes between theologians, cosmologists and evolutionists as to the implications of the still-unfolding revelation of modern science. Science fiction has used its own methods to explore a whole range of stances, incarnate in several of the acknowledged classics of the genre: James Blish's "A Case of Conscience"; Anthony Boucher's "The Quest for St. Aquin"; Arthur Clarke's "The Star"; and Walter Miller's *A Canticle for Leibowitz*. Speculative fiction by writers outside the genre, including C. S. Lewis and Franz Werfel, has added a significant further contribution to this problematic area of concern. Now that Walter Miller has died it will fall to Terry Bisson to overcome his interminable writer's block and bring the sequel to *A Canticle for Leibowitz* to its conclusion; in the meantime, the debut novel by anthropologist Mary Doria Russell, *The Sparrow* (Villard, 1996) will obtain wide circulation by virtue of being taken up by the Book-of-the-Month Club. We have come a long way since Horace Gold rejected "A Case of Conscience" because he ran "a family magazine"—which, by virtue of that definition, had no place for "all that religious jazz".

To sf readers *The Sparrow* will inevitably seem like a second take on "A Case of Conscience". Its central character is a Jesuit who becomes part of the team appointed to make first contact with an alien species but finds that the manifest reality of alien society puts a severe strain on his faith. When Blish, in the guise of William Atheling Jr, reviewed his own story he complained that the ending was not sufficiently ambiguous—a criticism that leads me to conclude that he would have loved *The Sparrow* and envied its author the availability of a marketplace willing to tolerate such devastating ambiguity. What Mary Doria Russell might think of "A Case of Conscience", if she even knows of its existence, I can only guess, but I suspect that she would find it insufficiently Jesuitical—a judgment that would, in a suitably wry fashion, praise it with faint damnation.

The Sparrow looks back, as an anthropologist's novel would, to all the "first contacts" that have taken place in the last five hundred and ten years (the last of them in the early years of this century). It is built on the knowledge that the arrival of ambassadors of Western civilization, however well-intentioned, has always been disastrous for the cultures thus contacted—all of which have been obliterated or altered out of all recognition in the aftermath of contact. It is built, too, on the recognition that Jesuits were almost always among the first wave of contactors, and that their ambassadors very often took the brunt of any violent backlash generated by the contacts. Russell's hypothetical ambassadors, being without exception good and knowledgeable people, want to do better than their predecessors. They go where no man has gone before, boldly determined to commit no sins; they are meek, and they are as pure in heart as it is possible for humans to be—the author goes to great pains to establish this fact in her slow but effective build-up—but their mission nevertheless goes horribly wrong, in a fashion that rings horribly true.

The Sparrow (whose title comes from the observation that although no sparrow ever falls without God's knowledge and pity, the sparrow nevertheless falls) is a carefully-crafted mystery story, which hoards until the last few of its 380 pages the revelation of exactly what happened to Emilio Sandoz, S.J. on the alien world. At times the reader may feel a trifle impatient with his reluctance to spell out the causes of his utter abjection, but it is done in a good cause, because the real point at issue is not what was done, but what ought to be inferred from what was done, within the context of Emilio's religious faith and the organization to which he belongs. The Gordian intricacy of that problem requires extraordinarily elaborate establishment, in terms of the characterization of both the Jesuit and non-Jesuit characters, and once properly established, there is no way that the knot can be brutally severed by the kind of device that Blish felt obliged to deploy in his tale. Here, conscience has to go the full distance, with no ready-made refuge in sight.

I must admit to a certain surprise that the Book-of-the-Month Club picked up this book, although the decision has my wholehearted endorsement. The novel's prose is exceptionally well-crafted, the characterization exceptionally detailed, the story exceptionally gripping and the climax exceptionally moving, but it is nevertheless a conscientious science fiction novel, which does not skimp on its careful explanation of how an interstellar expedition might be mounted. Nor is it in any way a comforting book—and its selectors must have been aware that America has a good number of strident interest groups whose members will find much in it to deplore. Even those who approve of its moral conclusions—and it is not obvious that the Vatican would pronounce them orthodox, although they are certainly respectful of Catholic faith and Catholic ambition—will inevitably find much to unsettle them along the route by which those conclusions are attained. *The Sparrow* is, in essence, a challenging book—which is, in my view, the best kind, although it is a kind that has not traditionally been favored by populist book clubs.

I doubt that Mary Doria Russell will be able to compete with Lois McMaster Bujold for next year's Hugo award, and I dare say that many of the field's critics will hail this fact as further evidence of the popular genre's moral and aesthetic bankruptcy, but those sorts of games are played according to its own rules. As TV assumes command of the genre label, squeezing out from beneath its protective umbrella the last fugitive vestiges of intellectual seriousness, there will be some readers who will find great relief in the news that books like *The Sparrow* can now be packaged and successfully sold as literary novels. It is a book that everyone with a serious interest in sciencefictional thought-experiments ought to read.

Babes in the Wilderness

Fantasy fiction can be formularized because it has in its secure custody a number of elementary story-structures that can stand any amount of repetition. Repetition is an advantage rather than a handicap when it attains the functions of ritual, each movement reaffirming some fundamental aspect of our social consciousness—which stands, of course, in constant need of reaffirmation by virtue of being something shared. One such elementary story-structure is the tale of an individual who moves from a milieu whose rules are understood and internalized to one which is unfamiliar and problematic. In many versions the movement is from civilization to barbarism but, even if it is the other way around, it is still a brave venture into moral wilderness where the old norms do not apply—a journey in which the wisdom of adulthood is devalued and the painful uncertainties of childhood return in full force, all the more agonizing for their seeming impropriety.

This pattern is extraordinarily elastic, capable of many different manifestations. In Terri Windling's novel *The Wood Wife* (Tor, 1996) the mover is a citified writer who inherits a house on the edge of the Arizona desert, and finds the surrounding land inhabited by archetypal magical forces, given a particular form by the previous owners' artistic genius. In Jeff VanderMeer's novella *Dradin in Love* (Buzzcity Press, 1996) the mover is an out-of-work missionary who returns to the decadent city of Ambergris as Festival time approaches, and enlists a direly unreliable go-between to assist in his courtship of a lovely woman glimpsed through a high window. In the Forkbeard Fantasy company's *The Fall of the House of Usherettes* (The Lyric Studio and eighteen other venues throughout the UK, 1996) the mover is film buff Bernard von Earlobe, who comes to the decaying Empire Picture Palace in search of the secret of liquid film, and finds himself entrapped in the phantasmagoric world of Roderick Lilyhair and his three sinister sisters.

In terms of their style and method it would be hard to imagine three works of art more different than these, and their similarity of structure certainly does not suffice to make them peas in a pod. Even so, they all share a common and vital purpose: to dramatize and celebrate the anxiety and exhilaration of entering the unknown—and they are all, according to their different lights, excellent.

Terri Windling's novel is, as might be expected, the weightiest and most earnest of the three. Having long established herself within the field as an artist and an editor of considerable influence—for whose vision, ambition and ingenuity genre fantasy already has much to be thankful—she must have felt that her first novel carried a fearful burden of expectation. Any slight failure of elegance or intelligence would have seemed glaring. Fortunately, there is none; the characters are well-wrought, to the extent that one can believe in them as artists as well as human beings, and the tale is carefully built to its vivid and compelling climax. Here, as befits a fantasy with authentic *gravitas*, the mover adapts herself to her wilderness, not by taming it but by learning enough of its hidden workings to negate its worst threats and draw profit from its most generous opportunities.

Jeff VanderMeer's novella—the work of a prolific poet and short story writer whose work has so far mostly appeared in respectable but unprofitable small press publications—rejoices in the freedom of relative esotericism. Its sly jokes and off-hand references are unrepentantly varied and blithely recherché; the book carries a dedication to "the late Angela Stalker", preferring that author's maiden name to the signature she used on her books. In such a work as this there is no need, and perhaps no possibility, of the kind of adaptation that Windling's heroine was honor-bound to win. Poor Dradin, victim of a *fin de siècle* sensibility, is bound to find the wilderness of excessive artifice cold, inhospitable and wounding—as all truly sensitive souls must. The author's prose is delicate and ornate, but the narrative has force and wit in plenty. The book is, incidentally, a remarkably well-produced volume with handsome illustrations by Michael Shores, and it is an auspicious debut for its publisher, who also edits the excellent small press magazine *The Silver Web*.

Forkbeard Fantasy's dramatic collage, which has five parts but only three actors (Ed Jobling, Chris Britton and Tim Britton), is an out-and-out comedy stuffed with nudging references to the more Poesque aspects of cinematic history. The stage-set is a masterpiece of ingenuity and its possibilities are exploited to the full as live performance and filmed inserts are neatly woven together into a fast-moving and intricate plot, whose climax is a fine *coup de théâtre*. In comedy, of course, the true horror of the wilderness may become unapologetically apparent and the predicament of the central character can be reduced to the simple alternatives of escape and annihilation. Neither adaptation nor a tragic failure to adapt can be applicable in an extravaganza of this kind. (For those unfortunate enough to miss the play while it tours the length and breadth of the land, there is a tabloid comic book based on Tim Britton's storyboard).

None of us is immune from the responsibility of moving from the social situations we know into ones which are new—and, by virtue of being new, puzzling, threatening and challenging. Anyone who was immune from such movements would hardly be enviable on that account, because they would be existentially stagnant. We have every reason, therefore, to be grateful for such analyses of the predicament as these, not because they tell us how to do it—we must, of necessity, already know that—but because they tell us exactly what the achievement is worth, in terms of the only currencies that really matters. We need the earnest versions almost as much as we need the ironic ones, which we need almost as much as we need the comic ones—which, in their paradoxical turn, we need almost as much as the earnest ones. As Johan Huizinga has observed, play is the most serious activity in which we can indulge ourselves.

But the Platitudes Linger

Ronald Wright's *A Scientific Romance* (Anchor, 1997) is exactly what it says it is: a calculated continuation of the tradition of British futuristic fiction, which was overwhelmed and obscured after World War II by the importation of American science fiction. It pays homage to two of its predecessors in titling its first two parts "The Wells Device" and "After London", and mentions two more *en passant*, albeit obliquely, when its hero wryly compares his means of transportation to those employed by the heroes of Mary Shelley's *The Last Man* and M. P. Shiel's *The Purple Cloud*. Its closest parallel texts are, however, two that the author almost certainly did not read, and of which he has probably never even heard: Edward Shanks's *The People of the Ruins* and Cicely Hamilton's *Theodore Savage*. The similarity arises not from any direct influence but from a sometimes-uncanny resonance of concern, method and tone—and this is what places Wright's book at the very heart of its fugitive genre.

The distinctive attributes of the British tradition were never entirely lost, of course, not only because some British sf writers remained insistent on tracing their lines of influence from H. G. Wells and Olaf Stapledon instead of, or as well as, *Amazing Stories* and *Astounding Science Fiction*, but because certain typical elements of scientific romance resisted dissolution by the ideological acids of the American Dream. Scientific romance was always, first and foremost, an apocalyptic art-form, whose principal spur was the fear of wars and natural disasters to come. It was the imaginative fiction of an empire in terminal decline, of a world whose frontiers were collapsing inwards rather than expanding outwards. It was never devoid of hope, but once the Great War of 1914-18 had revealed to everyone that modern warfare had no real victors, its basic emotional spectrum ranged from the plaintively elegiac via the bitterly sarcastic to the madly hysterical.

The People of the Ruins (1920) and *Theodore Savage* (1922) were among the first scientific romances to be produced in the aftermath of the Great War, when the conviction was strongest that another such conflict would mean the end of civilization, and the belief was widespread that this was the direction in which our collective passions would inevitably lead us. The similar anxieties extrapolated by Wright do not relate to war *per se*, but to the possible ecocatastrophic effects of new diseases; the HIV epidemic is the event that seems to him to be the decisive omen of our impending doom. His hero, who fears that he has been afflicted by Creutzfeldt-Jakob disease, takes delivery of an empty time machine built by a contemporary of Wells, which seems to have returned from the year 2500. He sets off for the same year and finds London empty of all human life, reclaimed by tropical jungle. Like Mary Shelley's Verney and Shiel's Adam Jeffson, he sets off on an odyssey through the empty world, traveling on motorways overlaid by a kind of Astroturf, which has rendered them immune to colonization by real plants.

Wright's hero does, in the end, find a community of people living on the shores of Loch Ness; their culture still in decline and full of wretched ironies (this section of the text is called "The Scottish Play" and features a suitably peculiar Laird and Lady MacBeth). The visitor from the past knows that the new barbarians have no possibility of recovering what their ancestors had and threw away; he is an archaeologist who understands well enough that excavation is destruction, and that civilization "ploughed up the rails behind" when it stripped away the world's reserves of coal and oil. "We had at best one chance to get it right", he says—and that has always been the underlying message of scientific romance, more lachrymose than alarmist in its delivery. Wright's lachrymosity is more modern in its mannerisms than Edward Shanks's or Cicely Hamilton's, but tears are tears, no matter how one tries to dignify the business of weeping.

It was not until the aftermath of World War II that Americans realized, by the grace of Stalin's spies, that even they could no longer deem themselves invulnerable to the effects of war. While the all-conquering flood-tide of coca-colonization was all-but-drowning scientific romance, therefore, science fiction took on an apocalyptic edge of its own. That edge was, however, always blunted by science fiction's own precious variant of the American Dream: the conquest of space. Who the hell cared that Earthly civilization was doomed, so long as the final frontier was there to welcome the most enterprising of its refugees?

The lachrymosity of such classic works of sf as *The Martian Chronicles* and *A Canticle for Leibowitz* was decisively altered by virtue of the fact that the weepers' eyes were, at the end if not the beginning, raised heavenwards. Awareness of impending ecocatastrophe has been countered in much the same way by more recent sf, which has produced multitudinous images of Edenic other worlds. Would-be alarmists have found it frustratingly difficult to sweep aside that ridiculous litter and bring home the realization that there will be nowhere to fly when we have irredeemably fouled our nest. Fortunately, the most effective response to frustration is to try harder and to cut deeper, and that is what sf's skeptics have done. It is arguable that there has never been a science fiction novel that cuts quite as deep as Michael Swanwick's *Jack Faust* (Millennium, 1997).

Like *A Scientific Romance*, *Jack Faust* is exactly what it says it is: a version of Faust recast for the twentieth century. It imagines that the ambitious scholar really did discover a reliable source of knowledge, which volunteered to tell him anything—provided only that he would consent to listen. This exceptionally well-informed alien Mephistopheles is honest enough to tell his victim exactly why he wants Faust to listen—because it wishes to see humankind annihilated and is confident that knowledge is a sure route to self-destruction—but poor vainglorious Faust thinks he knows better. The entire heritage of scientific knowledge and technology is promptly laid before him, to communicate to his fellows as best he can. Then Swanwick proceeds with great flair and conviction (not to mention monumental sarcasm) to map out a high road of good intention that heads straight for Hell, astroturfed for convenience every step of the way.

Jack Faust is, in a sense, a perfectly horrid book. It flatly contradicts the tacit assumption of the entire tradition of American science fiction that Enlightenment is the ultimate good: that knowledge and reason are the only things that can, and very probably will, save us from the worst effects of our collective passions. Swanwick argues the contrary case: that our collective passions are so powerful and so inescapable that Enlightenment only increases the probability that our enmities will have fatal consequences, not merely for our enemies but for ourselves. This is exactly what Bertrand Russell argued, in *Icarus; or, the Future of Science*, in response to J. B. S. Haldane's *Daedalus; or, Science and the Future* (both issued in 1924), but it has never been argued as cleverly, as elegantly or as powerfully as it is in *Jack Faust*.

The legend of Faust was no sooner introduced to literary analysis than it was entangled by the apologetics of Literary Satanism; Marlowe may not have been fully aware that he was of the Devil's party but Goethe certainly was, and was determined that it was where he wanted to be. If I had been asked my opinion a week ago, I might well have opined that there was no way back from Goethe's ringing defense of Faustian ambition, but Swanwick does not even take leave to abandon those elements of the legend that were added by Goethe to facilitate the rescue. Margarete is in *Jack Faust* to leaven Faust's ambition with love, and he loves her as fervently—if not quite as honestly and boldly—as she loves him. Their love retains its strength and depth even when the time comes for poor Margarete to make some final account of the consequences of her affections and ambitions, but it cannot save either of them and its only ultimate effect is to hasten Faust along his highway to Hell. Even in the blackest nightmares previously produced by American science fiction, love was allowed some redemptive value, but *Jack Faust* is relentless, and persuasively so. In Swanwick's reckoning, passion is passion, and all of it leads to destruction.

What hope is left, then, for the futures of science fiction? Can the desire to believe that true Enlightenment still lurks at the bottom of Pandora's Box bear any but withered and poison fruit? If it can, we must look to writers more ingenious than those who have so far formed the backbone of the genre. If there is any real hope for future salvation it must be found in robust myths of cosmic escape that make a determined and effective attempt to avoid the traps so blackly laid out in *Jack Faust*. Perhaps it is not surprising that the one man who seems capable of that, at present, is neither British nor American, but Australian, thus set to stand outside both of the opposed traditions of scientific romance and science fiction. There is a certain delicious irony in the fact that *Jack Faust* is scheduled for UK publication on the same day, and from the same source, as Greg Egan's *Diaspora* (Millennium, 1997).

Although *Diaspora* is not a misleading title, it is not nearly as exact as *A Scientific Romance* or *Jack Faust*; writers who find their true vocation within sf usually cultivate a certain expertise in the art of telling understatement. The novel is indeed an account of a diaspora forced on the inhabitants of Earth by the discovery that a burst of gamma rays released by a collapsing binary star is about to devastate the Earth's ecosphere, but the news is brought to the last "flesher" remnants of humankind by the inhabitants of a polis (a community of conscious software), who have received it from a gleisner (a flesher-shaped robot). The fleshers react exactly as the kind of individuals for whom *Jack Faust* is an apt allegorical symbol might be expected to react. First they refuse to believe it, then they go ape (except, of course, for the "dream apes" who have already surrendered the burden of intelligence in order to return to the Edenic womb of thought).

The only fleshers who survive *Diaspora*'s ecocatastrophe are those who are unceremoniously dragged into the polises by means of Introdus software; no black MacBeths are left behind to measure the grisly failure of humankind's vaulting ambition. In Egan's imperious view, however, this hardly matters. The heritage of human knowledge and wisdom passes to those who were always best-fitted to receive and appreciate it: the software folk. Happily, they are also far better equipped to withstand the emotional rigors of interstellar travel than their unreformed ancestors.

In each of Egan's first three novels—*Quarantine, Permutation City*, and *Distress*—human beings occupied a very special place in the universe, by virtue of being its observers, but *Diaspora* represents a crucial break with the anthropic principle. Here, observation is impotent in the face of a haphazard disaster that is brutally objective in its reality. Contemporary physics is not only impotent to prevent or predict the sudden collapse of Lacerta G-1, but impotent to produce the sort of wormhole that might provide a short cut to the stars. When it eventually turns out that the galactic core is about to go the same way as Lac G-1, thus sterilizing the entire galaxy, extreme measures are required to facilitate a further escape.

Even though they have purged themselves of all the old passions, transforming themselves into the kind of community that could have welcomed Jack Faust with open arms, Egan's polises still require a Mephistopheles to take them by the metaphorical hand and show them the signposts that lead to the macroverse—and then further on, and on, and on, not quite *ad infinitum* but far enough to convince even the most atavistic among them that the best way to be is to commit oneself to solitary, dispassionate labor in the Truth Mines. This is not a Heaven that would be attractive to everyone—but it is, in its own sweet way, every bit as magnificent as Jack Faust's Hell. In any case, what other salvation is now imaginable? If our machines cannot replace and redeem us, what hope can we possibly have of any kind of immortality?

Those who can find no consolation in Egan's Utopia still have a few alternative brands waiting on the supermarket shelves. One reason why Egan has abandoned his clever variations on the theme of the anthropic principle is that such explorations have already been taken to their extreme by Frank Tipler in *The Physics of Immortality*, which suggests that it does not matter a damn what we do to the Earth or to ourselves, because we will all be saved in the end by the ultimate computer, which will reincarnate each and every one of us at the Omega Point, as a sideline to the job of redesigning the universe so that the next Big Bang won't be quite as messy as the last one. Re-creation has the advantage of unlimited flexibility, implying, on the one hand, that we can be re-created without our troublesome warts, and, on the other, that if wartiness were still required, we could have it in spades.

In Tipler's scheme, it is not only our humankind that can be reproduced but all conceivable humankinds. This is his gift both to the despairing man in the street and the despairing science fiction writer, who has already seen the popularity of fantasy devour his marketplace as avidly as the universally-anticipated ecocatastrophe will devour the world. There comes a time in the life of every marginalized science fiction writer (in this instance the British are marginalized by definition) when he realizes that if he hopes to make any money he had better try to disguise his next magnum opus as a fantasy trilogy. Thus, Brian Aldiss wrote *Helliconia Spring et al*, Bob Shaw *The Ragged Astronauts et al.*, Ian Watson *The Book of the River et al*, and now Paul J. McAuley has written *Child of the River: The First Book of Confluence* (Gollancz, 1997).

Child of the River offers us a Utopia far less sterile than the one in *Diaspora*, whose inhabitants are fortunate enough to be able to spend all such time as they do not devote to the search for the secrets of their genetic heritage in hitting one another with crude but sometimes magical weapons. This enables their story to zip along at a fair old pace, drenched in melodrama every step of the way—thus ensuring (hopefully, at least) that they do not lose the attention and interest of the better kind of reader. (From the point of view of the writer, the better kind of reader is, of course, the more numerous kind.)

Being a writer of good conscience as well as some artistry, McAuley does take the trouble to inform us that the miscellaneous barbarians distributed along the shores of his exceedingly long river are not actually living in Heaven, because Heaven lies on the other side of the black hole into which the Preservers disappeared. What remains in the artificial milieu of Confluence is a kind of Purgatory, which is almost, but not quite, beyond redemption—and the hero of the story is the lucky superman who just might be its redeemer. We shall have to wait until volume 3 to find out, but that's the way the game is played. I have every confidence that McAuley—who is not the kind of "make it up as you go" writer who is likely to be caught with his pants down when the time comes to fabricate a conclusion—will make a much better fist of it than Philip José Farmer did in the Riverworld series.

I wish that I could like *Child of the River* more than I do, but when it is set beside *Jack Faust* and *Diaspora* it seems to me to be clinging too hard to conventional narrative props—so hard, in fact, that the props have become crutches and the real story's legs are in danger of wasting away. On the whole, however, I am very glad to have been sent all four of these books in a single batch, because it is very unlikely that the remainder of the year's production could produce another quartet half as impressive. If *Jack Faust* and *Diaspora* fail to win awards it will be because they are too uncomfortable for the voters to bear, and although *A Scientific Romance* and *Child of the River* stick more tightly to the tried-and-true conventions of their respective genres, they are sufficiently thoughtful and sufficiently elegant in expression to act as efficient counterweights to the more challenging texts.

There is a crucial moment in *Diaspora* when citizens of a polis go to the rescue of the fleshers of Atlanta, only to be rudely rebuffed. The flesher who responds to their appeal gazes at his would-be saviors "with a kind of fascinated loathing". His rant in defense of his right to remain untroubled concludes: "We humans are fallen creatures; we'll never come crawling on our bellies into your ersatz Garden of Eden. I tell you this: there will always be flesh, there will always be sin, there will always be dreams and madness, war and famine, torture and slavery." (p. 92)

A Scientific Romance, Jack Faust, Diaspora and *Child of the River* agree with every element of this tirade save one, which they consider self-contradictory; the one thing they all agree upon is that while there are sin, dreams, madness, war, famine, torture and slavery, then flesh cannot endure forever. Only *Diaspora*, however, offers us an authentic alternative; only *Diaspora* subjects the flesher rant to scathingly casual dismissal in order that the plot can get on with other and further business.

"I thought religion was long gone, even among the statics," is one software person's amazed response to the flesher's imbecility.

"God is dead," agrees the other, sadly, "but the platitudes linger."

The Endurance of Edgar Allan Poe

The program for the London Actors Theatre Company production of Sophia Kingshill's *The Murder of Edgar Allan Poe* (Finborough Theatre, October 1-25, 1998) reproduces, among other interesting documents, the obituary of Poe penned by Rufus W. Griswold for *The New York Tribune*. It reads, in its entirety: "Edgar Allan Poe is dead. He died in Baltimore the day before yesterday. The announcement will startle many, but few will be grieved by it. The poet was well known, personally and by reputation, in all this country; he had readers in England, and in several of the states of Continental Europe, but he had no friends."

Actually, Poe was apparently under the impression he had at least one friend, that being the man he appointed as his literary executor. Given that the man in question was Rufus W. Griswold, he might have been mistaken, but I suspect that he knew exactly what he was doing. The biography Griswold wrote of Poe waxed lyrical on the subject of his neurotic debility and his dipsomania, making him (in the words of the *Penguin Companion to Literature*) "an almost Satanic figure". Many Poe scholars have assumed that this was a combination of rank ingratitude—Griswold made his own name after taking over the editorial post that Poe vacated when he left Philadelphia for New York in 1844—and sheer viciousness, but no such scholar should ever forget Poe's great love of hoaxes. Only "The Balloon Hoax" is nowadays frankly recorded as such, but "The Philosophy of Composition" is a blatant hoax too, and so is "The Facts in the Case of M. Valdemar", and there is an element of wry deception in dozens of other pieces, even (perhaps especially) the visionary masterpiece *Eureka*.

If I had to bet—and who will deny me the right?—I would wager that the obituary Griswold signed had earlier been dictated, word for word, by Poe himself. There is no doubt at all that Griswold's biographical demonization worked far better to preserve Poe's name and work than any exercise in conventional apologetics could ever have done—and there is no doubt that Poe would have known that it would. Poe left us, in his poetry and prose, not much more than enough work to fill a single volume, but if it really was his own imp of perversity that pulled Griswold's strings, he also left us a legend to illuminate every page of that volume with an eerie radiance that made every line catch fire.

In the English-speaking world (unlike France) Poe has never been reckoned a writer of the first rank, but that has not inhibited his precious notoriety, nor has it diminished his influence. There is, now more than ever before, a veritable legion of writers occupied in the business of adapting Poe to every other medium, new and old, displaying him as a key character in their own reflections on the barbarism of the past, and casting metaphorical nets in a ceaseless attempt to land, gut and fillet the essence of his artistry and significance. Sophia Kingshill's play attempts all three of these tasks, and succeeds in all three—aided by zestful performances by her actors and clever employment of the confined space of the Finborough Theatre stage by director Joe Cushley.

The plot of the play imagines Poe—who is flat broke and desperate to procure food and medicine for his dying wife—being caught up in a little war between two rival newspapers: James Gordon Bennett's *New York Herald*, forerunner of William Randolph Heart's "yellow press", and Horace Greeley's pious *Tribune*, founded to oppose Bennett's muck-raking. Bennett is a character in the play but the *Tribune* is represented by one of its more interesting contributors, the pioneering feminist Margaret Fuller. When an Irishman named Richard Robinson is arrested for the axe-murder of a whore, Bennett, determined to help the story run and run, decides that it will play better if Robinson is acquitted and another murderer found; he therefore offers Poe the princely sum of $50 if Poe can turn his fabled skill in detection to producing that end. Despite Fuller's censure—which he feels keenly, having accepted her charity—Poe endeavors to do what has been asked of him, but his enquiry does not proceed smoothly. Try as he might to follow the precepts of C. Auguste Dupin, the truth he is avid to find insists on twisting itself into hallucinatory knots, within which the identities of all the participants in the drama become inextricably confused. Circumstances continually conspire to tip him out of the detective story that he is trying to act out into one or other (or even several at the same time) of his paranoid fantasies of guilt-made-manifest.

Act One of the play is virtually stolen by a newsgirl who delivers a running commentary on the plot in a hectic mixture of raucous hawking-cries and plaintive songs. Liza Hayden plays the part magnificently, all the more so when she is required to metamorphose into a whore during the first phase of Poe's investigation; her *multum in parvo* cleavage is as expansive as her voice and I have rarely seen anyone display an armpit with such languid provocation. Largely thanks to her good work, the second act can proceed without the aid of such forthright devices. Here Eamonn Clarke, who plays Poe and Robinson, comes into his own with two fine set pieces (one in each character) and Eve Hopkins (Virginia and "Ligeia") secures the delicate balance of her own spectral ambiguity. As the voice of sanity and cynicism Victoria Willing (Margaret Fuller and a whore) and Chris Tranchell (James Gordon Bennett and, briefly, a lout) have less opportunity to make an individual impact but they provide the sturdy framework that supports the others in their characterizational gymnastics, ably assisted by Erika Poole (Virginia's mother and the brothel-keeper).

Like many ingenious efforts of this general stripe *The Murder of Edgar Allan Poe* is what the *Guardian*'s weekly guide calls "Fringe Theatre". The same was true of Ian Mackenzie's remarkable one-man show, which played at the Steiner Theatre two years ago, and of the portmanteau production of *The Masque of the Red Death* with which the London Actors Theatre Company is bracketing the Kingshill play. Poe would almost certainly have approved; although it would be assuming too much to assert that he preferred the margin of American culture to its mainstream, he was certainly the kind of man who, once that sentence was passed upon him, did everything in his power to assert and demonstrate that the margin was the better place to be. When fate and fortune cast deep shadows over his life, he flatly refused to run for the sunlight; instead he set about proving, as best he could, that any worthwhile artist was bound to love the obscurity of Stygian gloom and to despise the golden light of fame and academic respect. That is a message which cannot become dated—and that is why Edgar Allan Poe continues to speak to us today as intimately, as wisely and (in an admittedly perverse fashion) as reassuringly as he ever did.

Poe did have friends, and he still does: friends who love him well enough to sustain as best they can the legend of his madness, his intoxication, his notoriety and—above all else—his uncanny powers of perception.

Phantasmagoria Revisited

Forkbeard Fantasy, whose touring production of *The Fall of the House of Usherettes* I reviewed in IZ 116, have taken to the road with their new production, *The Barbers of Surreal*, which will finish its run in Liverpool on June 19th 1998. Like its many predecessors, *The Barbers of Surreal* is a multimedia production in which the company's three actors synchronize their performances—especially their entrances and exits—with video sequences, one of which displays events happening beyond a window and another the far side of a magic mirror. This allows the various characters played by each actor to interact in a marvelously complicated fashion; the wonderful intricacy of the piece is brilliantly contrived by writer Tim Britton, and expertly sustained by the performers.

Tim Britton plays Salvador, a barber who has become a qualified genetic engineer in order to bring about a revolution in the art of hair-styling, pioneering the production and development of organic toupees. Salvador has also bought the disused Museum of Childhood next to his salon, within which his brother Flabberjay (played by Britton's brother Chris) has embarked upon a far more adventurous series of experiments, and from which Salvador has removed a strangely-clouded looking-glass. Although their new ventures in hairdressing are welcomed by such independently-minded clients as Squigglehair and Madame de Range the brothers' other endeavors are of some concern to Salvador's assistant Yacob (Ed Jobling)—who cannot understand why everyone treats him as a child, although he believes himself to be thirty-two. Salvador's dog, Andalou, becomes a nervous wreck after glimpsing something in the looking-glass, and spends the entire play all a-quiver—and who can blame the poor wee thing, when every wig in the salon is apt to start wandering around when no one is paying attention?

Yacob's ominous anxieties reach a new pitch when Salvador acquires a new assistant from the Institute of Anthropomorphism—and even Salvador begins to get a little nervous when he catches glimpses of an old crone in a blue dress, who seems intent on reaching the mist-shrouded world beyond the looking-glass. In a climax even more hectic than the awe-inspiring finale of *The Fall of the House of Usherettes*, the fruits of Flabberjay's experiments are revealed—albeit fleetingly—in all their phantasmagorical glory. While the audience sits entranced, like the prisoners in Plato's cave, all manner of variously-formulated shadows move across the virtual landscape beyond the bright-lit stage. The effect is hilarious, but there is a depth to the comedy that adds an echo of authentic wonder to every laugh.

The seed from which *The Barbers of Surreal* grew is the notion that genetic engineering offers opportunities for real-izing the surreal—which is to say, bringing into tangible actuality things that have previously belonged to the realm of the imagination. The strong stem from which its lush dramatic foliage is generated is, however, the link between the imagination and the culture of childhood: the particular surreality of Lewis Carroll's nonsense-worlds. The program notes liken the show's recipe to the list of ingredients in egg shampoo—where the "natural" and the artificial are cleverly compounded for efficacy and showmanship alike—and the comparison is very apt.

The delight that the Forkbeard ensemble take in their endeavors is similar in spirit to that of George Méliès, the theatrical illusionist who became one of the great pioneers of the early cinema. For Méliès, film was a kind of stage magic, a means of manufacturing better and bolder illusions; as the quality of filmic illusion increased, however, subsequent movie-makers became far more interested in film as synthetic experience, and mostly employed the tricks of the trade to cultivate the particular illusion that what the audience could see was really happening; cinematic surrealism was largely banished to the realm of animation. By moving their performances back and forth across what they call "the Celluloid Divide" the Brittons and Jobling are restoring a kind of illusionist artistry to the deployment of video—in collaboration with animation and conventional stage magic—which serves to remind us that the history of film has allowed all manner of possibilities and potentialities to decay into disuse and pass almost unheeded.

It is extremely unlikely that 1998 will throw up any other work of absurdist science fiction to compare with *The Barbers of Surreal*, and it is a shame that there is no award within the field for which it could be seriously considered. It is unlikely, too, that there will be many theatrical productions visiting such humble venues as the Merlin Theatre, Frome and the Bridport Arts Centre that are as extravagantly innovative and inventive as this one. Because of the limitations of visibility associated with such devices as the "mirror", the caged manikin and the peripatetic toupees, the production requires an intimate space, and it would be very difficult to reshape it for a full-sized auditorium, but work of this ingenuity and importance really deserves a far greater audience than its present circumstances permit.

In addition to touring with *The Barbers of Surreal*, Forkbeard will be mounting an exhibition of "animated paraphernalia" at Cheltenham Art Galley from July to September and will be running workshops in connection with the Cheltenham Music Festival. It is worth making every effort to see any and all of their productions if you can; they are among the most artistically-significant endeavors in contemporary fantasy, and the time will surely come when it will be reckoned a considerable privilege to have seen them in their original form.

PART THREE

Reviews from *Foundation*

Meeting in Infinity **by John Kessel, Arkham House, 1992**

"Literature is a political tool used by ruling elites to ensure their hegemony," says one of the alien Krel in John Kessel's story "Invaders". "Anyone who denies that is a fish who can't see the water it swims in." Given that the Krel are not very nice people, it is not entirely clear that this statement has full authorial backing, but "Invaders" is definitely a story that sets out to tell the brutal truth, the whole brutal truth and nothing but the brutal truth, so it wouldn't be at all surprising if it had. "Invaders" tells the story of Pizarro's destruction of Atahualpa's empire, in parallel with the story of the Krel, who perform much the same task of cultural devastation upon us by less violent means, callously fouling everything your average US college teacher of American Literature and Creative Writing considers sacred.

A particularly telling strand of the cynical morality play is built around the fact that what the Krel like best about Earth is the crack (cocaine, that is—they have no expertise in Anglo-Irish slang). Cocaine was, of course, one of the main discoveries made by Pizarro's conquistadores while they were setting about the serious business of obliterating Incan culture and civilization. Lest the reader should fail to be discomfited by this scalding attack on everything John Kessel despises, "Invaders" also includes a third series of inserts, in which the author refers to his own endeavor in writing the story, which climaxes with the observation that most science fiction is "as much an evasion of reality as any mind-distorting drug" and goes on to catalogue the alleged similarities between the phenomena of addiction to sf and addiction to crack. By this means, Kessel betrays in advance the casually happy ending which he then appends to his story, excusing its hollow upbeatness with the observation that: "Having been an SF user myself, however, I have to say that, living in a world of cruelty, immersed in a culture that grinds people into fish meal like some brutal machine, with histories of destruction stretching back to the Pleistocene, I find it hard to sneer at the desire to escape. Even if escape is delusion."

Actually, as *Meeting in Infinity* demonstrates, Kessel doesn't find it all that hard to sneer; it's just that he likes to ameliorate his sneers with big dollops of sentimentality, after the customary fashion of American Dreamers. In America, story values demand that bleakness always comes with a strong seasoning of sugar, which—given that literature is a political tool used by elites to maintain their hegemony—may well be one of the reasons why Americans in general, and American sf fans in particular, so frequently fall victim to obesity.

I think it was Terry Carr who once published an anthology called *Science Fiction for People Who Hate Science Fiction*. That was back in the '60s, when the genre was begging to be taken more seriously by the Literary Establishment (whose core membership was presumed to be made up of people who taught American Literature and Creative Writing in colleges). The anthology presumably sank without trace, but the cause it espoused was eventually half-won. Nowadays, a good deal of science fiction is not only read, but also written, by people who hate science fiction. John Kessel is a cardinal example, because of the consistency of his viewpoint and because he is very good at it. It is probable that there has never been such a skilful and effective writer of the kind of sf that people who hate sf are likely to adore. He has all of the necessary qualifications: he knows next-to-nothing about science and—being on the cushy side of the Two Cultures gap—is proud of the fact; he deploys items from the vocabulary of ideas that SF writers have built up, but he does so without any extrapolative or exploratory purpose; he uses them instead as metaphors to dramatize a human condition which (knowing next-to-nothing about science) he considers eternal and inevitable; the stocks of knowledge that he assumes to be common between himself and his reader, upon which he draws in order to establish a stream of meaningful communication, are mostly literary (readers are assumed to have read and rightly admired *Moby Dick*, to have read and incorrectly admired Raymond Chandler, and to have heard of and overrated H. G. Wells), with occasional excursions into the cinematic and the musical (the only previously-unpublished story, "Faustfeathers", is *The Tragical History of Dr. Faustus* as interpreted by the Marx Brothers; it is the only story in the book with an unbetrayed happy ending).

The earliest story here, "Not Responsible! Park and Lock It!" (1981), is an allegory with robots. It describes a world in which all humanity is driving along an endless westbound highway, getting nowhere. An adolescent boy, who feels that there ought to be more to life than sitting in a back seat, begins a trek across the "Median" in search of the legendary eastbound carriageway, but is intercepted by a robot, which lists all the good reasons why he should turn back (pseudo-logical, religious and straightforwardly threatening); in the end his father brings him back and buys him his own car in order to set him on the right road. As a satirical examination of the futility of trying to escape the limitations of social conformity, the story is neat and effective, although it is not quite as vivid as the novella "Another Orphan" (1982), in which a modern man wakes up to discover that he is a crewman on the Pequod, and must adjust to its rigors while wondering whether he can figure out which of his crewmates is "Ishmael" and whether Ahab can be deflected from his obsessive quest before everyone aboard goes to their destined destruction. The story conscientiously leaves such matters unsettled, or at least undescribed, and deftly understates its back-references to the central character's distortively-mirrored "real" life; its climax is a brilliantly effective monologue, in which Ahab tries hard to persuade the protagonist to give up the ridiculous delusion that he is or ever could be anything other than what he appears to be. "Another Orphan" won a Nebula Award, which offers a telling clue as to why the Science Fiction Writers of America has now redefined itself as the Science Fiction and Fantasy Writers of America, having accumulated over the years a majority of members who only like the kind of science fiction that people who hate science fiction find it possible to like.

Meeting in Infinity kicks off with "The Pure Product", which would be an odd choice for anyone but a teacher, given that it is the worst story in the book. It recommends itself to teachers, however, because it is essentially a heartfelt wail about the failures of modern education. If things go on, it argues, the people of the future will all be psychopaths who have no values at all, and if they ever discover the secret of time travel, they will make us suffer for our mistake. "The Pure Product" is followed by a little parable called "Mrs. Shummel Exits a Winner", which coldly informs us that everybody in the world hates winners so much that no sensible nonentity would want to become one. I can think of no higher praise for a story of this kind than to say that if Jesus had thought of it, he would probably have used it. This is followed by "The Big Dream", which places Raymond Chandler at the heart of one of his own plots in order to instruct us that he was (a) a screwed-up shit, and (b) a lousy writer, which is followed in its turn by "The Lecturer", another self-conscious allegory, which sarcastically puts the boot into the kind of teacher of whom Politically Correct teachers are nowadays required to disapprove. Even these relatively lackluster materials are well-crafted, but they are easily surpassed in power by the stories hoarded for the latter part of the collection.

"Hearts Do Not in Eyes Shine" is, consciously or unconsciously, a careful updating of Edward Bellamy's *Dr. Heidenhoff's Process* (1880), in which an attempt to dispose of the legacy of past misfortunes by getting rid of the relevant memories inevitably goes sadly awry. "Faustfeathers" is silly but fun, and provides a welcome change of pace. "A Clean Escape" is about an escape into delusion which—readers will by this time be utterly unsurprised to learn—is far from clean and, in the end, not really much of an escape. "Not Responsible! Park it and Lock It!" is followed by the similarly allegorical "Man", which imports a clever contemporary twist into the age-old *doppelgänger* motif. "Invaders" is followed by the similarly dour fable "Judgment Call", whose moral is that we should never be tempted to take credit for being lucky, and by the phantasmagorically flippant "Buddha Nostril Bird", which is perhaps the only story in the book that has the advantage of being slightly out of the author's scrupulously careful and conscious control. Instead of saving "Another Orphan" for last, Kessel allows sentimentality to dictate that he give that honour to "Buffalo", in which he imagines a meeting between his father and H. G. Wells, when the two of them understandably f-f-f-fail to communicate, although each of them finds separate solace in the background music (obligingly provided by no less than Duke Ellington). This fade from the pretentiously philosophical to the pretentiously personal is the kind of move that any college teacher of American Literature would consider appropriate.

The blurb describes *Meeting in Infinity* as a "midcareer retrospective", which may or may not indicate that Kessel intends to abandon writing in another ten or twelve years. I assume that it is his own description, because I cannot quite imagine a humble in-house copywriter composing a blurb like this on anyone else's behalf; it begins with a long explanation of the cover picture, from which the title of the book has been borrowed: "In his 1899 woodcut *Meeting in Infinity*, which appears on the jacket to this book, Edvard Munch presents two transitory human beings who intersect—but do not really unite—within the eternal rhythms of the infinite. As the man assumes an attitude of abject despair, the luxuriantly coiffured femme fatale floats imperiously past. Through this reductive tableau, Munch conveys the psychic resonances of modern man: the simultaneity of pleasure and pain, of alienation and ecstasy, of ephemeral human icons cast adrift among the immutable." So there we have it: John Kessel, mid-career, identifies with Edvard Munch as interpreted by an overweeningly posy critic, and he is doing his bit for the great cause of trying to turn science fiction into something that literary critics might consider Respectable-with-a-capital-R.

Meeting in Infinity is in many ways a very impressive book, and not merely because it is as handsomely produced as Arkham House collections invariably are, with first-rate illustrations by J. K. Potter. The stories in it are unusually articulate and unusually persuasive, and I am offering a sincere compliment when I say that their principal effect on me was to make me painfully aware of how much I loathe the ideologies on behalf of which their persuasive power is exercised. Reading it has helped me more fully to realize the extent to which the science fiction label has been hijacked by writers who have determinedly set themselves against everything that the early American prophets of the genre proposed that it should stand for: celebration of the dynamic force of scientific and technological progress; appreciation of the fact that there are no solutions to human problems save technological ones; confidence in the hope that science might be the main instrument of our self-delivery from evil. But what can one expect, after all, given that literature is a political tool used by ruling elites to ensure their hegemony, and that the very idea of "Literature" is a political tool used by cultural elites to maintain their intellectual hegemony? I never fully understood, until I read John Kessel, how much I sympathize, in the deepest layers of my problematic psyche, with Hugo Gernsback.

John Kessel teaches American Literature and Creative Writing at North Carolina State University. There is a photograph of him on the back flap of *Meeting in Infinity* in which he is not smiling.

The Barber of Aldebaran by William Moy Russell, Janus, 1995

Way back in 1954, *The Observer* offered a first prize of £200 and twenty runners-up prizes of £20 each for unpublished stories of not more than 3,000 words set in the year 2500. Two thousand two hundred and forty entries were received (two hundred pounds was a lot of money in those days, when the paperback companies producing almost all British sf were paying £25 for 50,000-word novels). The judges chose a short list of three, which were published in the newspaper so that the readers could decide the winner by ballot; that winner and the twenty runners-up were published by Heinemann in a book called A.D. 2500, together with an introduction by Angus

Wilson. So far as I am aware, nothing more was ever heard of the competition winner, E. L. Malpass. Arthur C. Clarke's "The Star", later to be enshrined in the Science Fiction Hall of Fame, failed to make the last twenty-one, but Brian W. Aldiss and Arthur Sellings both did.

Among the other eighteen prize-winners, few seem to have achieved any subsequent celebrity. Robert Wells sold a single short story to *Science Fantasy* ten years later. D. A. C. Morrison might or might not be the Alex Morrison who sold a story to *Authentic* the following year. Stephen Earl went on to write a very boring travel book called *The Hills of the Boasting Woman* (not many people know that, but it happens that Stephen Earl was an old boy of my school, and I once had to sit through his slide-show of those very same hills). One who did acquire a certain modest fame was, however, William Moy Russell, a man of many parts—pioneer of humane animal research, sometime radio star, etc., etc.—who is well-known to readers of *Foundation* as W. M. S. Russell, emeritus professor of Sociology at the University of Reading, ex-President of the Folklore Society and polymathic author of such fine essays as "Folktales and Science Fiction" (F25) and "Voltaire, Science and Fiction: a Tercentenary Tribute" (F62).

The Barber of Aldebaran is a novel compounded out of two novellas, which Russell wrote in the wake of his success in the Observer competition, in 1954 and 1955. It is not at all obvious why they failed to find a market at the time, given that they are cleverly-constructed, deftly-written and briskly-paced comedy adventure stories that are a joy to read. Perhaps the editors of the day were wary of publishing work that was not in deadly earnest, and might be construed as poking fun at the genre, or perhaps they felt that the occasional references to opera might be wasted on the teenagers who formed the bulk of the burgeoning genre's readership. Whatever the reason, it was the genre's loss; had the two stories been published their author might have been disposed to write more, and they would very probably have got cleverer and cleverer as well as funnier and funnier.

The protagonist of *The Barber of Aldebaran* is Harri Balsam, a young executive at Robotics Incorporated, who is fortunate enough to stumble on an ironically ingenious solution to the awful incompetence of the corporation's products. His brainwave revitalizes his own personal robot attendant to spectacular effect (albeit with a few unlooked-for side-effects, which is where the operatic barbers come in) and sets in train a revolution in his world's affairs. The plot moves with the rapidity of a Whitehall farce, and has many of the same preoccupations, not to mention one or two of the same stock characters. (Professor Russell is, however, well-known for his feminist views, so the character of the winsome but ruthlessly acquisitive Cutie-pie should not be held against him.)

The elements of theatrical farce move further to the fore in the second part of the story, when Harri becomes a reluctant ambassador to Toxicurara, a world whose inhabitants take inhospitability to unprecedented lengths. The plot is moved and levered by the multifarious pheromonal secretions of an unassuming alien life-form called the flit—perhaps after the well-known fly-spray?—whose eventual salvation from threatened extinction must count as a triumph to gladden the hearts of environmentalists everywhere.

It has to be admitted that *The Barber of Aldebaran* does show its age in certain respects; given that nothing else dates as fast as images of the future, its antiquity could hardly be concealed. For that very reason, however, it will be a godsend to all those readers who spend their time lamenting the fact that modern writers don't write sf the way they used to; such readers might well regard it as a precious fragment of the Golden Age miraculously preserved in amber. It is worth bearing in mind, too, that we now live in an era when comedy science fiction has finally been accepted as a worthwhile pastime, at least by readers outside the genre; gone are the days when Robert Sheckley was a lonely figure haunting the fringes of the field,while R. A. Lafferty was its token eccentric and Ron Goulart its champion bore; nowadays, writers who wear the label proudly are forced to look enviously upon the spectacular successes of Douglas Adams and Grant Naylor. Thanks to the successes of these writers—aided and abetted by Terry Pratchett's best-selling comic fantasies—there is now an audience of comedy sf connoisseurs, who will not mind at all that this book is haphazardly displaced from its own time, because they will only be interested in the aspects that are essentially timeless. There *are* aspects of it that are essentially timeless, and it is very funny. The slight effort that may be required to seek it out is well worth making.

Voyage by Stephen Baxter, HarperCollins, 1996

Alternative histories are, by virtue of their nature, committed to identifying the most crucial moments in human history: the moments at which a single decision, had it been made differently, might have wrought a drastic and dramatic change in the unfolding pattern of history. It is not surprising that the principal nodal points, which have attracted great noisy flocks of alternative historians, have been wars and assassinations. There is, however, a significant minority report compiled by writers of a less orthodox stripe, which is dismissive of the cardinal importance of bullets and battles. In L. Sprague de Camp's excellent *Lest Darkness Fall*, Martin Padway eventually discovers that it is not his attempt to alter the outcome of a crucial battle that has subverted the Dark Ages, but the seemingly-insignificant technologies he has introduced in order to make a comfortable day-to-day living. In the classic anthology *If it had Happened Otherwise*, edited by J. C. Squire, we find—alongside all the expectable speculations about the non-expulsion of the Moors from Spain, the escapes of Napoleon and Lincoln, and the harmless passing of that fateful moment in Sarajevo—G. K. Chesterton's "If Don John of Austria had Married Mary Queen of Scots", which blithely suggests that the moral uplift of a single Good Example might work more to the benefit of mankind than a change in the livery of a million casualties of war.

Stephen Baxter's *Voyage* offers a tokenistic feint in the direction of the orthodox school of thought by commencing the divergence of his alternative history in 1963, when Lee Harvey Oswald's bullets kill Jackie Kennedy while leaving JFK crippled but alive. His true allegiance is, however, to the other side. In his scheme of things, as in Sprague de Camp's, politics is peripheral; Kennedy's survival is important only insofar as it offers the tiniest of nudges to the development of the space program, helping to tilt a knife-edge decision as to whether NASA is committed by its paymasters to the Shuttle program or to the planning and execution of a manned mission to Mars. Unlike de Camp, however, Baxter is not concerned to suggest that what hangs on this decision is the advancement of utilitarian kinds of technology that make a considerable difference to the patterns of everyday life. His true counterpart within the great tradition of alternative history stories is G. K. Chesterton; his fundamental argument is all to do with the moral uplift that might be offered by a glorious Good Example.

Baxter has already established a secure reputation as an assiduous and expert literary craftsman. He does his research very thoroughly, and he deploys it with consummate artistry. His prefatory note to *Voyage* concludes with the assurance that "it really would have been like this", and the text that follows never falters in its support of that claim. Every detail, technical or political, is in place; as an account of events that might have happened, it is thoroughly convincing. This is, in itself, a very considerable achievement—all the more so when one bears in mind that some individuals still living in our world had to be replaced or sidelined for reasons of diplomacy. There might be some readers who will find the sheer abundance of authoritative detail wearisome, and a few who will long for less authority and more action, but within its niche market, the book will certainly secure the admiration of connoisseurs. To the proposition that "it really would have been like this" the text offers as firm a *quod erat demonstrandum* as any that has ever been provided by an alternative historian. Nor is the story unduly lacking in action and dramatic incident; the disasters it admits, and the heroic triumphs it celebrates, are authentically touching by virtue of taking place within such a compelling context.

Unsurprisingly, given the purpose for which blurbs are designed, the copy on the jacket flap of the HarperCollins edition of *Voyage* is noticeably less modest than the text. The blurb ends with a formula similar to that employed at the end of the prefatory note, except that it uses the word *should*—uncompromisingly emphasized—rather than the word "would". It may be a mere advertisement, written by someone other than the author of he text, but that subtle slide from technical to moral judgment is the real heart of the argument. If this whole exercise has any point to it, all the telling detail and all the narrative authority must be reckoned as a means rather than an end. It is no small achievement to convince us that it would have happen this way, but it is an essentially preparatory achievement. The real question is, what does this hypothetical history have to tell us about our own? Did we get it wrong?

The judgment of the author seems, on the surface, to be that we did get it wrong. His afterword implies as much, although it is careful not to say so explicitly. "What went wrong in 1969?" he asks, rhetorically—and concludes his explanation with the judgment that "in the end, we cannot help but regret the loss of the great spectacle that we would have enjoyed had Natalie York walked on Mars...in 1986". As surfaces go, however, this is noticeably less firm underfoot than it might have been.

The caution of that last sentence might seem to many True Believers in the Conquest of Space to be unduly half-hearted in merely regretting the loss of a "spectacle", but it is an honest admission of the true weight of the text's *quod erat demonstrandum*. I have to admit that I never believed for a moment that, if Don John of Austria had married Mary Queen of Scots, their Good Example would have uplifted all Europe, and I don't really believe that G. K. Chesterton, in his heart of hearts, believed it either. Having read *Voyage*, and having allowed myself to be convinced by every detail of its alternative history, I can't believe for a moment that it has made a damn of difference to anything that actually matters that nobody went to Mars in 1986—and I don't really believe that Stephen Baxter, in his heart of hearts, believes it either. Perhaps he did when he set out to write *Voyage*, but once having written it, he surely must have felt compelled to accept the results of his own enquiry.

If asked "was it worth it?" the characters in *Voyage*—with one token exception, who is abruptly shuffled off to the sidelines as soon as he defects, lest he embarrass everybody else—would declare emphatically that it was, even though it cost them their careers, marriages, friends and—in sum—lives....but they would have to say that, wouldn't they? The authorial voice is, however, forced by its own authority to judge that they are, without exception, "near-psychotic"—and that no mission of this kind could possibly be accomplished by individuals who were not. All progress, as George Bernard Shaw pointed out, depends on the unreasonable man, but that sometimes has the effect of making progress itself unreasonable—not always, but sometimes. I presume that Baxter set forth on his own mission in order to argue that his hypothetical mission to Mars would not have been an unreasonable element of progress, but what his text actually implies, by virtue of its awesome scrupulousness, is that it would.

In 1905 Anatole France argued that H. G. Wells was the only futurist who had ever set forth as an explorer prepared to be surprised by what he found, rather than a dogmatist intent on painting his hopes and fears upon the *tabula rasa* of possibility. (It is, of course, rather ironic that, by the time France made that judgment, Wells had become a dutiful dogmatist just like all the rest.) Stephen Baxter has already demonstrated, in *The Time Ships*, that there is no one more worthy than he to walk in the footsteps of the great pioneer of scientific romance; perhaps *Voyage* ought to be assessed as a further demonstration of his worthiness. In concluding his bold and brilliantly-executed experiment with the assertion that we cannot help but regret the loss of a "great spectacle" he damns the enterprise of his characters with conspicuously faint praise—and he is, as he will hopefully remain, perfectly accurate in his summation of the real implications of his work.

The Gaia Websters by Kim Antieau, Roc, 1997

C. S. Lewis once observed that readers occasionally react to certain kinds of texts with an instantaneous horror and loathing so powerful that it warrants comparison with a phobia. Such a reaction tends to obliterate critical distance, thus precluding the possibility of accurate critical judgment. It is arguable that no one subject to such a side-effect should attempt to review a book that produces it but I must confess that I have always found the reaction itself interesting, in a quasi-medical fashion, and it is also arguable that all reviews reveal as much about the reviewer as they do about the book under consideration, so I shall take the reckless step of attempting to define what it is about *The Gaia Websters* that triggered my allergic detestation. I am content to accept that the text cannot actually be as frankly abysmal as it seems to me to be, or no editor on earth could ever have bought it, and even if the reviewer for the *Vancouver Columbian* had been deeply in love with Kim Antieau, he or she could never have thought her worthy of such a hyperbolic claim as the that quoted on the front cover, to the effect that she is "comparable to Ursula le Guin and Margaret Atwood".

The amnesiac heroine of *The Gaia Websters* calls herself Gloria Stone because she thinks the name suits her. She is possessed of a miraculous ability to heal any and all diseases and injuries by the mere laying on of hands, although she is coy about accepting the title of "soothsayer" lest she attract the attention of itinerant witch-hunters (who are said to be around but never actually appear). Gloria is the resident healer of Coyote Creek, Arizona—a mysteriously self-sufficient village (mysteriously, at least, to me, or any other reader interested in its ecology and economy) in a post-catastrophe world that has learned to hate and fear all technology. The grounds for this hatred are not so much that technology caused the Fall that has returned human society to a quasi-Medieval level—there is nothing particularly nasty, brutish or short about a life whose fundamental comforts are sustained and continually renewed by magical healers—but that the continued use of a few battered and unreproducible artifacts might somehow bring back the bad old days. Echoes of the bad old days in question still persist, however, in the remnants of its political order (Arizona has a governor) and the fact that the majority of human males are still sneeringly macho, while the majority of their female kin are equally relentless in their humble martyrdom as they await the salvation of True Love.

Like many an amnesiac heroine before her, Gloria eventually turns out to be a product of evil technology herself: a left-over instrument of male power-games and male lust, who has had to survive greater abuses than the author can bring herself to describe or explain. This is unsurprising, given that the only things the author does feel competent to describe are woeful sentiments and desolate landscapes, while the very concept of "explanation" seems utterly alien to her. Following conventional advice to abuse-survivors, however, Gloria does her heroic best to shrug off the awful burden of her heritage, to forget (yet again) what needs to be forgotten, and to get on with the serious business of healing people and finding True Love.

The principal reason for my extremely negative response to this plot and its many analogues is that its attitude to technology seems to me to be mind-bogglingly stupid. Even Kim Antieau knows full well that, when Mother Nature had her way with us, the way in question was paved with the Black Death, smallpox, Spanish flu, malnourishment, direly inadequate housing and frightful toilet facilities, but the proposition that the answer to these difficulties lies in the simple power of wish-fulfillment seems to me to be as inept as it is inadequate.

Antieau is, of course, by no means alone in suggesting that the downside of our ever-increasing dependence on technology might ultimately be overcome by cultivating mental powers that would cut out the inconvenient mechanical middlemen. Even John W. Campbell Jr. succumbed to the seductive attraction of this myth in his Don A. Stuart days, and never made a full recovery. The careful way in which Antieau reserves the privilege of healing power to female abuse-survivors still forced to struggle against evil ingratitude also has its nobler precedents, in the Kleenex school of science fiction pioneered by Zenna Henderson. Antieau's repetition of this well-worn cliché seems to me, however, to be far weaker than its antecedents, to the extent of being actually childish. If the comparison with le Guin and Atwood were not already absurd, on the grounds that neither of those writers are idiot enough to embrace such a worldview, it would founder on the rock of their adult exactitude. *The Gaia Websters* is one of the vaguest texts I have ever encountered; its every half-hearted attempt to tie its various elements together into any kind of rational or aesthetic whole is shrouded in a dense cotton-wool of uncontrolled gushing and uneasy circumlocution.

Given that Kim Antieau clearly believes, along with John Gray, that men are from "Mars" and women from "Venus", she might not be astonished by the strength or polarity of my reaction to her attitude to technology or the manner of its expression. Nor, I suspect, would her editor; there is clearly someone at Roc USA who has a strong liking for anti-masculine fantasy, given that the same publisher has issued works by Gael Baudino and Felicity Savage that similarly seem to take pride in extending the imaginative limits of New Age feminism. Although I do not actually like either of these other writers, however, they do not excite the same allergic response. This is partly attributable to the compensating literary virtues which they possess—Baudino, for instance, is capable of robust plotting and is much better able than Antieau to realize her settings—but only partly; there remains something about Antieau that I find uniquely excruciating. I think, on due consideration, that it is her appalling conceit.

I am well aware, of course, that a modest author is a contradiction in terms, but Antieau's vanity is not the familiar kind of exaggerated self-confidence that so easily grows into cavalier arrogance. Nor is it the quaintly wistful hopefulness that allowed Zenna Henderson to pretend—at least for a while, once now and again—that all the problems of the world might be solved by elementary schoolteachers, if they only had the right tools for the job. It is a particular, and to my mind rather peculiar, kind of narcissism, which not only allows the author to project an image of heroic endeavor that is as silly as it is insipid, but also allows her to remain blithely oblivious of the absurdity of her own magniloquence—a magniloquence that easily overrides the aesthetics of conventional grammar, syntax and meaning.

Consider, for instance, these brief excerpts from the novel's climactic summation of its heroine's achievements:

> "The light was all consuming. I plunged straight into it and found the groove. Suddenly I was filled with something strange and beautiful, so relaxing I wanted to fall into it, did fall into it, and splashed it all over myself. The feeling pushed Church's memories open. I wanted to laugh. How ridiculous that I had ever felt disconnected, not belonging....
>
> "I reached out to the other soothsayers and they reached for me, all over the Earth, weaving a web around the planet, the connections pulsing with my discoveries and all their memories and knowledge. We were the new web, the new weavers. We were here for the planet and all her creatures...." (pp. 228-9)

This remarkable combination of the imagery of TV commercials and TV sitcoms, stitched together with a literary analogue of the kind of *non sequiturs* that TV's rapid cuts have now established as the common currency of everyday experience, seems to me to confirm all the warnings Harold Innis and his better-known disciple, Marshall McLuhan, issued in the 1950s and 1960s about the inhospitability of electronic media to linear (and hence to logical) thought. It is bad enough to hear the infuriating introductory jingle of *Friends* continually assuring the world that the essence of the ideal social relationship is to "be here for you"; to see that amplified into the assertion that the essence of individual worth and the ultimate expression of individual wish-fulfillment is to be "here for the planet" surely qualifies as an aesthetic as well as a logical atrocity. The philosophy of composition underlying *The Gaia Websters* seems to me to be no kind of thought at all, but rather a kind of anti-thought (and such is my determination to be both fair and serious that I will nobly resist the terrible temptation I feel at this juncture to make puns on the author's name).

Although crass ecological mysticism of the kind displayed in *The Gaia Websters* is often accompanied nowadays by fervent pro-Venereal and anti-Martial rhetoric there is nothing essentially feminist (or even feminine) about it, and I do not think that my response to the book can be dismissed as a trivial symptom of male backlash. My objection to Kim Antieau's vision of a Gloria Stone capable of healing men, women, loyal coyotes and Mother Gaia herself by the pressure of gentle hands and the power of soppy wish-fulfillment is not that it seems so very obviously female but that it seems even more obviously to be a myopic, glaucomatic and astigmatic vision. And yet, it must have some appeal, or its editor could not have liked it enough to put it into print (although claiming, as the back cover blurb does, that its author is "pushing her unique talents to even greater limits" does smack of leading with one's chin).

I have not read Antieau's first novel, *The Jigsaw Woman*, but it could not have reaped the praise quoted on the flyleaf if it were half as bad as *The Gaia Websters*, so I am tempted to wonder whether the present offering might be an earlier work considered unpublishable until it became commercially desirable to follow up the success of *The Jigsaw Woman*, but the fact remains that it has been published with an accompanying fanfare. Evidently the editor believes—perhaps with some justification—that there are sufficiently large numbers of TV-socialized New Age-inclined readers out there to make this kind of text saleable—and saleable, moreover, under the science fiction label.

All fantasies are, of course, images of impossible worlds. Good fantasies are, however, ones whose impossibility refers back in interesting ways to the world as it is and the world as it might be. It seems to me that The Gaia *Websters* not only fails dismally in that ambition, but constitutes a blatant insult to the intelligence of its readers—but it is, after all, only a book, as inappropriate an object of horror and loathing as a spider in the bath.

Earthquake Weather by Tim Powers, Legend, 1997

In *The Birth of Tragedy* (1872) Friedrich Nietzsche distinguished between the "Apollinian" genius of careful measure and restraint, which drew out the ordered harmonies of Greek art and philosophy, and the irrationally passionate "Dionysian" verve, which had to be domesticated and set in harness in order to energize that art and philosophy. Tragedy, he argued, was a child of the union of the Apollinian and the Dionysian—a child subsequently slain by rationalism, and unrisen from the dead until modern times. In his later work, Nietzsche employed the figure of Dionysus to symbolize the precious synthesis of the Dionysian with the Apollinian as well as that which was more narrowly Dionysian, and hence to signify a joyous affirmation of the life of the flesh and the world, which he frequently opposed to the unproductive otherworldliness of Christ and Christianity.

It is still easy, in today's pluralistic culture, to make distinctions between the Apollinian and the Dionysian. They are as obvious in fantastic literature as they are elsewhere, although the hardened Apollinians mostly work in the broad lakes of the literary mainstream and children's fiction, while the greater number of wholehearted Dionysians are crowded into generic backwaters (among the several American writers who fuse the two most cleverly, James Morrow and John Crowley have recently seemed the most effective). To date, Tim Powers has had to be reckoned among the most vividly accomplished of the Dionysians, although *The Stress of her Regard* offered clear testimony to the fact that he harbored some Apollinian ambitions. Both *Last Call* and *Expiration Date* offered brilliantly ingenious and deliriously hectic narratives, which toyed with eccentric scholarship in much the same way that *The Anubis Gates* had done, but neither aspired to be anything more than rousing entertainment of the very finest quality. *Last Call* deservedly won the World Fantasy Award, but its masterful melodrama never aspired to the kind of profundity that might have invited comparison with authentic tragedy. *Earthquake Weather* is a sequel to both of these texts, and it continues their stories in the same ingenious and hectic vein, but it adds a further layer of complexity to the Gordian tangle that results from the combination of their (initially independent) metaphysical schemes, and it also discovers, in its oblique portrayal of the god Dionysus, the darker depths of feeling and of meaning that entitle it to be considered Dionysian in Nietzsche's later sense of the term.

It must be admitted that many readers approaching *Earthquake Weather* are likely to find it rather confusing. The blurb attached to the Legend edition includes no notification of the fact that it carries forward the stories of *Last Call* and *Expiration Date* (perhaps because one or both of those volumes were issued in the UK by rival publishers). The fact is, however, that only readers who have read and remembered both of those works will quickly find their feet within the new text, and even they might find it something of a strain. The two central characters of the present work—"Scant" Cochran and Janis Cordelia Plumtree—are new, as is the villainous Dr. Armentrout, in whose mental asylum they are brought together, but the remainder of the cast is second-hand. More importantly, the highly idiosyncratic world in which they move is concocted by combining the worlds within the two earlier texts, adding a whole fleet of subsidiary hypotheses in order to stitch them together, and then extending its syncretic reach even further and more ambitiously.

Readers who have not previously met Pete and Angelica Sullivan and Koot Hoomie Parganas in *Expiration Date* will probably find it difficult to become attached to them now, and readers who did not share the appalling tribulations suffered by Scott Crane in becoming the Fisher King of the western USA in *Last Call* may not be able to feel the urgency of the quest to resurrect him that supplies the plot of *Earthquake Weather*. Even readers who do remember Sherman Oaks from *Expiration Date* will probably have difficulty relating to Long John Beach, and those who recall Arky Mavranos from *Last Call* might not find his older and wiser incarnation altogether recognizable, but without the groundwork secured by earlier reading, obtaining identificatory toeholds with the minor characters in the new texts is likely to be well-nigh impossible. Even the minor characters have vital roles to play in meeting the challenges laid down by the plot, in which the central problem of Scott's resurrection is monstrously complicated by the multitude of possibilities opened up by his—and, to a lesser extent, everybody else's—death. As if the fates and fortunes of ghosts outlined in *Expiration Date* were not enough, they are more intensively recomplicated here; again, the work done by the earlier volumes is largely taken for granted in *Earthquake Weather*, in spite of all the careful reminders sown into the story.

When the hurdles of sorting out the characters and the exotic possibilities of life-after-death have been taken, there still remains to the reader of *Earthquake Weather* the difficulty of getting to grips with a metahistorical framework that is every bit as complicated as the one underlying Umberto Eco's *Foucault's Pendulum* but nowhere near as neatly laid out. Eco's Templar conspiracy was, after all, a fundamentally Apollinian construct, whose main aim was to impose stern order on seeming chaos; Powers' account of the travails of Dionysus in the wake of the French Revolution and the various treasons of his Californian brides is a metamorphic process in which order and chaos are engaged in an intricate dance every bit as disturbing as a earthquake and as wayward as the weather. (Eco's Templars do appear briefly in Powers' scheme, only to be dismissed by a casual throwaway gesture as a matter of merely marginal significance.)

The texts that provide most of the headquotes mapping out *Earthquake Weather*'s progress, as well as allegedly encoding its metaphysical framework, are Shakespeare's *Troilus and Cressida* and Dickens's *A Tale of Two Cities*, both of which are here represented as ideative descendants and extensions of the most enigmatically Classical of Greek tragedies, *The Bacchae*. The allegorical contortions of the text's conceptual topology are virtually unequalled in modern literature. Just as Powers' recapitulation of Jessie Weston's thesis in *Last Call* made David Lodge's in *Small World* seem so straightforward as almost to be shallow, so *Earthquake Weather* makes *Last Call* seem so perfect a model of analogical rectitude as to be almost pellucid; "bizarre" is far too feeble a word to capture its convoluted exoticism.

Powers' work has always seemed intoxicated in a light-hearted sort of way. His villains have usually been exceedingly nasty and authentically scary, but he has offered more than adequate compensation in the vigor and courage of his heroes. Mellow bonhomie and cavalier braggadocio were never submerged for long, even in the darkest phases of *The Anubis Gates* and *On Stranger Tides*, and that rule held good as far as *Expiration Date*—but *Earthquake Weather* takes its intoxication into a deeper and more paranoid phase.

Scant Cochran is an uncharacteristically impotent figure, who cannot bear up under the weight of his own troubles and has no significant resources to add to those of the good guys carried forward from the earlier texts. It is not simply that he is fallible—all Powers' heroes have been human enough to make barely-forgivable errors—but that he is indecisive, as unclear in his ambitions as he is dubious in his competence. He never properly figures out, even as the story gathers force in nearing its end, exactly what he ought to do, or how; in consequence, it is left to the other characters to meet the dead king's most vital needs, while he only supplies the key to one of several awkward locks. Cochran's relative impotence is precisely mirrored by the stubbornly peripheral status and ever-declining energy of Armentrout, whose villainy never comes close to matching the tortuous pressure exerted by Scott's father in *Last Call* or Sherman Oaks and his female counterpart in *Expiration Date*. Armentrout's own campaign runs out of steam long before the climax of the book, by which time he is merely one more clownish victim of ironic misfortune, to be battered, bruised and ultimately turned inside-out by the plot. If one argues, as one certainly could, that the real hero and villain of the book are contained—along with several others—within the Multiple Personality Disorder of Janis Cordelia Plumtree, they are even further weakened in their narrative authority by the necessity of sharing space in the same confused and permanently drunken brain.

In *Earthquake Weather*, unlike any of Powers' previous novels, it is the general narrative scheme rather than the particular predicaments of enthusiastically-pursued heroes that must take on the Herculean task of engaging the reader's interest and towing the reader through the text. It is mainly by virtue of this deflection of attention that the intoxication of the text becomes absolute. All connection with sobriety is lost, and the rule of Dionysus—ever-present but rarely glimpsed—is totalitarian in its oppression. This Dionysus is, however, no mere sot, subsidiary in his implication to Zeus the All-Father and promiscuously fecund Pan; this Dionysus is a figure of cardinal importance, the very linch-pin of the hypothetical universal scheme that enfolds, defines and awards meaning to human life and human endeavor. He is, in *Earthquake Weather*, not merely *a* god but *the* god, unique in his significance if not his existence.

Difficult as it may be for the unsuspecting and unsympathetic reader, *Earthquake Weather* is undoubtedly a masterpiece, awesome in its achievement as well as its complexity. It is delirious in its narrative thrust, haemorrhagic in its inventiveness, and calculatedly insane in its reinterpretations of literature, myth and occult symbolism, but it never consents to revel in its own disorderliness and accept its own eventual inexplicability. It never lets go of the responsibility to make ultimate sense, to bind up its plethora of treasures into some kind of logically- and aesthetically-satisfactory whole. It is serious in its intensity, as fascinated by the necessity for beginnings and ends to meet and fuse as its myriad ghosts are by the palindromes that capture and confine them. It sacrifices the melodrama of heroism and villainy in order to reach beyond their scope, to authentic tragedy, not in the trivial sense that it has a downbeat ending, but in the true sense that it recognizes the limitations of human action and human ambition, and the awful difficulty that afflicts the winning of life's smallest but most precious victories. It takes a harsh and tacitly pagan view of the politics of redemption, but a keen awareness of the necessity of redemption, from painful grief as well as sinful guilt, always frames the centre-stage action, never to be forgotten for an instant.

Earthquake Weather is a book to be shelved alongside *Little, Big* and *Blameless in Abaddon*, even if that decision sets it inconveniently above its unidentical twin preludes *Last Call* and *Expiration Date*. No one should attempt to read it without having first read its predecessors, but no one who has read it predecessors should delay before capitalizng on their fortunate expertise. *Earthquake Weather* will reach parts of them that the earlier books did not reach, and it will nourish those parts with intelligence and imagination of a rare vintage.

The Twentieth Century by Albert Robida, translated by Philippe Willems, Wesleyan University Press, 2004

There is a certain perversity in the fact that English readers have had to wait until the entire twentieth century has vanished into the past before gaining access to Albert Robida's 1882 account of its early progress. This English edition is now more than fifty years "late," since the book's story is almost entirely set in 1952 and ends with the characters looking forward optimistically to what 1960 might bring. Fortunately, thanks to the recent advent of the steampunk subgenre, sf enthusiasts have now become used to taking delight in fanciful visions of antique futures-that-never-were, so this edition has a timeliness of its own, and might even be reckoned more durably up-to-date now than it must have seemed a year after its original publication, when the Decadent Movement became all the rage in Paris.

It may seem surprising that not a word of Albert Robida's work was translated into English in the 1880s, given that France's other leading sf writer of the era, Jules Verne, was routinely and successfully translated. In Britain, however, Verne was regarded as a writer of "boys' books"—masculine adventure stories fit (once the anti-English sentiments had been censored) for the education of young imperialists. Although Robida began his career with an affectionate pastiche of Vernian adventure fiction, a five-part series of *Voyages très extraordinaires de Saturnin Farandoul dans les 5 ou 6 parties du monde et dans tous les pays connus et même inconnus de M. Jules Verne*, he could never take the adventure component seriously and tended to give it a blatantly farcical slant. *The Twentieth Cen-*

tury has only a tokenistic adventure component, which does not intrude until chapter 9 of part 3, and if that were not enough, the fact that it has a female hero places it far beyond the pale of boys' book fiction. The more famous compendium with which Robida followed it up, *La Guerre au vingtième siècle* (1867-68 in magazine form; book 1887), was even less suitable for young imperialists, by virtue of its subtle but unmistakable pacifism.

The plot of *The Twentieth Century* is a mere device on which to hang a tour of the institutions, folkways and international relations of Paris in 1952. Its hero, Hélène Colobry, has just left school and is instructed by her guardian, the billionaire banker Raphaël Ponto, to find a means of earning a living. She tries out the law, politics and journalism before finally deciding that she is so generally incompetent that she will have to face the ultimate ignominy of shopping around for a husband instead. Although Philippe Willems' introduction is careful not to overstate the novel's feminist credentials, and all of this is part of Robida's light satire, he is far too polite a writer to make the underlying egalitarian philosophy of this notion seem anything but entirely natural.

The avoidance of melodrama in favor of detailed descriptions of everyday domestic and social life inevitably makes *The Twentieth Century* seem as much documentary as drama, and the fact that Robida is forced to rely on his wit to provide the narrative energy thus sacrificed also makes it seem calculatedly trivial, but modern readers can probably see far better than nineteenth-century ones that the triviality is a mask protecting some serious arguments. The violence of *La Guerre au vingtième siecle* is here reduced to a few passing observations—the "great wars" of 1920 are a distant memory here, as is the utter spoliation of Russia by nihilist terrorism—but its legacy survives, subtly interwoven into the texture of world peace.

Twenty years after the publication of *The Twentieth Century*—by which time he also had such extravagantly earnest examples as Camille Flammarion's *La Fin du monde* (1895) and Gabriel Tarde's *Fragment d'histoire future* (1896) to consider—Anatole France regretfully observed in *Sur la pierre blanche* (1905) that writers tended to use the literary future not as a medium for open-ended exploration but as a canvas on which to paint their hopes or fears. He would doubtless have included Robida's most august predecessor as a futuristic satirist, Emile Souvestre, in the latter category, because—despite its wit—Souvestre's *Le Monde tel qu'il sera* (1846), is effectively a dystopia. Robida is, however, much harder to pin down in this way, and has more exploratory spirit than France had apparently observed. Although any nineteenth-century reader, looking at *The Twentieth Century* through the lenses of his or her own hopes and fears, could easily identify Utopian and dystopian elements in it, they are mere by-products of Robida's method and assumptions.

What Robida was doing—and it remains surprisingly rare, even today—was neither to predict the twentieth century, nor to prescribe for it, nor to issue warnings regarding its direr possibilities, but simply to establish one of the points that Anatole France was trying to make: that in the future, things would be different, and that no matter how odd or immoral that different state of being might seem to the idol-infested eyes of the present, it would seem perfectly normal to those living in it. The great strength of *The Twentieth Century*, which makes it an authentic literary classic, is that all the amusing drawings and the jokes in the text are laid upon the fundamental assumption that the moral condition of the future will be and ought to be judged on its own terms, not ours. The fact that any honest image of the future is bound to seem rather shocking and/or silly to present-day readers is their failure, not that of the image. Robida understood that, although the majority of his readers never have—and that is one reason why Robida became so disenchanted with futuristic fiction that he eventually gave up on it, although few of his admirers understood what he was getting so upset about, given that he was only a cartoonist.

Now that *The Twentieth Century* is no longer a work of futuristic fiction, of course, modern readers cannot possibly find anything shocking in it, and its silliness is likely seem further inflated and enhanced by quaintness. It is now a utopia in the purest sense: a no-place whose absolute desertion by the actual course of history has proved that it was a world that never could have been—not merely a jest but an essentially empty jest. Perhaps we should remember, however, that the world is literally what we make it, and that—as Albert Robida was one of the first to observe, in *Jadis chez aujourd'hui* (1890) and *L'Horloge des siècles* (1902)—we really could turn the clock back if we wanted to, and sideways too if we were prepared to be ingenious.

If we wanted to, we really could live, as Hélène does, in a world where the outcome of court cases depended exclusively on emotional appeals to the prejudices of jurors, and prisons were pleasant retreats where criminals could be rehabilitated in harmonious tranquility. We could live, as she does, in a world in which women routinely run for parliament and in which loyal monitors keep a close watch on the public's representatives to make sure that political corruption and mendacity stays within approved bounds. We really could live, as she does, in a world in which journalists are routinely called out for duels by anyone who takes offence at what is written about them. Living in a world dominated by aerial transport would be more difficult, but we could surely do it if we really tried hard. And it would all seem perfectly normal; the prospect of Posh and Becks fighting back-to-back duels with Max Clifford and Piers Morgan, using AK-47s at twenty paces or rocket-propelled grenades at forty, would seem no sillier to us than current tabloid headlines, and just as entertaining.

This, I think, is the spirit in which *The Twentieth Century* should be read—and if it is read in that way, it is just as educational and inspiring today as it would have been in 1882, to anyone who could see past the fog in his or her ideological lenses. We could still build that sixth continent, or turn Italy into a theme park, and the idea of redefining France as a limited company, in which the people would be shareholders rather than taxpayers, might still be worth considering, no matter how absurd it seemed in 1882, even to Robida—whose citizens of 1952 reject the notion out of hand—that the twentieth century might allow rampant capitalism to evolve to ridiculous extremes.

The Wesleyan edition of *The Twentieth Century* is a thoroughly readable translation, and the illustrations have lost nothing of their élan and éclat, even if the combination of the reproductive processes of 1882 and 2004 has occasionally blurred their lines a little. Every serious science fiction reader should have a copy. Happily, we shall soon be able to see a little more of its native context, as Wesleyan intends to follow it up with its most august predecessor, Souvestre's *The World as it Shall Be*, and has already produced a new version of Cousin de Grainville's *Le Dernier homme* (1805) as *The Last Man*.

Robida is enjoying a long-overdue renaissance in France, where Jean-Pierre Moumon's Apex has produced facsimile reprints of several of his lesser-known works, including the last element of his "future history series," *Un Potache en 1950* (1917; a potache is a student*)*, *Jadis chez aujourd'hui* and two books in which Robida provided illustrations to accompany texts by other hands, Octave Uzanne's *La Locomotion future* (1895) and Pierre Giffard's *La Guerre infernale* (1908)—the latter a magnificent version of the feuilleton, including all the color covers. More English translations will undoubtedly follow; I. F. Clarke has already done a version of the text of *La Guerre au vingtième siècle* (1887) for his Liverpool University Press anthology *The Tale of the Next Great War*, so it is entirely probable that an illustrated edition similar to the Wesleyan Twentieth Century will eventually appear. My own translation of the first of Saturnin Farandoul's adventures has been in the hands of the Battered Silicon Dispatch Box for over a year now, but I have no idea when (or whether) it will appear—the trouble with the future is that one never knows what isn't going to happen.

[Note. My translation of the entire 200,000-word text of *The Adventures of Saturnin Farandoul* has now been published by Black Coat Press, as has my translation of *The Clock of the Centuries*, which also includes "Yesterday Now". *Chalet in the Sky*, including "A Student in 1950", will follow soon.]

The World as It Shall Be by Émile Souvestre; translated by Margaret Clarke; edited with an introduction by I. F. Clarke, Wesleyan University Press, 2004

This volume in the excellent Wesleyan University Press series of "Early Classics of Science Fiction"—which follows up the Clarkes' version of Jean-Baptiste Cousin de Grainville's *Le Dernier homme* (1805), translated as *The Last Man*—is a work of considerable historical importance. The early history of futuristic fiction is entirely dominated by French works but Louis Sébastien Mercier's *L'An deux mille quatre cent quarante* (1771) was the only one of the four most crucial foundation-stones laid by French writers easily available in English before the new translation of Cousin's *The Last Man*—and that was in an awkwardly unsatisfactory translation (as *Memoirs of the Year 2500*) first issued in 1795, whose obsolete typography made the fascsimile edition issued by the Gregg Press in 1977 even more difficult to read. Now that *Le Monde tel qu'il sera* (1846) is available as *The World As it Shall Be*, only Félix Bodin's *Le Roman de l'avenir* (1834) remains to complete the set.

It is, of course, entirely natural that the first great strides in futuristic fiction should have been taken in France, because it was in France that the philosophy of progress was first propounded by Anne-Robert-Jacques Turgot and the Marquis de Condorect, arguing that technological improvements and social improvements went hand in hand, and that both were bound to accelerate in the future. All of the pioneering exercises in futuristic fiction were meditations on the idea of progress and crucial question of whether—or to what extent—technological improvements assisted the revolutionary ideals of liberty, equality and fraternity.

Two of the four landmark texts cited above—Mercier and Bodin—are sympathetic to the basic Turgot/Condorcet thesis, although they retain certain reservations about the manner of its potential unfolding; the other two are much more suspicious of it, although they acknowledge certain strengths in the argument. Cousin's objection to the progressive account of human improvement is based in religious doctrine—*Le Dernier homme* is essentially a religious fantasy, in which God calls a halt to the world's development when material progress has achieved its climacteric—but Souvestre's is based in a more general religious sentiment, divorced from any particular dogma. In *The World as It Shall Be* there is no prospect of divine intervention in the world's affairs; its fundamental assumption is that material progress—in the absence of adequate sentimental checks—is bound to create a world that is the converse of the long-anticipated millennial Kingdom of God.

In consequence of its skeptical pessimism, Souvestre's novel is the first dystopian satire; its comic element is, however, so magnificently grotesque and so ludicrously exaggerated that it is by no means grim. Its title is a calculated echo of the first of Voltaire's famous *contes philosophiques*, "Le Monde comme il va" [The World as It Is] (1746), whose centenary it celebrates, and it sets out deliberately to outdo Voltaire in terms of flamboyant black comedy. In further elaborating the Voltairean method, however, Souvestre clearly had Félix Bodin's more recent precedent—especially Bodin's explicit criticisms of Mercier—in the forefront of his mind.

Bodin, although supportive of Mercier's daring in using the future as a narrative space, had complained that Mercier's method of so doing left much to be desired. *L'An 2440* is virtually unreadable, mainly because its slim first edition was augmented in subsequent printings by the patchwork addition of further footnotes and the expansion of those already included, so that the supportive commentary eventually outgrew the text, forcing readers to perform mental and digital acrobatics in search of a clear and coherent argumentative sequence. Bodin was prepared to forgive Mercier a certain amount of hasty improvisation, in recognition of the difficulties he faced as the author of an unstamped (i.e., illegally circulated) book that built up a tremendous pressure of demand—whose mere existence put him at risk of losing his liberty, and whose continued re-embellishment was a continual provocation—but felt that the real problem with the text was rooted in the necessity that had generated the footnotes in the first place.

L'An 2440 is a static Utopia, more essay than fiction in spite of the apologetic strategy that formulates it as a dream; Bodin, as his own title suggests, was seriously interested in the possibility of writing an authentic *roman* [novel] of the future; in addition to his exemplary attempt to do that, his book contains an essay admitting the methodological problems facing any such project but urging its necessity, on the grounds that *stories* set in the future, illustrating progress in a "picturesque, narrative and dramatic way" would be far more effective as ideative propaganda than Mercieresque depiction. (Bodin is equally critical of Cousineque "apocalypses," on methodological as well as ideological grounds.) Souvestre had obviously read this essay, and had taken note of the manner in which Bodin had attempted to practice what he preached, importing conflict into his plot by providing two exemplary pairs of characters, one committed and one opposed to the progress of civilization, the former representing the "positive" attitude of mind (in the Comtean sense) and the latter the "poetic" or "anti-prosaic" descendants of the world's military conquerors.

Souvestre disagreed with Bodin as to the merits of positivism, and considered Bodin's association of the poetic and the military to be a slur; he also considered the balanced symmetry of Bodin's characteriological exemplification drastically oversimplified. He also considered Bodin's depiction of future world-government and transportation—the latter involving a vast expansion of aerial traffic—over-optimistic. He too uses characters as exemplars, but his two innocents—champions of his own triple idealism of love, poetry and faith—are confronted with a vast array of opposites, all of them gross caricatures. (This edition, fortunately, reproduces the illustrations from the original, which supplement the verbal sketches with deft style and deadly accuracy and add considerably to the text's impact and enjoyment.) His depiction of future transportation, however, represents it as highly dangerous; its hazards occasionally read like an advance parody of Jules Verne, in its descriptions of cannon-fired ferries and a ramshackle submarine called the Dolphin Express. His description of future government is similarly cynical, and the world he describes is essentially turbulent (although he refuses to employ the melodramatic contrivances Bodin uses in order to import violence into a supposedly peaceful society: airborne pirates, neo-Amazons and freelance barbarian hosts).

Souvestre's story gets under way when the recently-wed Maurice and Marthe, understandably musing on what the future might hold for them, are greeted by the cheerful John Progrès, mounted upon a steam-powered flying machine, with a briefcase full of share certificates in his hand. Having arranged their passage from the present to the year 3000, however, this perennial Santa Claus leaves them to experience the multitudinous progeny that have adapted to every economic and cultural niche.

Maurice and Marthe discover that—as in Bodin's future, and in stark contrast to Mercier's—their beloved Paris has been consigned to the dustbin of history; global culture now has its center in Tahiti (in Bodin's *roman* it was a rebuilt Carthage). Indeed, all Europe has fallen into ignominious decay, while such emergent powers as Charcoal Island and Budget Island have taken up the torch of industrial revolution. These islands belong to no nation, the latter being the capital of United Interests, a global corporation of phenomenal efficiency and rapacity.

The first people the newcomers encounter in the year 3000 include M. Omnivore, of Omnivore and Company—which mines cultural resources much as its predecessors had mined natural ones—and the enterprising traveling salesman M. Blaguefort, but the person who takes them under his wing is, inevitable, a historian, named M. Atout. (Whereas the slang version of *blague* [trick] is adequately reflected in the English term "blag," there is no convenient English parallel for the way *atout*—a trump card—was used in nineteenth-century French to mean something along the lines of "Gotcha!" or "Take that!") This series of introductions and the subsequent journey to the city of Sans-Pair is, however, merely a prelude to a much more extensive series of encounters, as the visitors are taken on a conducted tour of the educational, medicinal and communications systems of the world that progress has made, discovering that all three of their own key ideals have been sacrificed on the altar of progress, with results that are extreme in their absurdity.

Looking back from a vantage point beyond the twentieth century, one can easily see that neither Bodin nor Souvestre solved the problem of equipping the novel of the future with a plot, even to the limited and jerry-built extent that H. G. Wells contrived in *The Time Machine*, *When the Sleeper Wakes* or "A Story of the Days to Come". Like any author forced to introduce readers to a whole new world, Souvestre has no alternative but to present them with a kind of travelogue, enlivened to the best of his ability by obstacles to surmount and puzzles to solve—and, like many another, he attempts to make up for the lack of conventional melodramatic resources by exploiting the narrative energy of comedy. The result is blatantly farcical, and there is a sense in which the grafting of such slapstick bodywork on to such an earnestly anxious chassis is bizarrely chimerical, but in its own arcane fashion it does work.

The World as It Shall Be is a far-ranging book, which fires off shots in every possible direction. Its funniest passages are perhaps those concerning the popular press of the year 3000 and the future society's image of the nineteenth-century. The latter is built on the method of using the literature of the day as a mirror to society, and Souvestre takes care to include a few of his own novels along with numerous highly-colored items by Balzac and Eugène Sue as he compiles an account of marriage, murder and general misbehavior as recorded in popular fiction.

All this is, however, situated after a swingeing denunciation of the ideals of modern political economy (one of the intellectual advantages Souvestre has over Mercier is that he is writing after the displacement of the theories of the French "physiocrats" by the new economic theories of Adam Smith and David Ricardo) and it cannot help seeming trivial and a trifle superfluous—a fact that the author obviously came to appreciate rather too keenly, cutting his text abruptly short well before the travelogue's third part has reached a length equivalent to its predecessors, thus condemning it to a conspicuously lame ending. Perhaps, if he had had the benefit of hindsight, he would have planned the sequence of revelations differently. The whole point of the book, however, and its crucial importance as a historical artifact, is that it was a bold foray into unknown territory, undertaken at furious pace without the benefit of a chart. As such, it is magnificent, even in its flaws.

Margaret Clarke's translation is excellent, rendering a difficult text very readable and thus making a valuable book readily accessible. Everyone with an interest in the history of futuristic fiction will welcome it, and *The World as It Shall Be* is an essential addition to any serious British or American library of science fiction. Casual readers will find much in it that is amusing, and much that is entertainingly prophetic, so it has something to offer everyone—even those who feel (as we all surely should) that its savage treatment of the positive is as horridly unfair as Félix Bodin's previous treatment of the poetic.

That is, however, the function of satire: to venture to the farthest extremes in order to obtain a clearer view of the location and layout of the middle ground.

[Note: Félix Bodin's *The Novel of the Future* is now available in English translation from Black Coat Press.]

PART FOUR

Miscellaneous Reviews

"What Sweet Music They Make...." (Thee Vampire Guild, 1995)

Thee Vampire Guild's compilation CD *"What Sweet Music They Make...."*—which advertises itself as "the Ultimate Compilation of Vampire/Goth Music" but will soon be supplemented by a second collection—represents the culmination of a remarkable trend. Although song lyrics about vampires have been around for some time on a small scale, Blue Oyster Cult's "Nosferatu" (on *Spectres*, 1977) being one of the most significant precedents, the last three or four years has seen an astonishingly rapid proliferation of such lyrics. The meager handful assembled in the previous three decades has suddenly grown by an order of magnitude, developing a rich imagery that is both complex and idiosyncratic.

To some extent, this phenomenon is simply the onward roll of a wave of fashionability that has already borne spectacular fruit in "dark fantasy" fiction and in the cinema, but it cannot be considered a mere echo of no intrinsic interest. Such movements of subject matter across the media landscape are never passive; any transition of this kind necessarily involves a transfiguration as great as that which is involved in the translation of vampire fiction to the cinema screen. There is an obvious reduction involved—just as the Dracula of the movies is far less rich and complex than the Dracula of Bram Stoker's novel, the vampire of a song lyric is bound to be even more abbreviated—but the shrinkage is not straightforward or simple. Any process of imagistic reduction is also a matter of narrower, and hence more intense, focusing—and is therefore a qualitative rather than a merely quantitative transformation. For this reason, if for no other, the adaptation of the vampire icon to the environment of "Goth music" is of interest as a new and distinct phase of an interesting evolutionary schema.

"What Sweet Music They Make...." (which opens with the famous snatch of dialogue from Tod Browning's *Dracula* in which Bela Lugosi refers to wolves as "children of the night" and adds the oft-misquoted comment "What music they make!") features fourteen tracks by nine bands from five different nations, thus offering eloquent testimony to the fact that although the Goth subculture might be thinly spread, it covers a lot of territory. The music is various in style, reflecting differences between the represented nations as well as the eclectic tendencies of the Goth subgenre—which is diffuse by comparison with, for example, "industrial" or "jungle" music—but it has a fairly consistent underlying feel by virtue of its unifying subject-matter. The composers represented here have a reasonably clear idea of how to use rhythm and melody to signify their subject-matter, which is not entirely attributable to direct imitation. One proximal source of this common musical "language" is, of course, the cinema, which has been using specific kinds of music to heighten viewer response to vampire films for some considerable time, but there is a propriety already built into the cinematic use of musical effects, which these songwriters are exploiting and carrying further forward.

The propriety of musical representation is a difficult thing to pin down—the ways in which music can reflect and enhance emotional experience are complicated and to some extent mysterious—but there is no harm in trying to venture a few speculative comments, or pointing out a few interesting connections. In particular, it might be appropriate to explore the links between the ways in which music can be used to enhance the emotional resonance of the lyrically-concentrated icon of the vampire and the ways in which that icon can nowadays be incorporated into "lifestyle fantasies".

(It might be politic to note at this point that all lifestyle is to some extent fantasy, and that "lifestyle fantasy" should not be construed as a pejorative term. No matter what vulgar humor may allege, there are very few lifestyle fantasists in lunatic asylums; even the most exotically inventive are quite sane. Anyone with the slightest comprehension of the utility of fantasy in literature and interior life ought to understand perfectly well that there is no particular merit in those lifestyles that are constructed under the pressure of overt and covert media advertising by consumers intent on obsessive conformity to the most widely-sanctioned social norms; such behavior might occasionally be excused in the terminally middle-aged, but it is entirely inappropriate to the young and the intelligent.)

* * * * * * *

The great majority of habitual readers of vampire fiction and aficionados of the cinematic vampire relate to the material as mere observers, whose "identification" with characters in the narratives is a temporary affair put aside as soon as the book is laid down or the film ended. It has been noticeable for some time, however, that Anne Rice, Chelsea Quinn Yarbro, P. N. Elrod, and many other writers in the same revisionist vein have so enhanced the charisma of the vampire that, for a small minority of enthusiasts, identification with vampires has begun to spill over into lifestyle fantasy. Few such lifestyle fantasists actually elect to represent themselves as vampires (and most of those who do have their tongues in their cheeks) but imaginative identification with the vampire's particular outsider status has enabled many people to present themselves—if only in private daydreams or within the relatively safe haven of the Vampire Lestat Society and its analogues—as "fellow travellers" of vampirekind.

To individuals of this stripe the works of Anne Rice *et al.*— because rather than in spite of the fact that they are fantastic— provide a uniquely apt metaphorical account of the tribulations of sensitive souls suffering in a tortuous wilderness of mediocrity. For readers such as these, the distinctively modern kind of vampire fiction that concentrates its attention on the uncomfortable existential plight of heliophobic more-or-less-guilt-ridden drinkers of human blood is a diffuse Jeremiad with which they can wholeheartedly empathize. However odd it may seem to unsympathetic bystanders, the lamentations of the undead seem to this sector of their audience to constitute a meaningful and understandable exaggeration of their own alienated sense of being.

The majority of people who listen to the kind of music featured on *"What Sweet Music They Make...."* are, of course, consumers after the straightforward fashion of most consumers of vampire novels and vampire films. To a far greater extent than books or films, however, subgenres of music are identified with manifest subcultures, and the "Goth" subgenre is no exception. The people who listen to Goth music, especially those who go to see bands play live, are likely to observe a particular dress-code and to have a reasonably well-developed sense of community with others of their kind. Even if their contact with other members of the community is fairly infrequent (or even virtually non-existent) such people know what it means to be a Goth, and they are highly likely to assert that Goth is not merely a style of dress or a musical subgenre but "a way of life". To the limited extent that the Goth subculture has taken up the particular fascination with vampires whose formulation may be credited to the novels of Anne Rice *et al*, therefore, it has done so in a relatively wholehearted fashion. Those who feel that Goth is a way of life may well feel that it needs no further embellishment, and that its essence and dignity might be imperiled by more extreme adventures in lifestyle fantasy, but those most powerfully drawn to the vampire icon are inevitably more likely than people outside the subculture to incorporate an element of lifestyle fantasy into their appreciation.

Because lyrics are much more compact than films or books, throwing their motifs into much sharper relief than more extended narrative forms, that fascination which has recently made vampire fiction a literary subgenre in its own right becomes much more blatant in its musical manifestations. The latest generation of vampire novels has provided an elaborate decoding and a careful recomplication of the sexual symbolism lurking within the "classic" literary vampires, and it has added an extraordinary depth of feeling to its extrapolations and analyses of the existentialist plight of the "undead", but song lyrics are compelled to strip these matters down to their essentials. Having done that, though, the songs then re-dress the lyrical essentials in the emotionally-loaded clothing of melody, rhythm and percussion, thus adding an extra factor to the focusing process.

The fact that music has strong subcultural associations serves to enhance this focusing effect even further. It is certainly not the case that *"What Sweet Music They Make...."* consists entirely of music made by lifestyle fantasists for lifestyle fantasists, but it is noticeable that several of the bands featured have taken aboard some elements of lifestyle fantasy in their self-representations, and that the majority of the songs involve an imaginative identification of singer and subject-matter that is fervent even when it is ironic or manifestly playful.

If we desire to cut to the heart of the fascination that the contemporary literary/cinematic vampire has for so many people, it might well be the case that the most direct route is via the lyrics of such songs as these. Here, more clearly than anywhere else, is the fundamental emotional configuration of that fascination laid bare. It may be as well, though, to begin with some preliminary remarks about the subculture that has played host to the rapid proliferation of vampire imagery.

* * * * * * *

The British punk "revolution" of the late 1970s spawned a whole host of new styles of self-presentation, most of which sought to display a down-at-heel grotesquerie (many of them are on display as I write in the "Streetstyle" exhibition organized by Ted Polhemus for the Victoria and Albert Museum). In general, the kinds of outfits and ornamentation favored by high street shops were automatically out, while eccentric mélanges, body-piercing and miscellaneous things of threads and patches were in; one exception to this rule was, however, the appearance that the reportage of the day called "Gothic punk" and which later became simply "Goth". Although the other manifestations of punk quickly faded away, after the usual fashion of such fads, Goth proved surprisingly persistent, and it has not yet shown any obvious signs of terminal decline.

The Goth dress-code involves all-black attire, ameliorated by the occasional dash of red or purple velvet in its female versions, and more-or-less lavish decoration with robust imitation-silver jewelry. Dyed-black hair is *de rigeur*, if not quite compulsory, and tends to be splayed in all directions; female eye make-up tends to be lavish and garish, and lipstick is usually very dark or vivid red, contrasting sharply with complexions whose pallor may be artificially enhanced.

The early models on whom this look was based were Siouxsie Sioux of Siouxsie and the Banshees and Robert Smith of The Cure, but as these bands evolved away from their punk origins they adopted musical styles rather different from the one that became definitive of the hard core of Goth music. The British band that played the leading role in establishing the baseline of Goth music in the early 1980s was the Leeds-based Sisters of Mercy, whose singer/songwriter Andrew Eldritch defined both the mood of the music and its characteristic style of presentation. The black-clad band played in near-darkness, further obscured by the liberal outpourings of a smoke-machine, while Eldritch—often wearing a hat to shadow his pallid face from the spotlight, if one were used—intoned his usually mournful and sometimes anguished lyrics in a deep and conspicuously raw baritone voice.

Other bands favored by the early Goths included Sex Gang Children—who were associated with the London scene based in a club called the Batcave rather than the Northern cities where Goths were (and still are) more numerous—and the avantgardist Bauhaus. It was, however, The Sisters of Mercy who became the most definitive Goth band; insofar as one can speak of a typical "career structure" for British Goth bands it takes the form of early imitation of The Sisters of Mercy—sometimes to the point of blatant pastiche—

followed by the gradual but insistent development of a more distinctive style. One can see this pattern in the career path of The Mission (whose founding singer/songwriter Wayne Hussey had earlier played guitar for Eldritch), Fields of the Nephilim and Rosetta Stone.

The Gothic style of dress and the associated taste culture were exported on a limited scale to America, where Bauhaus were very popular and the quasi-Gothic punk band Christian Death established a domestic base. The Sisters of Mercy were less central as an influence in the USA, although they did inspire imitators like The Wake. Gothic imagery was taken up on a much more prolific scale in Germany, which nowadays probably has more bands that describe themselves as "Gothic" or "Dark Wave" than Britain. These include such Sisters of Mercy clones as Love Like Blood but they span a wide range of musical styles, from the quasi-orchestral adventures of Sopor Aeternus, Ghosting and Engelsstaub to the near-industrial sound of Girls Under Glass. There are notable Goth groups in France (*e.g.* Corpus Delicti and Lucie Cries) and Italy (*e.g.* Ataraxia and the Deviate Ladies), and isolated examples can be found further afield, in Switzerland (Panic on the Titanic) and Finland (Two Witches). Relatively few of these bands sing in their native languages; English remains the language of preference for any European band hoping to find a sizeable audience, although many of the above-named groups do include at least some non-English tracks on their albums.

His pseudonym notwithstanding, Andrew Eldritch's lyrics have never exhibited any conspicuous or consistent interest in fantastic material, and the same is true of most of the other bands that were favored by the Goths in the early '80s. The principal exception was Bauhaus, who drew upon the imagery of fantastic cinema in such tracks as "The Man with X-Ray Eyes", set a sarcastic deal-with-the-devil story to music in "Party of the First Part" and—perhaps most significantly—gave great prominence in their performances to the ironic nine-minute anthem "Bela Lugosi is Dead" (from *Press the Eject and Give Me the Tape*, 1982) and its chanted chorus: "Undead! Undead! Undead!" As Goth groups diversified, however, several were drawn to fantastic imagery of a more earnest stripe. The Mission and Fields of the Nephilim both gravitated towards a kind of syncretic mysticism, which became the inspiration of one of the subculture's classic albums, Fields of the Nephilim's *Elizium*. Continuing this trend, many bands of more recent provenance have elected to be "Gothic" through and through, basing almost all their material in dark fantasy imagery and often addressing such imagery in an extravagantly Decadent manner.

Although they mostly retain the basics of the Eldritch mode of presentation, some of the newer British Goth bands embellish it with gaudier displays. Some, including the members of Nosferatu, have cultivated a dress code that might initially have been borrowed from David Vanian, the singer of proto-Gothic punk band The Damned, echoing if not actually mirroring the costume of cinematic vampires. Almost all Nosferatu's lyrics deploy fantasy imagery, as do the unusually articulate lyrics of Incubus Succubus—which are delivered with crystal clarity by the charismatic Candia McKormack, whose trained voice and exuberant style of presentation contrast sharply with the Eldritchesque norm. The members of Incubus Succubus are assertive in their declared paganism, and their lyrics are equally assertive as celebrations of pagan imagery. Other recently-emergent British Goth bands whose lyrics are consistently and deeply steeped in fantastic imagery include Witching Hour, Son of William, and The Whores of Babylon.

* * * * * * *

The chains of influence that link the more recent British Goth bands to horror fiction and films, and to vampires in particular, are evident enough in their music, but they are even more blatant in the fanzines that follow and map the genre. Many of these are produced by societies whose primary focus is vampirism. Thee Vampire Guild produces *Crimson*, while one Vampyre Society produces a fanzine called *The Velvet Vampyre* and another produces *For the Blood is the Life*. One of the longest-running current Gothic fanzines is *Bats and Red Velvet*, which used to issue from "the House of Dracula". Nosferatu's marketing arm is a one of Britain's two Gothic Societies; it produces a fanzine called *The Grimoire*.

There are subtle differences of complexion between these organizations and periodicals, some of which are intensely suspicious of the more wholehearted lifestyle fantasists while others are quite fascinated by them. *Erebus Rising* declares its function to be "the logical analysis of the vampire as a reality", although its contents also include material about Goth bands and fiction reviews. Articles on "real" vampires—including interviews, confessional pieces and anecdotes of the "believe it or not" variety—are to be found in most of these periodicals but they are not the only manifestation of lifestyle fantasy affectations. The metaphorical language-code used in contact ads permits some people advertising for correspondents to identify themselves as vampires without any danger of being taken too literally; such ads can be found in generalized youth culture magazines like *The Zine* as well as the specialist fanzines.

Some Goth fanzines that avoid use of the vampire as a definitive icon are nevertheless replete with more generalized fantastic imagery; one such is *The Penny Dreadfull*, whose essays on fiction sometimes show considerable theoretical insight. In addition to all this, Goth subculture has, of course, produced one very significant addition to the ranks of British fantasy writers in Storm Constantine, who manages the band Empyrean as a sideline to her successful literary career.

Exactly how and why so many Gothic fanzines suddenly developed this fascination with vampires is unclear. Many older Goths of the "Batcave generation" regard it as a freakish and faddish aberration of no more interest or consequence than the marginal overlapping of Gothic dress-codes with those of sadomasochistic fetishism (a phenomenon that is linked to it by virtue of the sadomasochistic aspects of the kind of vampirism which was identified as a sexual perversion by Krafft-Ebing). Even some of the people involved with these fanzines regard it as a mere coincidence that a substantial number of people who like Gothic music also happen to like horror films and Anne Rice novels, thus bringing about an accidental convergence of interests in the fanzines that has naturally been reflected in the concerns of bands whose roots lie within the fan community.

There are also some Goth bands whose members regard the vampire invasion as a joke to be sent up. The title-track of Paralysed Age's *Bloodsucker* E.P. (1994) is mockingly sarcastic, while the packaging of Vampyre State Building's eponymous debut E.P. (1994)—which is boxed with a miniature red-tipped stake and a poster depicting the band in overblown theatrical costumes—spares no effort in slyly assuring buyers that the entire enterprise is as calculatedly silly as it is possible to be. Nevertheless, the magnitude and the complexity of the phenomenon do seem amply sufficient to warrant further exploration, and there does seem to be strong circumstantial evidence supporting the case that there must be some kind of natural affinity between the musical moods and methods of Goth music and the emotional resonances that give rise to vampiric lifestyle fantasies.

* * * * * * *

Of the bands featured on *"What Sweet Music They Make...."* the one that makes the most copious and the most various use of supernatural imagery in its work is Incubus Succubus. The band is doubly represented on the compilation by "Vampyres" and "I Am the One", both of which are taken from *Belladonna and Aconite* (1993). The former lyric is by Candia McKormack, the latter a collaboration between Candia and Tony McKormack. "Vampyres" is a rousing dance-track whose chorus joyously celebrates the fact that "So much can change with a single kiss"—the "fatal kiss of exquisite bliss" in question being, of course, a vampire's bite. "I Am the One" is a ballad, albeit of an uncharacteristically assertive kind, which begins:

> I am the one
> From the dark side of your dreams
> I am the one
> The one who hears your screams
> I am the one, I am the one
> I am a vampyre a calling for your love
> I am the fire that burns within your blood
> I am the one, I am the one.

This is, of course, metaphorical—and vampirism is by no means the only metaphor upon which Candia McKormack draws in writing the intensely-fantasized love-songs of which she is very fond—but the metaphor in question is one whose elasticity readily lends itself to further exploration. Another of the band's songs credited to her alone is "Vampyre's Kiss", which includes the verse:

> Let me hold you,
> Open up your love to me,
> Feel my caresses,
> Open up your heart to me,
> Where in this life would you
> find a lover like I can be
> I will destroy you,
> Open up your soul to me!

Compared with the customary vocabulary deployed by popular music this is not merely unusual in its assertiveness but also—more importantly—in staking a claim to a unique intimacy. Bloodlust is not here deployed as a substitute for mundane sexual attraction, but as a supplementation that symbolizes and guarantees a special intensity.

This kind of vivid eroticization of vampirism is only one aspect of the deployment of the motif in Goth music, but it is perhaps the most intriguing one and the one most firmly linked to the lifestyle fantasy aspects of Gothic subculture. All writing about sexual love tends towards supernaturalization, because we have no other vocabulary with which to attempt description of the power of erotic attraction; writing about it in these terms is a new phase in a familiar process of evolution, by which metaphors that were once used to express sexual anxiety and dread are usurped for the nobler purpose of expressing a kind of passion that is both honest and reckless.

Given that the orthodox vocabulary of romantic expression makes such lavish use of such terms as "eternity" and "forever", tacitly supported by the notion that "true"—*i.e.*, faithful—love will endure beyond death in a Christian Heaven, it is logical that a vocabulary conceived in opposition to that tradition should avidly seize upon alternative and quite different notions of eternal togetherness. The fact that any such pose is unsupportable by real belief is quite irrelevant; the vast majority of the users of the traditional vocabulary cannot possibly believe that love really does endure forever, on earth or in Heaven (and the minority that does is just as seriously and pathetically misled as people who really do believe in vampires). In view of the fervent tenor of the anti-Christian lyrics written for Incubus Succubus by Tony McKormack—which include such vitriolic condemnations as "Church of Madness" and "All the Devil's Men"—it is not surprising that his wife should resort to the calculatedly unorthodox representations that she deploys in her own work.

There is a strong element of irony in all this, but there is also a defiant seriousness that is heavily emphasized, not merely by the pattern of Candia McKormack's lyrics, but by the way these are set to music. Tony McKormack's melodies are robust and insistent, mostly facilitating an exuberant kind of dancing, but they do retain the haunting, rather plaintive quality that is typical of Goth music. ("Haunting" usually suggests a kind of effete frailty, but the distinctiveness of such paradigm examples as *Elizium* lies in their artful combination of an ethereal dreaminess with rich multilayered instrumentation and a driving drumbeat.) The dance-rhythms employed by Incubus Succubus are uninhibited, but they are not interminably repetitive after the fashion of the music featured in contemporary dance charts; they include deft changes of pace in the direction of a more contemplative mood—a mood-switching device that is used to good effect in such hymnal pastiches as "Samhain" and the title-track of their second CD album, *Wytches* (1994).

* * * * * * *

The flagrant romanticism of Candia McKormack's lyrics stands at one pole of the spectrum of moods represented on *"What Sweet Music They Make...."*. At the other pole, expressing a sexuality that is nakedly aggressive as well as assertive, are two mildly masochistic but nevertheless conspicuously masculine songs written by Jyrki Virtanen, singer with the Finnish band Two Witches. "The Hungry Eyes" and "Mircalla" are both taken from the band's first album, *Agony of the Undead Vampire* (1992), all but one of whose tracks were subsequently reissued on *The Vampire's Kiss* (1993). The former song, addressed to a "teenage whore" with "hungry eyes", proceeds by conscientiously melodramatic stages to the imploring chorus lines "Be my Carmilla!" and "Please bite me again!" The second also refers to the heroine of Sheridan le Fanu's famous novella "Carmilla" (1872), who was fond of deploying anagrammatic variations of her name.

Although many singers within the subgenre employ a hoarse and guttural singing style, this is most pronounced of all in those bands whose musical style is stridently Teutonic. It is, of course, a style of presentation well-suited to Germanic languages, whose phonetic forms facilitate—if they do not actually demand—a kind of jagged huskiness. (Such a style sounds far less unusual to German audiences than the Anglo-American ones, which might be one reason why the Eldritchesque manner of presentation has been so successful there.) At any rate, in these two tracks Jyrki Virtanen—who sings in English although the band's record company is German—takes this rawness to an extreme only matched by the singers with the two German bands represented on the CD; the contrast between his presentation and Candia McKormack's serves to emphasize in no uncertain terms the difference in emotional tone between their lyrics.

Like Incubus Succubus, Two Witches make extensive use in their work of other dark fantasy imagery, and several more of their lyrics deal with vampirism, including two of the tracks on their recent E.P. *Bloody Kisses* (1994): "Bites and Bloody Kisses" and "Requiem". The sleeve-notes unfortunately reverse the credits relating to these two songs, but the former was written by Jyrki Virtanen and is a more extensive exercise in much the same style as "The Hungry Eyes" and "Mircalla"; it is more adventurous musically but it retains the same starkly physical attitude to vampiric intercourse. The latter, by contrast, features a lyric written by Donna Crow, the editor of *Erebus Rising*, and is cast in a much more contemplative vein. Interestingly, however, "Requiem" has no truck with the kind of romanticism found in Candia McKormack's lyrics, de-emphasizing the sexuality of vampirism in favor of the kind of impassioned existential guilt trip that Anne Rice regularly credits to her reluctantly predatory anti-heroes.

The plaintively regretful lyric of "Requiem" laments the lives sacrificed to the singer's bloodlust and yearns for release from the curse of eternal life, whose chorus—"Deliver us from evil/Forgive us our sins/ For we are god's creation/Condemned and chained by him"—significantly shifts in its last rendition so that the final line becomes "But an earthly reflection of him". The concentration here is not on vampirism as a kind of hypersexual relationship capable of achieving a unique intimacy, but on the state of "undeath" as an unusually complicated and comprehensive species of alienation.

The music featured on *Bloody Kisses* is a recognizable development of that featured on *The Vampire's Kiss* and *Phaeriemagick* (1993) but the staccato style of songs like "The Hungry Eyes" is softened and ultra-cinematic melodramatic chords give way to a more liquid musical accompaniment. The other tracks on the E.P. both have lyrics by Jyrki Virtanen but they have more in common with "Requiem" than "Bites and Bloody Kisses". Although it is not about vampires in any obvious sense "Dreamworld (Doomed to Infinity)" provides a further example of what might be called "vampiric angst": the imagination of a state of being in which the conditional removal of the threat of death is no better—and perhaps worse—than the awareness of mortality, which (according to Martin Heidegger and other existentialist philosophers) undermines and spoils ordinary conscious existence.

* * * * * * *

The vampire as predator is no less extensively featured on *"What Sweet Music They Make...."* than the vampire as lover. The only track on the album whose lyric is not sung in English is German band Umbra et Imago's "Vampir Song", but this makes such evocative use of cinematic sound effects—including "literal" fleeing footsteps as well as metaphorical heartbeat-echoing percussion—that it makes sense whether one can understand the words or not. This is the longest track on the album, and the one that seems most traditional in its presentation of the vampire as a horrific and threatening presence, but, like the films whose essence it attempts to capture, it is possessed by a feverish excitement. This excitement—which the music insistently builds in dialectical opposition to the harsh words—reminds us that fear is a stimulant, whose emotional arousal can be negotiated, if we are clever enough to work the alchemical trick, into other kinds of arousal.

A more anguished kind of predatory impulse is displayed in starkly melodramatic style by the other German contributor to the compilation, Sopor Aeternus and the Ensemble of Shadows. "The Feast of Blood" is even more staccato in its musical expression than "The Hungry Eyes", and its singer affects a screechy falsetto voice, which is no smoother than Jyrki Virtanen's but rather more eerie in its effect. The song moves swiftly and relentlessly to a hoarse mantra-like chant, which repeats the lines "And the feast/will never end/until we all descend" several times before finally adding the punch-line "in Hell".

The singer/songwriter responsible for "The Feast of Blood" employs the *nom de guerre* "Varney", although one suspects that he may not be entirely familiar with the content, tenor and downmarket reputation of James Malcolm Rymer's penny part-work *Varney the Vampyre; or, The Feast of Blood*, from which the name is presumably borrowed. Varney provides one of the most extreme and most interesting examples of exotic self-representation to be found in the subgenre. In the band's publicity material and occasional interviews he is enthusiastic to pose as a reincarnate soul working off some very heavy bad karma. Indistinct photographs show him white-masked, dressed in a penitent's robe, and his answers to questions subtly imply that he looks not unlike Max Schreck's version of Nosferatu.

All this might seem like comedy in the camp vein of Vincent Price's portrayals of the Abominable Dr. Phibes, were it not for the fact that "The Feast of Blood" is so very atypical of the band's work. It does not appear on the CD *Sopor Aeternus* (1994), which is a wonderfully atmospheric collection of mournful songs—some sung in German and some in English—making adept use of modern musical technology to construct a dignified Schopenhauerian soundscape redolent with melancholy keening and soulful pessimism.

The two longest tracks on *Sopor Aeternus*, "Im Garden des Nichts (Secret Light in the Garden of my Void" and "Time Stands Still...(...But Stops for No-One)" are remarkable extensions of the idea of existence prolonged as a kind of purgatorial curse. Again, the adjective that first springs to mind in any attempt to describe the musical quality of these tracks is "haunting", and again it is necessary to add the caveat that this in no way implies that they are simplistic or effete. A verse from "The Devil's Instrument", a lyric from the forthcoming Time Heals Nothing, will suffice to give the flavor of the world-view extended in these songs:

> In a cradle of mercy we are sleeping
> the half-sleep of oblivion
> no holy water could ash away our faults
> nor benedictions purify our souls.
> The gates remain locked
> for the Wingless Children of Wrath
> so long ago splintered and trodden down
> as children of glass....
>
> Please my Lord extinguish the light
> the illumination hurts my eyes
> my choice was wrong. so wrong
> (I am your slave)
> truly everything is pain....

* * * * * * *

Although "The Feast of Blood" addresses the subject-matter of vampirism more directly and more immediately than Varney's other work, *"What Sweet Music They Make...."* could have extended its musical range by using a more representative track. Instead, the compilation fills in the relevant part of the spectrum by including two tracks by the French band Corpus Delicti, which has similar avantgardist tendencies and likewise favors lyrics extrapolating this peculiar kind of "alternative angst". The two tracks in question are "Firelight" and "Staring", both from *Twilight* (1993). Like the great majority of the lyrics on *Twilight* and *Sylphes* (1994)—which are all in English—these are unusually sophisticated for a writer employing a second language; although not entirely free from infelicities, the remarkable set comprised by the songs on these two albums is a considerable achievement on the part of lyricist Sebastian. The band's music, somewhat influenced by Bauhaus, is also exceptional in its capacity to reflect the mood of the songs.

"Firelight" is the more dramatic of the inclusions on *"What Sweet Music They Make...."*, and compiler Phill White showed good judgment in choosing it to lead off his musical anthology, but "Staring" is the more intricate, and perhaps the more interesting lyrically. Its reflective verses are variations on a theme, continually repeating the Proustian phrase "I used to....":

I used to get caught in the clouds
With blood on my face, with the strangest smile
Hoping for the wind to carry me away
Wishing for a wave to be another day
I used to climb above the walls
Made by the sound of the voices, cold
I used to try to touch the air
But always found a deep despair

The conclusion to which the verses eventually lead is:

Awake in a gloomy world
With killing mirrors that never glitter
Now, I'm fed up with staring
At the black sky, suffering
There's a coffin waiting for me somewhere
With nothing to see inside and no reason to stare
And the Devil is waiting for me somewhere
I'm coming
I don't know where
I close the door...

Lyrics such as these invert the customary philosophical analyses linking existential angst to the awareness of mortality, and which construe the horrific threat of "nothingness" as the inevitability of death. Here, as in Varney's more thoughtful work, it is a hypothetical immortality (linked by necessity to darkness and alienation) that becomes a prospect direly difficult to contemplate, while extinction is redefined as a kind of merciful release—a consummation devoutly to be wished. This theme is further extrapolated, with the aid of other kinds of imagery, elsewhere in the band's work—most notably in the title-track of *Sylphes*. "Sylphes" is not Eldritchesque but it certainly warrants description as eldritch; the lyric celebrates death as a kind of ecstatic dissolution into nature, its narrative voice declaring that "Entering into the forest I have the most beautiful death/The most beautiful death".

* * * * * * *

There are echoes of the vampiric angst that is most explicitly deployed by Corpus Delicti in almost all of the tracks on *"What Sweet Music They Make...."*, but the element of anguish is usually offset by some contrasting element carefully alloyed with it. The eroticism used to offset it in "I Am the One" is also deployed, with feeling and delicacy, in the compilation's concluding track, Depeche

Mode's "One Caress", while the calculated exuberance of "Vampyres" is reproduced in one of two tracks by the American band *The Dark Theater*, "Vampyre's Dance". A similar assertiveness is to be found in two tracks by the Scottish band Dream Disciples, whose "Crimson White" and "Resting Place" are built on skirling guitar-riffs similar to those employed by other Scottish bands like Simple Minds and Big Country to import the hectic pace of traditional highland dances into contemporary rock music.

The Dark Theater's other contribution to the compilation, "At Love with the Gods (Movement III)" is a new version of a song whose original title was "Undead". It is more complex musically than "Vampyre's Dance" and darker in mood, representing a directional development that is similar in kind to the one undertaken by Two Witches. "At Love with the Gods (Movement III)" develops a kind of Romanticism that values exoticism for its own sake—one which is very much in tune with the tenor of that American dark fantasy whose tradition is rooted in the *Weird Tales* school of fiction. The Dark Theater's marketing arm, Screem Jams Productions, produces a fanzine called *Screem in the Dark*, which contains a good deal of vampire material presented in a jauntily lurid style entirely suited to its cultural context. A not-dissimilar spirit of unashamed Romanticism is displayed in Nosferatu's contribution to the compilation, "The Keeper's Call", whose ornately enigmatic lyric represents conversion to vampirism as the beginning of a great adventure. The Dark Theater and Nosferatu both have band-members called Vlad, but in neither case is the element of lifestyle fantasy involved in this nomenclature as conscientiously extrapolated as that of Sopor Aeternus' Varney. The Dark Theater's Vlad and his wife (and fellow band-member) Lynda are, however, frequent guests on American TV talk shows.

"The Keeper's Call" is from Nosferatu's *Savage Kiss* E. P. (1993), whose contents are reproduced on their second album *The Prophecy* (1994). This continues the process of evolution already evident on their first album *Rise* (1993), whereby the band has moved away from its Eldritchesque beginnings toward a more melodic musical style and the use of lyrics which borrow from a wide range of literary sources. *The Prophecy* features several other tracks celebrating exoticism *per se*, including "Time of Legends", which sweeps through an assortment of heroic fantasy motifs, and "Farewell my Little Earth", which is sentimental science fiction. The lyricist responsible for both these items and for "The Keeper's Call", Niall Murphy, is also responsible for "Savage Kiss"—a curious hymn to aggressive female sexuality, which refers to vamps of an entirely natural variety—but the album's final track, "The Enchanted Tower", has a lyric by *Grimoire* editor Sapphire Aurora. "The Enchanted Tower" draws its imagery from a series of prose pieces published in the fanzine which follow the exploits of a female vampire based on Erszabet Bathory; as with Donna Crow's lyric for Two Witches, it adopts a more languidly reflective mood than most of the band's other materials.

* * * * * * *

If one considers the fourteen tracks of *"What Sweet Music They Make...."* as a semi-coherent set, therefore, it is easy enough to discern two partly-entwined connecting threads that bind that set together: the existential and the erotic. The existential thread involves a virtual inversion of traditional existentialist characterizations of angst, but it is further complicated by the way in which that reconfigured angst is alleviated or ameliorated by more assertive elements. The erotic thread is, in its purest form, a celebration of the heightening of erotic excitement which can be achieved by certain kinds of exoticism, but that too is further complicated by the awareness that this particular kind of sexual exoticism is implicitly predatory or sacrificial (depending upon the point of view). The two threads are interestingly interlinked by virtue of the fact that the sadomasochistic aspects of vampiric sexual relationships are not seen in terms of destruction but rather in terms of recruitment, the threat of extinction being largely displaced by that of a perpetuation which is partly—but not wholly—misfortunate.

Leaving aside such satirically-inclined pieces as Paralysed Age's "Bloodsucker", most other vampire-related Goth music can be slotted into this pattern fairly readily. For instance, "Slave to the Night" and "Kissed by Death" on Witching Hour's *Exhumation* (1994) are calculatedly melodramatic pieces emphasizing the existential thread, with particular emphasis on the alienation of the vampire, although the latter calls attention to the sexual transmission of the blight. This is in harmony with most of the band's other work, including their two versions of "Carnival of Souls". The Marionettes' elliptical "Like Christabel" (on *Ave Dementia*, 1992), on the other hand, echoes the erotic imagery of the Coleridge poem on which it is presumably based, although its mood stands in stark contrast. Whereas Coleridge's "Christabel" is Gothic in the original sense, "Like Christabel" maintains a flirtatious ironic ebullience of a kind that is more extravagantly elaborated in the band's extraordinary necrophiliac anthem "Play Dead", which might be regarded as the very epitome of contemporary Gothicism.

Some Goth bands that only employ vampire imagery peripherally or en passant can also be related fairly easily to the pattern evident on *"What Sweet Music They Make...."*. For example, Engelsstaub's *Malleus Maleficarum* (1993) further extends the angst-ridden avantgardism of Corpus Delicti and Sopor Aeternus; although it is most blatant in "The Eden of Pain or Pleasure" and "Sacrificium" (he latter lyric being one of two written by the band's female singer Lilith) the entire album thrives on the calculated confusion of such opposites as Heaven/Hell, pain/pleasure and life/death, culminating in an epilogue in which the bands other lyricist—billed as GODkrist—claims to have deduced logically that Satan is God. The Whores of Babylon's highly distinctive and musically inventive *Metropolis* (1994) contains occasional intrusions of vampiric imagery, in "Lamia" and in the dance remix of "Carnal Desires", which reiterates the half-line "True as blood is wine" several times before adding the completing phrase ("you'll feel my pain"). The longest track on the album is, however, the magisterial "Oblivion", the painstakingly-built and munificent orchestral backing of which supports a lyric that both eroticizes and Romanticizes a plaint which can now be seen as characteristic of this whole structure of feeling:

> Look into my eyes, can you see my soul
> adorned like a grave, with no-one here to save me
> dying is easy, it's living I can't bear
> beyond the anguish, I feel and long to share
> of sweet serenity, I dream our worlds collide
> beneath my water's edge, you long to be my bride
> in harmony with all I am, I feel the tendency to walk beside my own
> Oblivion

* * * * * * *

All this is, of course, pure fantasy. Although there is a kind of vampirism that is perfectly possible, and easily available to anyone who cares to take it up and can find a compliant partner, the kind of vampirism to which these songs refer is much more ambitious. The lyrics featured on *"What Sweet Music They Make...."* and in similar songs are not about blood-drinking *per se*, but about blood-drinking as a kind of unholy communion, which promises both an advanced form of sexual intimacy and privileged access to a different state of being, to which common notions of life and death cannot be applied. There is nothing particularly surprising about this combination of promises, however odd the resultant compound may seem, given that the mythology of romantic love which currently possesses (or at least obsesses) Western sexual relationships does its damnedest to pretend that the state of being "in love" is indeed a heady transportation to a higher state of being.

Given that even the blood-drinkers among us are condemned to mortality, there might seem to be little enough to be gained from imaginative identification with immortals of any kind. There might also seem to be little point in raising the question of why the contemplation of one particular (and peculiarly problematic) kind of immortality should have become so popular with certain audiences as to have rapidly overspilled the literary subgenre that pioneered its redevelopment into a musical subgenre which had previously manifested no conspicuous literary connections. It is, however, the case that we live as much in our fantasies as in the real world, and that there are certain aspects of our experience—of which the erotic is the most obvious—to which the contributions of fantasy are far more important than those of sensation and rational analysis.

What is more, if existentialist philosophers are right about the inevitability of conscious life being haunted by the kind of unease or dread which Heidegger called angst, and about the essential inadequacy of all mental strategies that we might devise to counter that unease, then we ought not to despise any means that might enable us to stand aside—if only for a moment—from that awful pressure. Even if such a sidestep is merely a temporary release, it is surely worthwhile; if it provides an opportunity for productive reappraisal it is doubly valuable.

It was always difficult, even for ostensibly-devout writers like Sheridan le Fanu and Bram Stoker, to take it for granted that the condition of vampirism was a kind of damnation. No matter how stubbornly they asserted that undeath was a fate worse than death, it never became obvious, and the fact that their classic works made such a blatant connection between the habits of the undead and another "fate worse than death"—sexual spoliation—weakened their case still further. Film adaptations of Dracula tried hard to maintain both the insistence and the equivalence, pandering to official censors who did all they could to make the cinema the last bastion of Victorian moral imbecility, but the nature of the film medium was against them. No matter how hard the scripts tried to insist that what the vampires were doing was utterly horrible, the audience could see perfectly well that it wasn't.

The "truth" that was long manifest in images on the cinema screen, in spite of the rhetoric of the narratives that contained them—and which only had to be seen to be believed—was that vampires were handsome and charismatic, and that they offered their "victims" a very special sexual frisson. Even the *deus ex machina* that disposed of the chastened vampire at the end of every film could easily be seen by an educated audience for what it really was—a mere punctuation mark, utterly impotent to prevent many happy returns of rampaging lust. It was only a matter of time before a new subgenre emerged in which writers blessed with an even-handed cynicism would begin to examine vampires as flawed heroes rather than villains. Where Pierre Kast, Fred Saberhagen and Anne Rice led in the mid-1970s, dozens of others inevitably rushed to follow.

The fascination of vampiric eroticism rests on a series of realizations about the nature of sexual experience. Once it became absurd to believe that the excitation of female sexuality—even nakedly exploitative excitation—constituted a fate worse than death, it became possible to wonder whether it could be placed on a simple linear scale of badness at all. The masochistic delights available to male victims in submitting to female vampires, which had been available for contemplation even in the nineteenth century in such tales as Gautier's "Clarimonde", were made potentially available to female victims of male vampires—and, of course, to same-sex victims of either variety. Once it became possible to speculate as to the myriad ways in which play-acting, ritual and a delicate seasoning of pain might enhance rather than demeaning sexual encounters, the poetics of sexual paradox—which had always been savored by the few—became far more easily available for the aesthetic appreciation of the many. The notion of the vampire kiss—at once uplifting and imperiling, draining and transforming—became far more widely available as an adept seduction of the imagination.

The manner in which vampires are deployed by recent Goth music is a logical continuation of this trend. The very essence of the cinematic vampire—the charismatic predator capable of arousing a uniquely ambivalent sexual thrill—is concentrated into the lyrics alongside (and sometimes cleverly intermingled with) the very essence of the new literary vampire, who contemplates his existential plight with similar ambivalence. At the very least, identification with some such existential plight can perform the elementary function of fantasy fiction which J. R. R. Tolkien called "Recovery"; by removing us from the most fundamental conditions of reality, it allows us to cease taking those fundamental conditions for granted, and thus helps us to see them more objectively and more clearly. This sidestep is not an easy move to master, but once we have been taught the art of it, by Anne Rice or some other writer in a similar vein, it may become sufficiently facile to be triggered by something as slight as a song—and if it is, the musical mood of the song may then become a significant assistant to the further cultivation of the new viewpoint.

There is a sense in which all fantasies are similar, in offering scope for a Tolkienian Recovery of a distanced view of reality, but the fact that they are similar does not make them equal. If the aspect of reality with which we are concerned is mortality, and the angst associated with awareness of mortality, removal to an imaginative standpoint from which mortality is banished (whether that of orthodox religion or that of sciencefictional immortality) is a simple and straightforward negation which is almost impossible to trust.

Any examination of the history of religion or science fiction will readily reveal that people have enormous difficulty in pledging their faith to anything as simple-mindedly optimistic as immortality, and are immediately driven to start worrying about whether any imaginable Heaven might, in fact, turn out to be a kind of Hell. The imaginative contemplation of vampiric undeath, on the other hand, has all kinds of problems already built in. It may well be that if we desire to get a clear sight of the angst which actually afflicts us—with a view, of course, to being better able to cope with it—the imaginative assumption of a markedly different but no less acute form of hypothetical angst might be far more serviceable than trying to envisage a state of being which us entirely angst-less.

We already know, of course, that the people most inclined to grapple with angst are adolescents; it is those newly situated on the threshold adult awareness and adult responsibility who come fresh to the age-old conflict. Young people are not the only ones who stand to benefit from the powerful kinds of Recovery which readily extend (if only tentatively) into lifestyle fantasy, but they are the ones with the most to gain.

It is only to be expected, therefore, that the most dedicated fans of Anne Rice novels and vampire films are young; it is only to be expected, too, that young people who undergo the kind of sentimental education offered by these cultural resources should delight in finding the education echoed in music—and not merely echoed but amplified, dramatized and made vivaciously melodic. It is entirely appropriate that the music involved should be haunting without being feeble, melancholy without being dreary, exotic without being esoteric, and insistently stimulating without being crudely repetitive.

All art, Walter Pater once asserted (with the kind of courage that does not fear overstatement), aspires to the condition of music—by which he meant that all art ought to value form over content. If there is truth in the claim, it must be as true of the art of vampirism as of all others, and there is surely a case to be made both for its truth and its applicability.

Literary vampires, however reconfigured, arrive with an enormous quantity of stubbornly irrational luggage, which continually threatens to make them look absurd. Cinematic vampires are condemned by hideously camp costumes and ludicrous dentistry to hover perpetually on the edge of farce. The vampires of Goth music, in contrast, are easily able to reduce such encumbrances to mere passing gestures, dissolving as they work their magic not into a puff of smoke, or a stuffed bat, or a clotted expository lump, but into chords of pure sensation. Who could possibly deny that it is an environment to which they are very well suited?

Acknowledgments

Lyrics of "I am the One" and "Vampire's Kiss" by Incubus Succubus are quoted by permission of Pagan Fire Music; lyrics of "The Devil's Instrument" are quoted by permission of Apocalyptic Vision; lyrics of "Staring" are quoted by permission of Corpus Delicti; lyrics of "Oblivion" are quoted by permission of The Whores of Babylon.

Incubus by Ann Arensberg, Alfred A. Knopf, 1999

The narrator of *Incubus*, Cora Whitman, introduces her account of what she calls "the Dry Falls entity"—which has been set down three and a half years after the actual events—with a brief description of her present circumstances. She and her husband, Henry Lieber, are now forty-two- and fifty-six-years-old respectively. Having left their former occupations behind, they have established—along with Henry's former secretary, Adele Manning—a "private foundation" called the Center for the Study of Anomalous Phenomena. The purpose of this organization is to collect case-studies of "outlandish" events, in the hope of discovering patterns that might help to explain the strange occurrences that blighted the summer of 1974, when Henry was rector of the Episcopalian Church of St. Anthony the Hermit in Dry Falls, Maine.

The Saint Anthony after whom the Dry Falls church is named was an Egyptian reputed to have lived from 251 to 356. Between 286 and 306 he lived in complete solitude in a deserted fort at Pispir, during which time he allegedly underwent an extraordinary series of temptations, which became a favorite topic of Medieval legend-mongers and Renaissance artists. Graphic representations of the supernaturally-beleaguered saint were painted by Pieter Brueghel the elder and Hieronymus Bosch. His visions also provided the basis of Gustave Flaubert's novel *The Temptation of Saint Anthony*, which exists in two versions, one written in 1849 and the other 1874, because the author was persuaded by his friends that the earlier one was too shocking (it was published posthumously in 1908). Skeptics sometimes attribute Anthony's afflictions to the hallucinogenic effects of ergot poisoning, whose after-effects became popularly known as St. Anthony's Fire.

Arensberg's novel is, in essence, a modern recapitulation of the legend of Saint Anthony, its central character being a thoroughly modern "hermit" subjected to a thoroughly modern series of exotic "temptations". The fact that Cora Whitman's belated account does not interpret what happens to her as a diabolical temptation, preferring to present it in a very different light, is both a measure of the extent to which she fell victim to the temptation and a measure of the extent to which modern skepticism has devalued the religious assumptions of old. This crucial ambiguity is minutely calculated and carefully displayed by Cora's creator, the novel's author.

Cora's introduction to her story takes care to stress that the Liebers' conversion to skepticism is as uncompromising as most conversions. She states explicitly that "We no longer trust what we see, hear, taste, smell or touch". Given this forewarning, the reader is bound to treat her account of the paranormal happenings with considerable suspicion. If Cora does not trust what she has seen, heard, tasted, smelled or touched, why should her readers? That lack of trust is bound to extend to her eventual judgment as to how the strange events ought to be explained. Psychologically-sophisticated readers can hardly help wondering whether Cora's steadfast refusal to entertain the hypothesis that the cause of these events is the Devil, in anything more than a symbolic sense, is a symptom of what analytical jargon calls "denial".

The modern "hermitage" in which Cora Whitman is living in 1974 is her comfortable marriage to Henry Lieber, whom she met while serving as his secretary—a position in which she has been replaced by Adele Manning. She has fled to this refuge from a former home that was troubled by constant conflict between her widowed mother Emily and her older sister Hannah, who remained a spinster after her intended bridegroom was killed by an accident shortly before the appointed wedding-day. Within the marriage's protective custody Cora is able to extend her two vocations, cooking and gardening. She has settled into this situation after serving brief stints as a guide escorting pregnant women to the shrine of St. Anne de Beaupré ("the Lourdes of Quebec") and at the Shaker Village on Sabbathday Pond. She also worked as an assistant editor on *Maine Heritage* magazine, producing a feature on "Maine Kitchens" that enabled her to establish a secondary career as a columnist of domestic matters; she has continued this kind of work within the marriage.

Henry Lieber's attachment to the faith represented by the church of which he is rector is only a little less tokenistic than his wife's, although he was initially moved to take up his vocation by a revelation born of his harrowing experiences in World War II. Henry may also qualifies as a metaphorical hermit, but, unlike Cora, he does not do battle for himself alone. He is compelled—at least until his conversion to skepticism—to engage himself more actively than Cora with the welfare of his parishioners and with the spiritual fallout of the sinister forces that lay siege to Dry Falls. When the unrelenting heat-wave turns the town into a literal as well as a metaphorical desert, and the supernatural manifestations become increasingly phantasmagorical, it is Cora's situation, not Henry's, which is most closely akin to St. Anthony's. She is the one subject to the fiercer temptation, and the one who must ultimately make a lonely stand against adversity.

Although the first shadowy glimpse of Dry Falls' unwelcome visitor is granted to two stray pupils of a local girls' school, Burridge Academy—which later becomes the setting for a more extensive and far more intimate invasion—the strangeness of the season is initially manifest in a series of absences. The protracted absence of spring rain shrivels the gardens of Dry Falls, much to the dismay of the over-sensitive Emily Whitman, whose seemingly-magical "green fingers" have never before failed to make its soil yield an abundant harvest. At the same time, the loyal wives of Dry Falls find themselves in the midst of a metaphorical drought, all its menfolk having completely lost interest in sexual intercourse. Even Cora, whose marriage is less passionate than many, is eventually driven to a fine pitch of frustration by this creeping desertification. This aspect of the unholy visitation is well-nigh invisible on the polite surface of society, but confessions taken by Henry supplement the sisterly gossip gathered by Cora, allowing them both to glimpse the actual magnitude of the problem.

The purpose of this plague of disinterest is to prepare the way for the visitation to assume the form given to it by the novel's title. By the time the incubus begins to live up to its name, the female characters, almost without exception, are well-primed for its seductions. Most of them yield readily enough to the possibility of relief, but they do not all respond in the same way. The more interesting case-studies are the exceptions to the rule, who include the church's cleaner, Mary Fran Rawls, and Hannah Whitman. These two and a few others seem able to resist orthodox seduction in spite of their frustration, because they insist on reinterpreting what is happening to them in such a way as to de-sexualize its implications.

Seen as a social collective, Dry Falls experiences a period of grateful remission when the manifestations first begin to formulate themselves in apparent sexual intercourse—but the remission does not last long before it begins, slowly but inexorably, to give way to a greater and more awkward distress. Cora hears from most of her friends and acquaintances how they have tacitly succumbed or stubbornly refused to recognize seduction, but this inside information does not help her much when her own turn finally comes and she has to make her own decision as to what she will consent to see, feel and understand. The explicit drought eventually ends, as real droughts often do, with the breaking of a spectacular storm, but it is the metaphorical storm that brings Cora's existential drought to an end that provides the novel's real climax.

The supernatural manifestations of *Incubus* are rather tame by comparison with those routinely displayed by best-selling horror novels by the likes of Stephen King and Dean R. Koontz, but Arensberg is not attempting to appal or terrify her readers. Her primary interest is in the various ways in which the traditions of religious faith have been compromised in adapting to the norms of that civilized and tolerant fraction of American society that lies outside the so-called Bible Belt. The best defense that Cora has against the horrid violation that threatens her voluntary isolation, when she finally engages the incubus in single combat, is to understate it: to substitute a more cerebral reaction for the blind panic that an authentic encounter with the Devil would necessitate. Her readers are left to make up their own minds as to what really happened, and whether the psychological strategy Cora employs in coping with it is really the best one available. The evidence that Arensberg provides for her readers is inadequate to allow them to reach any firm conclusion—but that is the situation in which Cora finds herself, and with which every faith-challenged person in the modern world has to deal, on a day-to-day basis.

The eleven sections of Cora's account of the Dry Falls visitation borrow their subtitles from an alleged eighth century Irish prayer called "St. Patrick's Breastplate", which is quoted in full on the novel's pre-title page. As if it were describing the elements of a suit of armor, the prayer lists "Christ before us, Christ behind us, Christ within us," and so on. The preface and afterword that frame the core narrative are similarly associated with the second quote on the pre-title passage, which comes from *The Book of the Damned* (1919), by the pioneering collector of intriguing tidbits of eccentric reportage, Charles Fort.

Although Cora ends her account with a rather different and conspicuously banal moral, the argumentative thrust of her story is demarcated by the tension between these two quotes. The implication of the narrative course steered by the novel is that those of us who find St. Patrick's Breastplate too uncomfortable to wear have no alternative but to become Fortean hermits, obsessively engaged in the probably-futile mock-scientific collation of anecdotal reports of "anomalous phenomena".

Ann Arensberg's previous novels were *Sister Wolf*—which won the 1981 American Book Award—and *Group Sex*. *Incubus* carries forward the mildly ironic interest in female sexuality exhibited by the two earlier novels, exhibiting the same careful delicacy as well as the same earnest analytical fascination. The author of a novel whose primary subject-matter is the exposure of the hidden depths of a cozy community is bound to have difficulty conserving her own subtextual subtlety, but Arensberg succeeds very well; the narrative filtered through the eyes and mind of her unreliable narrator is neatly layered and deftly unconventional.

As a dabbler in the subject-matter of popular horror stories, Arensberg is following in a long tradition of American women novelists, which extends from Edith Wharton and May Sinclair to Joyce Carol Oates and Anne Rivers Siddons. Like those predecessors and contemporaries, she demonstrates that the language of the supernatural can be very useful in modeling and exploring the ways in which the conventional requirements of polite society are continually threatened and undercut by anxiety and the unruly forces of desire.

INDEX

Absolute Magnitude 62
Ace 40
Ackerman, Forrest J. 73
Adams, Douglas 125
Adventures of Saturnin Farandoul, The 141
Agony of the Undead Vampire, The 157
Aiken, John K. 74, 78, 81
Air Raid Precautions Handbook no. 2 89
Aldiss, Brian W, 41, 70-71, 75, 78-79, 81, 83-85, 87, 111, 124
Alexandre Humboldt-Fonteyne: La Collection Interdite 48-53
"All the Devil's Men" 156
Amazing Stories 73, 78, 106
Amis, Kingsley 75, 78, 82, 87
Analog 41, 52, 93
Anderson, Poul 31-36, 80, 82, 92
Anderton, James 101
An deux mille quatre cent quarante, L' 141-142
"Another Orphan" 121-122
"Anticipator, The" 93
Antieau, Kim 128-132
Anubis Gates, The 133, 135
Archette Guy 78
Arensberg, Ann 168-172
Arkham House 10-11, 39, 123
Asaro, Catherine 83-84
Ascent of Wonder, The: The Evolution of Hard SF 91-93
Asimov, Isaac 36-37, 53, 72-73, 79, 82, 86
Askew, Jackie 94-95
Astounding Science Fiction 40-41, 62, 72, 93, 106
Ataraxia 97-101, 152
Atheling, William Jr. 76, 87, 102
"At Love With the Gods (Movement III)" 162

Attebery, Brian 92
Attwood, Margaret 129
"Attitude" 62-64
Aurora, Sapphire 163
"Aurora in Four Voices" 84
Austin, Nick 90
Authentic Science Fiction 40, 124
Ave Dementia 163
Bacchae, The 135
Bacon, Francis 51
Baldwin, Stanley 89
"Ballads in 3/4Time" 27
Ballard, J. G. 83, 92
"Balloon Hoax, The" 51, 113
Balzac, Honoré de 145
Banks, Iain M. 79, 81, 83
Barber, Paul 96
Barber of Aldebaran, The 123-125
Barbers of Surreal, The 115-117
Bathory, Erszabet 163
Bats and Red Velvet 95, 153
Baudelaire, Charles 44
Baudino, Gael 130
Bauhaus 151-152, 160
Baxter, Stephen 85, 87, 125-128
Bayley, Barrington J. 40-42, 83
Beagle, Peter S. 20
"Bear Trap" 87
Beckham, David and Victoria 140
"Bela Lugosi is Dead" 152
Belladonna and Aconite 155
Bellamy, Edward 37, 122
Bennett, James Gordon 114
Benford, Gregory 13-17, 85, 92
Benson, Stella 25
Bester, Alfred 78, 92
Best of Hal Clement, The 62
Best of Science Fiction, The 91
Big Country 162
"Big Dream, The" 121-122
Billion Year Spree 75
Birth of Tragedy, The 133
Bisson, Terry 101

"Bites and Bloody Kisses" 157
Black Coat Press 145
Blameless in Abaddon 137
Blaylock, James P. 21
Blish, James 40, 42, 76-78, 80, 85, 101-102
"Bloodletting" 45, 47
Bloodsucker 154
"Bloodsucker" 163
Bloody Kisses 157-158
Blue Oyster Cult 147
Bodin, Félix 141-145
Bohm, David 44
Bond, Nelson 74, 77
Book of the Damned, The 172
Book of the River, The 111
"Bore, The" 76
Boss in the Wall, The 20-22
Boucher, Anthony 76, 78, 101
Bova, Ben 64
Brackett, Leigh 71, 75-76, 79-80, 84
Breath of Suspension, The 18
Bretnor, Reginald 72, 87
Brin, David 81
Britton, David 97, 99-101
Britton, Chris 105, 116-117
Britton, Tim 105, 115, 117
Brown, Fredric 80
Browning, Tod 147
Brueghel, Pieter 169
Brunner, John 83
Buchanan, Ginjer 66
"Buddha Nostril Bird" 122
"Buffalo" 122
"Bug, the Mouse and Chapter 24, The" 41
Bujold, Lois McMaster 79, 81, 103
"Bulge" 62
Bulmer, Kenneth 76, 82-83
Bullett, Gerald 23, 25
Burroughs, Edgar Rice 74, 80
Burroughs, William S. 23
Bush, Kate 98
Cabell, James Branch 23
Caesar's Column 37

Campbell, John W, Jr. 32, 40, 64, 70, 72-73, 92-93, 130
Campbell, Joseph 78-79, 85
Canticle for Leibowitz, A 101, 107
"Carmilla" 157
"Carnal Desires" 164
"Carnival of Souls" 163
Carr, Terry 120
Carroll, Lewis 116
Carter, Brandon 15
Carve the Sky 18-19
"Case of Conscience, A" 101
Centauri Device, The 83
Chadwick, Philip George 89-91
Chalet in the Sky 141
Chandler, A. Bertram 73
Chandler, Raymond 120-121
Chaney, Lon 97
Chanson de Roland, La 55-56, 58
"Charms of Space Opera, The" 74
Charwoman's Shadow, The 23
Chesterton, G. K. 126-127
Childhood's End 86
Child of the River: The First Book of Confluence 111-112
Choyce, Lesley 27
"Christabel" 163
Christian Death 152
"Chromatic Aberrations" 92
Churchill, Winston 89
"Church of Madness" 156
"Clarimonde" 166
Clarke, Arthur C. 36-37, 53, 86, 92-93, 101, 124
Clarke, Eamonn 114
Clarke, I. F. 140
Clarke, Margaret 145
Clash of the Star-Kings 20
"Clean Escape, A" 122
Clement, Hal 62-65, 92
Clifford, Max 140
Clock of the Centuries, The 141
Close to Critical 62
Clute, John 27, 70, 75
"Cold Front" 62
Coleridge, Samuel Taylor 163

Collier's 74
Comedians, The 100
Condorcet, Marquis de 141
Conklin, Groff 72, 79, 91
Constantine, Storm 95, 154
"Conversation of Eiros and Charmion, The" 51
Cook, Robin 28
Corpus Delicti 152, 160-161, 164, 168
Cosm 13-17
Count of Monte Cristo, The 78
Cousin de Grainville, Jean-Baptiste 140-143
Cramer, Kathryn 11, 69-87, 91-93
Crichton, Michael 28-29
Crime and Punishment 78
Crimson 95, 153
"Crimson White" 162
Crow, Donna 157, 163
Crowley, John 133
Cure, The 95, 151
Cushley, Joe 114
Cycle of Fire 64
Daedalus; or, Science and the Future 108
Dance in Blood Velvet, A 94
Daniel, Tony 87
Dark Theater, The 162
Datlow, Ellen 24
Davidson, Avram 20-22
Davis, Grania 20-22
Day of Wrath 90
Death Guard, The 89-91
"Death of Captain Future, The" 84
De Camp, L. Sprague 126
Dedman, Stephen 36-38
Deepdrive 18-20
Deep Range, The 5
Delany, Samuel R. 36, 38, 75, 81-82
del Rey, Judy-Lynn 71, 82-83
del Rey, Lester 71
Demolished Man, The 78
Depeche Mode 161-162
Dernier homme, Le 140-142
Deviate Ladies, The 152
"Devil's Instrument, The" 159, 168

Dewey, John 27
Diaspora 109-112
Dick, Philip K. 40, 92
Dickens, Charles 135
Dictionary of Literary Biography, The 23
Distress 110
Dr. Heidenhoff's Process 122
Donnelly, Ignatius 37-38
Donnelly, Marcos 45-48
Door into Summer, The 78
Dorsey, Candas Jane 27
Dostoyevsky, Fyodor 78
Double Star 78
Dracula 94
Dradin in Love 104-105
Drake, David 81
Dream Disciples 162
"Dreamworld (Doomed to Infinity)" 158
"Drode's Equations" 92
Drunkard's Endgame 42, 44
Dumas, Alexandre 78
Duncan, Dave 27
Dunsany, Lord 23, 25
Dyson, Freeman 44
Earl, Stephen 124
Earthquake Weather 11, 133-137
Eco, Umberto 21-22, 135
Eddy, Nelson 97
"Eden of Pain or Pleasure, The" 164
Egan, Greg, 109-111
Eldritch, Andrew 95, 151-153, 161
Elizium 152, 156
Ellington, Duke 122
Ellis, Edward S. 78
Elrod, P. N. 149
Empire Star 81
Empyrean 154
"Enchanted Tower, The" 163
"Enchantress of Venus, The" 80
Encyclopedia of Science Fiction, The 41, 70, 75
Enemy Stars, The 32
Engelsstaub 152, 164
Englund, Robert 97

Erebus Rising 154, 157
"Escape Route" 83
Escarpit, Robert 31-32
Eshbach, Lloyd Arthur 71, 87
Eternal Footman, The 46
Eureka 43, 51-52, 113
Exhumation 163
Expiration Date 133-137
Faber & Faber 41
"Facts in the Case of M. Valdemar, The" 52, 113
Fall of the House of Usherettes, The 104-105, 115-116
Fantasma dell'Opera, Il 97-100
Fantasy Review 73
"Farewell my Little Earth" 162
Farmer, Philip J. 111
Faust 98
"Faustfeathers" 120, 122
"Feast of Blood, The" 159-160
Fields of the Nephilim 152
Fin du monde, La 138
Firebird 41, 43
"Firelight" 160
Firestar 14
Five Gold Bands, The 75
Flammarion, Camille 138
Flaubert, Gustave 169
Flight into Yesterday 40, 43
Flood, Leslie 75
Flynn, Michael 13-17
"Folktales in Science Fiction" 124
"Fool's Errand" 85
Ford, John M. 92
Foreign Bodies 36-38
Forester, C. S. 84
Forkbeard Fantasy 104-105, 115-117
Fort, Charles 172
For the Blood is the Life 95, 153
Foucault's Pendulum 21-22, 135
Foundation 9, 11, 124
Four Days War 90
Fragment d'histoire future 138
France, Anatole 128, 138
Freud, Sigmund 68

Friends 132
Fuller, Margaret 114
Full Spectrum 3 45-46
Gaia Websters, The 128-132
Galactic Empires (Volumes I and II) 70, 81-82, 84, 87
Galaxy 70, 72, 74, 76-78
Galileo 51
Gaiman, Neil 23-26
"Game of Rat and Dragon, The" 81
Garcia y Robertson, R. 84
Gardner, Martin 44
Garments of Caean, The 83
Garrett, Randall 34
Gaulois, Le 97
Gautier, Théophile 166
Geier, Chester S. 78
Gernsback, Hugo 123
"Ghetto" 33-34
Ghosting 152
Giffard, Pierre 140
"Gift from the Culture, A" 81
Girls Under Glass 152
Gnome Press 39
Goethe, J. W. von 108-109
Gold, H. L. 76, 78, 102
"Goodly Creatures, The" 76-77
Gotisch 95
Gottlieb, Phyllis 27
Goulart, Ron 125
Gounod, Charles 98
Grant, Glenn 26-28
Grant, Richard 92
Gray, John 130
"Great Game, The" 85
Greeley, Horace 114
Greenland, Colin 83
Griffiths, Trevor 100
Grimoire, The (Gothic Society) 95, 153
Grimoire, The (Nosferatu) 163
"Grist" 87
Griswold, Rufus W. 112-113
Group Sex 172
Guardian, The 115

Guerre au vingtième siècle, La 138, 140
Guerre infernale, La 140
"Guest Law" 87
Haggard, H. Rider 75, 80, 82, 86
Haldane, J. B. S. 108
Half Life 62
"Halo" 62
Hamilton, Cicely 106-107
Hamilton, Edmond 72-73, 76-77, 79-80, 82, 86
Hamilton, Peter F. 83
Harness, Charles L. 39-44
Harrison, M. John 83
Hartwell, David G. 11, 26-28, 69-87, 91-93
Hawthorne, Nathaniel 92
Hayden, Liza 114
Hearst, William Randolph 114
"Hearts Do Not in Eyes Shine" 122
Heidegger, Martin 158, 165
Heinemann 123
Heinlein, Robert A. 38, 78, 86
Helliconia Spring 111
Henderson, Zenna 130
Hero with a Thousand Faces, The 79
"Hijo de Hernez, El" 45
Hill, Ken 97-98
Hills of the Boasting Woman, The 124
Hitchcock, Alfred 18
"Home by the Sea" 27
Hope, Anthony 77, 86
Hopkins, Eve 114
Horloge des siècles, L' 139
Hoyle, Fred 44
Hubbard, L. Ron 38, 74, 93
Huizinga, Johan 106
"Hungry Eyes, The" 157-159
Hussey, Wayne 152
"I Am the One" 155, 161, 168
Icarus; or, The Future of Science 108
Iceworld 62
"If Don John of Austria Had Married Mary, Queen of Scots" 126
If it Had Happened Otherwise 126
Imagination 76, 82
Imaginative Tales 76

"Im Garden des Nichts (a Secret Light in the Garden of my Void)" 159
"Impediment" 62, 64
Improper Apocalypse, An 45
Incubus 168-172
Incubus Succubus 153, 155-157, 168
"Indefatigable Frog, The" 92
Innis, Harold 131
Interzone 9, 11
"Invaders" 119, 122
Iron Heel, The 37
Irwin, Margaret 23, 25
Island Under the Earth, The 21
Isle of Lies, The 47
Issue at Hand, The 76, 87
Jablokov, Alexander 10, 18-20
Jadis chez aujourd'hui 139-140
Jack Faust 109-112
Jackson, Clive 80-81
Jigsaw Woman, The 132
Jobling, Ed 105, 116-117
"Judgment Call" 122
Jung, Carl 93
Kandel, Michael 85
Kast, Pierre 166
"Keeper's Call, The" 162
Kennedy, Jackie 126
Kennedy, John F. 126
Kepler, John 51
Kessel, John 10-11, 119-123
Kingdom of the Grail 55-61
King, Martin Luther 67
King, Stephen 171
King of Elfland's Daughter, The 23
Kingsbury, Donald 85
Kingshill, Sophia 112-114
Kingslayer, The 74
"Kissed by Death" 163
Kline, Otis Adelbert 74
Knight, Damon 42, 76-77
Knox, Calvin M. 82
Koontz, Dean R. 171
Kornbluth, C. M. 76

Krafft-Ebing 154
Kress, Nancy 28-31, 46
Krono 41
Lafferty, R. A. 21, 52, 125
"Lamia" 164
Lancelot Biggs, Spaceman 74
Last Call 133-137
Last Man, The (Cousin de Grainville) 141
Last Man, The (Shelley)106
"(Learning About) Machine Sex" 27
"Lecturer, The" 122
Legion of Space, The 71-73
Le Fanu, J. Sheridan 157, 165
Le Guin, Ursula K. 52, 85, 92, 129
Lem, Stanislaw 52
Leroux. Gaston 97-99
Lest Darkness Fall 126
Lewis. C. S. 23, 25, 84, 101, 128
"Like Christabel" 163
Little, Big 137
Living Alone 25
Lloyd-Webber, Andrew 97-98
Lockhard, Leonard 41
Locomotion Future, La 140
Lodge, David 135
"Logical Life, The" 62
Lom, Herbert 97
London, Jack 38
"Loneliness of the Long-Distance Writer, The" 27
"Longest Science Fiction Story Ever Written, The" 92-93
"Longline" 62-63
Lord Horror 101
Lord of the Rings, The 23
"Lost Sorceress of the Silent Citadel, The" 84
Love Like Blood 152
Lovelock, James 44
Lucie Cries 152
Lud-in-the-Mist 23
Lugosi, Bela 147
McAuley, Paul J. 85, 111
McCaffrey, Anne 92
McComas, J. Francis 76
MacDonald, George 25

McIntosh, J. T. 74
Mackenzie, Ian 115
McKormack, Candia 153, 155-158
McKormack, Tony 155-156
MacLean, Katherine 92
McLuhan, Marshall 131
Magazine of Fantasy & Science Fiction, The 11, 34, 45, 76-77
Malleus Maleficarum 164
Malpass, E. L. 124
"Man" 122
Manning, Bernard 100
"Man with the X-Ray Eyes, The" 152
Margulies, Leo 65
Marionettes, The 163-164
Mark of Zorro, The 43
Martian Chronicles, The 107
Marx, Karl 67
Marx Brothers, The 120
Mascetti, Manuela Dunn 96
Masque of the Red Death, The 115
Masters of the Maze 20
"Mechanic, The" 62
Meeting in Infinity (Kessel) 10-11, 119-123
Meeting in Infinity (Munch) 122-123
Megiddo's Ridge 90
Méliès, Georges 116
Memoirs of the Year 2500 141
Mercier, Louis-Sébastien 141-145
Meredith, Scott 77
Merritt, A. 80
Merwin, Sam Jr. 65, 72, 79
Metropolis 164
Meyers, Billy 75-76
"Micromegas" 51
Mightiest Machine, The 72
Miller, P. Schuyler 72, 79
Miller, Walter M. 101
"Mircalla" 157
Mirrlees, Hope 23, 25
Mission, The 152
Mission of Gravity 64
Mr. Godly Beside Himself 23
"Mrs. Shummel Exits a Winner" 121

"Ms. Midshipwoman Harrington" 83
Moby Dick 120
Modern Science Fiction: Its Meaning and its Future 72, 87
Monde comme il va, Le 142
Monde tel qu'il sera, Le 138
Moorcock, Michael 41, 76, 83-84
Moore, Brian 46
Moore, C. L. 80
More Issues at Hand 76-77, 87
Morgan, Piers 140
Morrison, Alex 124
Morrison, D. A. C. 124
Morrow, James 45-46, 133
Moskowitz, Sam 73, 79
Motherfuckers: The Auschwitz of OZ 97, 99-101
"Mother Lode" 27
Moumon, Jean-Pierre 140
"Movements of Her Eyes, The" 87
Munch, Edvard 122-123
Murder of Edgar Allan Poe, The 112-115
Murphy, Niall 162
Music of Many Spheres: The Essential Hal Clement Volume 2 62-65
"My Boyfriend's Name is Jello" 20
Natives of Space 62
Naylor, Grant 125
Needle 62
Neverwhere 24
New Atlantis 51
New Maps of Hell 75, 87
New Oxford Companion to Literature in French, The 55
News of the Black Feast 10
New Worlds 41, 75, 83
New York Herald 114
New York Review of Science Fiction, The 9, 11, 13, 93
New York Tribune 114
"Niche, A" 27
Nicholls, Peter 70
Nietzsche, Friedrich 19, 133
Nineteen Eighty-Four 17
Niven, Larry 92
Nomad 72, 74
Northern Stars 26-28
Norton Book of Science Fiction, The 92

Nosferatu 153, 162
"Nosferatu" 147
"Not Responsible! Park and Lock It!" 121-122
Novel of the Future, The 145
Oates, Joyce Carol 172
"Oblivion" 164, 168
Observer, The 123-124
Oceanspace 53-55
Of Worlds Beyond: The Science of Science Fiction Writing 71, 87
Olbers, Hans 43
"One Caress" 162
O'Neill, Joseph 90
On Stranger Tides 135
"Operation Afreet" 32, 34
Operation Chaos 34-35
"Operation Incubus" 34
Operation Luna 31-32, 34-36
"Operation Salamander" 34
Ornament to his Profession, An 39, 41-42
"Orphans of the Helix" 83-86
Orwell, George 17
Oswald, Lee Harvey 126
Other Worlds, The 73-74, 87
"Outlaw in the Sky" 78
Outsider, The 94
Pall Mall Gazette 89
Panic on the Titanic 152
Paradox Men, The 40-41
Paralysed Age 154, 163
Parrinder, Patrick 51
"Party of the First Part" 152
Pater, Walter 168
Pattern for Conquest 74
Penguin Companion to Literature, The 113
Penny Dreadfull, The 95, 154
People of the Ruins, The 106
Permutation City 110
Phaeriemagick 158
Phantom of Hollywood, The 97
Phantom of the Opera, The 97-98
Phantom of the Paradise, The 97
Phillifent, John T. 83
Physics of Immortality, The 110

"Pi Man, The" 92
"Planetfall" 62-63, 65
"Planet for Plunder, A" 65
Planet Stories 71, 80
"Play Dead" 164
Poe, Edgar Allan 43-44, 51, 112-115
Pohl, Frederik 44, 72, 79
Polhemus, Ted 151
Poole, Erika 114
Port of Peril 74
Potache en 1950, Un 140
Potter, J. K. 123
Powers, Tim 11, 133-137
Pratchett, Terry 125
Pratt, Fletcher 77
Press the Eject and Give Me the Tape 152
Price, Vincent 159
Prigogine, Ilya 44
"Prince of Space, The" 79
Prisoner of Zenda, The 77-78
Pritchard, John W. 40
"Probability Zero" 62
"Proof" 62-63
Prophecy, The 162
Prophets of the End Time 45
Prophets for the End of Time 45-48
Protect and Survive 89-90
"Pure Product, The" 121
Purple Cloud, The 106
Pynchon, Thomas 23
Quarantine 110
"Quest for Saint Aquin, The" 101
Rackham, John 83
Ragged Astronauts, The 111
"Raindrop" 62
Rains, Claude 97
"Ranks of Bronze" 81, 84
"Rappaccini's Daughter" 92
"Recording Angel" 85
Reed, Robert 85, 87
"Remember, the Dead Say" 27
"Remoras" 85
"Requiem" 157-158

"Resting Place" 162
Resurrection of Alonso Quijana" 45-46
Reynolds, Alastair 87
Reynolds, Mack 80
Ricardo, David 145
Rice, Anne 94-95, 149-150, 154, 158, 166-167
Ring of Ritornel, The 41, 43
"Ring Rats" 84
Rings 39-44
Roberts & Vinter 41
Roberts, Morley 93
Robida, Albert 137-140
Rogue Star 13-17
Roman de l'avenir, Le 141
"Rose, The" 40
Rose, The 41
Rosetta Stone 152
Russell, Bertrand 108
Russell, Mary Doria 101-103
Russell, William Moy (W. M. S. Russell) 123-125
Rymer, James Malcolm 159
Saberhagen, Fred 166
"Sacrificium" 164
St. Clair, Margaret 73-74
St. James Guide to Science Fiction, The 40
"St. Patrick's Breastplate" 172
"Samhain" 156
Satellite Science Fiction 65
Savage, Felicity 130
Savage Kiss 162
"Savage Kiss" 162
Sawyer, Robert J. 27
Schell, Maximilian 97
Schopenhauer, Arthur 19
Schreck, Max 159
Science-Fantasy 74
"Science-Fantasy and Translations" 76
Science Fiction Adventures 75-76, 82
Science Fiction Carnival 80
Science Fiction for People Who Hate Science Fiction 120
Science Fiction Quarterly 76
"Science in Science Fiction, The" 76
Scientific Romance, A 106-112

Scientific Romance in Britain, 1890-1950 90
Screem in the Dark 162
Sebastian 160
"Seesaw" 43
Seetee Shock 72-73
Sellings, Arthur 124
Sex Gang Children 151
Shakespeare, William 135
"Shall We Commit Suicide?" 87
Shanks, Edward 106-107
Shasta 39
Shaw, Bob 111
Sheckley, Robert 77, 81, 125
Sheffield, Charles 92
Shelley, Mary 106-107
Shiel, M. P. 47, 106-107
Shinn, Sharon 66-69
"Shobies' Story, The" 85
Siddons, Anne Rivers 172
Silverberg, Robert 75, 82
Silver Web, The 105
Simmons, Dan 83-85, 87
Simple Minds 162
Sinclair, May 172
Siouxsie and the Banshees 95, 151
Siouxsie Sioux 95, 151
Sisters of Mercy, The 95, 151
Sister Wolf 172
Skylark of Space, The 72
Skylark Three 72
Slan 42
"Slave to the Night" 163
Small Changes 62
Small World 135
Smith, Adam 145
Smith, Cordwainer 81-82
Smith, Edward E. 70-73, 75, 79
Smith, George O. 72, 74
Smith, Robert 95, 151
"Snowball Effect, The" 92
"Social Science Fiction" 82
Son of William 153
Sopor Aeternus 95, 159

Sopor Aeternus and the Ensemble of Shadows 95, 152, 159, 162, 164
Souvestre, Emile 138, 140-145
Space Odysseys 70, 87
Space Opera (Aldiss) 70, 87
"Space Opera" (Kandel) 85
Space Opera (Vance) 75
Space Opera Renaissance, The 11, 69-87
Sparrow, The 101-103
Spengler, Oswald 77
Spiegeleire, Michel de 48-53
"Spirey and the Queen" 87
Squire, J. C. 126
Stalker, Angela (Angela Carter) 105
Stalin, Josef 107
Stapledon, Olaf 106
"Star, The" 101, 124
Stardust 23-26
Starfarers 31-36
Starfish 53
"Staring" 160, 168
Star King, The 75
Star Kings, The 77 80
Star of Life, The 80
Stars my Destination, The 78
"Star Stealers, The" 79, 82, 84
Startling Stories 40, 72
Star Winds 83
"Status Symbol" 62
Steam-Man of the Prairies, The 78
Steele, Allen 53-55, 66, 84
Stengers, Isabelle 44
Still She Wished for Company 25
Stinger 28-31
Stoker, Bram 94, 147, 165
Stong, Phil 73-75, 87
"Story of the Days to Come, A" 144
Stress of Her Regard, The 133
Stross, Charles 87
Stuart, Don A. 130
"Stuck With It" 62
Sturgeon, Theodore 64-65
Sue, Eugène 145

Summers at Castle Auburn 66-69
SunDown SunRise 94-95
"Sun Spot" 62
Super Science Stories 72
Sur la pierre blanche 138
"Survivor, The" 85
Swanwick, Michael 20-21, 108-111
"Swordsman of Vardis, The" 80
Sylphes 160-161
Tale of the Next Great War, The 140
Tale of Two Cities, A 135
Tarde, Gabriel 138
Tarr, Judith 55-61
Taste of Blood Wine, A 94
"Technical Error" 62
"Temptation" 81
Temptations of Saint Anthony, The 169
Thee Vampire Guild 94-95, 147
Theodore Savage 106
These Mortals 23, 25
Thomas, Theodore L. 41
Three Hearts and Three Lions 34
Thrilling Wonder Stories 71
Time Heals Nothing 159
Time Machine, The 144
"Time of Legends" 162
Timescape 16
Time Ships, The 128
"Time Stands Still…(But Stops for No One)" 159
"Time Trap" 40-41
Tipler, Frank 44, 110
Tolkien, J. R. R. 166-167
Towing Jehovah 45
Toynbee, Arnold 43
"Tracking the Random Variable" 45
Tragical History of Dr. Faustus, The 120
Tranchell, Chris 114
Triplanetary 72
Troilus and Cressida 135
Trudel, Jean-Louis 27
Tubb, E. C. 76, 83
Tucker, Wilson 70, 73
Turgot, Anne-Robert-Jacques 141

EXOTIC ENCOUNTERS, BY BRIAN STABLEFORD * 191

Turner, James 10-11
Turner Diaries, The 38
Twentieth Century, The 137-140
Twenty Thousand Leagues Under the Sea 53
Twilight 160
Two Witches 152, 157, 162-163
Umbra et Imago 158
"Uncommon Sense" 62-63
"Under Another Moon" 27
Universe Makers, The 73, 87
Unknown 32, 34
Uzanne, Octave 140
Vampire: The Complete Guide to the World of the Undead 96
Vampires, Burial and Death: Folklore and Reality 96
Vampire's Kiss, The 157-158
"Vampir Song" 158
Vampyre State Building 154
"Vampyres" 155, 162
"Vampyre's Dance! 162
"Vampyre's Kiss" 155, 168
Vance, Jack 75, 80, 82
Vancouver Columbian, The 129
VanderMeer, Jeff 52, 104-105
Vanian, David 153
Van Vogt, A. E. 27, 40, 42-44, 80
Varney 159-162
Varney the Vampyre; or, The Feast of Blood 159
Velvet Vampyre, The 153
Verne, Jules 53, 137, 143
Vernes, Henri 48
"Very Slow Time Machine, The" 92
Vian, Boris 44
Virtanen, Jyrki 157-159
Voltaire 51, 142
"Voltaire, Science and Fiction: A Tercentenary Tribute" 124
Vonarburg, Elisabeth 27
Voyage 125-128
Voyages de Saturnin Farandoul dans les 5 ou 6 parties du monde et dans tout les pays connu et même inconnu de M. Jules Verne 137
Wake, The 152
Wallace, Ian 40, 42
Warrington, Freda 94-95
"Waterclap" 53

Watson, Ian 92, 111
Watts, Peter 27, 53
Weapon Shops of Isher, The 43
"Weatherman" 81
Weber, David 83-84
"We Have Fed Our Sea" 32-33
Weiner, Andrew 27
Weird Tales 80, 162
Wells, H. G. 93, 106-107, 120, 122, 128, 144
Wells, Robert 124
"Well-Wishers, The" 83
Werfel, Franz 101
Westerfeld, Scott 87
Weston, Jessie 135
"Weyr Search" 92
Wharton, Edith 172
"What Sweet Music They Make...." 94-95, 147-168
When the Sleeper Wakes 144
White, James 83
White, Phill 160
Whores of Babylon, The 153, 164, 168
Willems, Philippe 138
Williams, Paul 64-65
Williamson, Jack 32, 41, 71-73, 79
Willing, Victoria 114
Wilson, Colin 94
Wilson, Robert Charles 27
Witching Hour 153, 163
Windling, Terri 24, 104-105
Wolfe, Gene 92
Wollheim, Donald A. 20, 73, 79, 82-83, 87
Wood Wife, The 104-105
"World As It Is, The" 142
World as it Shall Be, The 140-145
World of Null-A, The 42, 44
"Worm in the Well, A" 85
Wright, John C. 87
Wright, Ronald 106-108
Wright. S. Fowler 90
Writer's Digest 73
"Wytches" 156
X-Files, The 22
Yarbro, Chelsea Quinn 149

"Yesterday Now" 141
Zebrowski, George 42
Zen Gun, The 83
Zettel, Sarah 85
Zine, The 154
"Zirn Left Unguarded, the Jenghik Palace in Flames, John Westerly Dead" 81

ABOUT THE AUTHOR

BRIAN STABLEFORD was born in Yorkshire in 1948. He taught at the University of Reading for several years, but is now a full-time writer. He has written many science fiction and fantasy novels, including *The Empire of Fear*, *The Werewolves of London*, *Year Zero*, *The Curse of the Coral Bride*, *The Stones of Camelot* and *Prelude to Eternity*. Collections of his short stories include a long series of *Tales of the Biotech Revolution*, and such idiosyncratic items as *Sheena and Other Gothic Tales* and The *Innnsmouth Heritage and Other Sequels*. He has written numerous nonfiction books, including *Scientific Romance in Britain, 1890-1950*, *Glorious Perversity: The Decline and Fall of Literary Decadence*, *Science Fact and Science Fiction: An Encyclopedia* and *The Devil's Party: A Brief History of Satanic Abuse*. He has contributed hundreds of biographical and critical entries to reference books, including both editions of *The Encyclopedia of Science Fiction* and several editions of the library guide, *Anatomy of Wonder*. He has also translated numerous novels from the French language, including several by the feuilletonist Paul Féval and numerous classics of French scientific romance by such writers as Albert Robida, Maurice Renard, and J. H. Rosny the Elder.